VACCINE COURT

Vaccine Court

The Law and Politics of Injury

Anna Kirkland

NEW YORK UNIVERSITY PRESS
New York

NEW YORK UNIVERSITY PRESS
New York
www.nyupress.org
© 2016 by New York University

Library of Congress Cataloging-in-Publication Data
Names: Kirkland, Anna (Anna Rutherford), author.
Title: Vaccine court : the law and politics of injury / Anna Kirkland.
Description: New York : New York University Press, [2016] | Also available as an ebook. | Includes bibliographical references and index.
Identifiers: LCCN 2016023901| ISBN 978-1-4798-7693-8 (cl ; alk. paper) | ISBN 1-4798-7693-3 (cl ; alk. paper)
Subjects: LCSH: Vaccination—Law and legislation—United States. | United States. Court of Federal Claims. Office of Special Masters. | Vaccination—Political aspects—United States. | Vaccination—Complications—United States. | Products liability—Vaccines—United States.
Classification: LCC KF3808 .K57 2016 | DDC 344.7304/3—dc23
LC record available at https://lccn.loc.gov/2016023901

New York University Press books are printed on acid-free paper, and their binding materials are chosen for strength and durability. We strive to use environmentally responsible suppliers and materials to the greatest extent possible in publishing our books.

Manufactured in the United States of America

10 9 8 7 6 5 4 3 2 1

Also available as an ebook

To the men and women of the vaccine court
and all who work for vaccine safety

CONTENTS

Acknowledgments   ix

Introduction: Our Immunization Social Order   1

1. How Are Vaccines Political?   33

2. The Solution of the Vaccine Court   65

3. Health and Rights in the Vaccine-Critical Movement   96

4. Knowing Vaccine Injury through Law   117

5. What Counts as Evidence?   146

6. The Autism Showdown   172

Conclusion: The Epistemic Politics of the Vaccine Court   199

Notes   217

Index   259

About the Author   273

ACKNOWLEDGMENTS

The chance to research interesting questions and then to write about them as part of an intellectual community is the great privilege of being a college professor. I realized when I could not stop reading and following the rulings of the vaccine court that it would just have to be the subject of my next book. This book would not have been possible without people being willing to talk to me about the vaccine court and their experiences within it, and I am deeply indebted to all of them. I did much of the research for this project as a fellow at the Law and Public Affairs Program at Princeton University in 2010–2011, where I enjoyed proximity to Washington, D.C., as well as the generous resources and stimulating conversations with my colleagues there, especially Kim Lane Scheppele, Paul Frymer, Leslie Gerwin, Elizabeth Mertz, Tanya Hernandez, Amy Lerman, Gordon Silverstein, Hendrik Hartog, Steven Wilf, and Keith Wailoo. The scholarly environment at the University of Michigan has nurtured me for my entire career. I am blessed with generous colleagues in the Science, Technology, and Society (STS) program who read and commented on sections of the book, especially Shobita Parthasarathy, Joel Howell, Gabrielle Hecht, Paul Edwards, Alexandra Stern, John Carson, Marty Pernick, Elizabeth Roberts, Joy Rohde, and Perrin Selcer. Sarah Fenstermaker and my colleagues at the Institute for Research on Women and Gender were especially caring in the final weeks of manuscript preparation. I also wish to thank Elizabeth Anderson, Roger Bernier, Carol Boyd, Art Caplan, Elizabeth Cole, Kevin Conway, Charles Epp, Geoffrey Evans, Eric Feldman, Patricia Segal Freeman, Sander Greenland, Colleen Grogan, Peter Jacobsen, Carla Keirns, Anders Kelto, Sandra Levitsky, Aaron Ley, Michael Lynch, Jonathan Metzl, Clark Miller, Jennifer Mnookin, Brendan Nyhan, Paul Offit, Lisa Prosser, Jennifer Reich, Dorit Reiss, Dorothy Roberts, Abigail Saguy, Dan Salmon, Jason Schwartz, Jeffrey Segal, Chloe Silverman, Sergio Sismundo, Emily Stopa, Beth Tarini, Curtis Webb, Elizabeth

Wingrove, and insightful anonymous reviewers for their help in thinking through the ideas in this book and for presenting me with new ones. Tom Burke has always been encouraging when it seemed like we were the only two people in all of political science who were interested in the vaccine court.

I presented papers that would become parts of this book and benefited from energetic audience participation at Northwestern University's Science in Human Culture Klopsteg lecture series, the American Bar Foundation, Vanderbilt University's Center for Medicine, Health, and Society, the University of Pennsylvania Health Law Students Association, the UCLA School of Law faculty lecture series, the University of Michigan Center for Ethics in Public Life, and the Child Health and Evaluation Research Unit at the University of Michigan School of Medicine. Anna Frick, Denise Lillvis, Lotus Seeley, and Courtney Shier (from Michigan's Undergraduate Research Opportunity Program) provided timely and helpful research assistance; Kathy Wood transcribed my interviews. I received research funding support from Princeton University, from the College of Literature, Science, and the Arts at the University of Michigan (Faculty Research Grant and Associate Professor's Fund), from the Women's Studies Department at Michigan, and from the Institute for Research on Women and Gender at Michigan (IRB #HUM00031641). I received no funding from any private corporation or from any government grant, and I have no conflicts of interest. My discussions of vaccine policy trends in the states are based on research first done with Denise Lillvis and adapted here from our article "Power and Persuasion in the Vaccine Debates: An Analysis of Political Efforts and Outcomes in the States, 1998–2012," with Denise Lillvis (first author) and Anna Frick, *Milbank Quarterly* 92, no. 3 (September 2014): 475–508. A version of Chapter 6 was published as "Credibility Battles in the Autism Litigation," *Social Studies of Science* 42, no. 2 (April 2012): 237–61. Chapter 3 on vaccine critics shares some material from "The Legitimacy of Vaccine Critics: What's Left after Autism?," *Journal of Health Policy, Politics and Law* 37, no. 1 (February 2012): 69–97, copyrighted at Duke University Press, and I first worked on the political account of vaccines that now constitutes Chapter 1 while composing my entry on childhood vaccines for Brent Steel's *Science and Politics: An A to Z Guide to Issues and Controversies*

(CQ Press/Sage, 2014). I thank all these publishers for permission to reuse these prior publications.

My family and friends have been a steadfast source of joy and support. I am very grateful to my network of caregivers whose labor created the time for me to write this book, especially Hannah Jones, Noreen Smith, Sarah Wizinsky, and the staff and teachers at the Ann Arbor Jewish Community Center.

Introduction

Our Immunization Social Order

Vaccine Injury and the Immunization Social Order

When parents hesitate or refuse to vaccinate their children, it is often because they have doubts about vaccine safety.[1] They fear vaccine injuries. They have heard that vaccines can cause autism, allergies, immune problems, or attention-deficit disorder, for example. Vaccine injuries do happen, though the scientific consensus is that none of these conditions are among them. More obscure conditions, such as thrombocytopenic purpura, a very rare and transient condition characterized by low platelets and excessive bleeding and bruising, are agreed-upon adverse events after vaccination (in this case, the measles-mumps-rubella or MMR vaccine). The tetanus vaccine can cause brachial neuritis, an inflammation of the nerves in the hand, arm, and shoulder; the rubella vaccine can cause arthritis, particularly in women; and the measles vaccine can cause encephalitis, a potentially very serious irritation and swelling of the brain. I always watch my children carefully in the few minutes after they receive a vaccine because anaphylaxis and fainting are also rare but possible reactions to injections. We have very personal, embodied experiences within the broader political and legal context of vaccination policy in the contemporary United States.[2]

Vaccine injuries are a complex and fascinating problem. They expose tensions between parents and professional experts, between certainty and doubt, and between different ways of knowing and being sure. Vaccine injuries display the inevitability of the meeting between science, politics, and the law, giving us a case to explore how well our democracy manages this tense and productive collaboration. Experts and activists have widely divergent ideas about what vaccine injuries are and how to recognize them, and recent decades have seen a strong social movement mobilized around injury claims. American vaccines are embedded within a robust private pharmaceutical economy, state-level vaccination requirements to enroll in school, a federal regulatory and safety monitoring regime, and an extensive health and medical research system. When vaccines cause injury, U.S. citizens can petition for legal compensation at a special court known simply as the vaccine court. A successful legal claim validates the harm, gives the injured person a sense of being heard, affirms governmental responsibility, and provides a proper ethical and financial response from the community.[3]

Throughout this book, I explore all the ways that we come to recognize a vaccine injury in the contemporary United States, asking who knows, how they know, how they prove it, who has the power to recognize it and how, and what they do about it. I place our vaccine court at the center of my analysis as the site where parents, activists, researchers, doctors, lawyers, and health bureaucrats come together to wrangle over what vaccine injuries really are. Our vaccine court is a useful institution for handling the recognition of vaccine injuries given that we regard them as posing simultaneously scientific, political, ethical, and legal problems. The vaccine court offers a desirable balance between openness to challenge and the stability of vetted expertise; it encourages peaceful social movement activism that must be presented as knowledge-driven, questioning, and public-spirited; and its design has allowed the vaccine court judges (called special masters) to give as much recognition as possible to people bringing claims while maintaining sufficient scientific credibility. The operation of our vaccine court since its first hearings in 1988 shows how rights claims and social movement activism are thoroughly intertwined with knowledge claims. Courts have always dealt in knowledge claims, of course, but the case of vaccine injuries shows exactly how legal actors work at the center of multiple knowledge sites to uphold and help constitute what I call the *immunization social order* in the contemporary United States.

Our immunization social order is the set of institutions, laws, pharmaceutical biotechnologies, and social practices that work together to produce high levels of vaccine coverage to prevent a wide range of diseases. It is both the freedom from vaccine-preventable diseases that we enjoy as well as the investments and social control necessary to maintain it. The Centers for Disease Control and Prevention (CDC) estimates that vaccination will prevent 322 million illnesses, 21 million hospitalizations, and 732,000 deaths during the lifetimes of the children born in the United States between 1994 and 2013.[4] During the time period 1994 to 2013, the U.S. government funded a consolidated effort to vaccinate uninsured and underinsured children. The CDC estimated that these immunizations saved $295 billion in direct costs and $1.38 trillion in total societal costs.[5] A starting assumption for this book is that this widespread freedom from illness, worry, and death is a precious achievement that we often fail to credit adequately because it is an absence rather than a presence. No parent recalls the time she did not have to sit with her sick child in the hospital. Instead, contested power relations among resistant activists and those who uphold the vaccine policies of our immunization social order have emphasized the costs and compulsions behind our immunization social order. Sociolegal scholars have long observed that law and legal institutions are the primary ways of maintaining social order, and thus my focus here is the role of law in channeling social movement conflict and resolving the challenges that vaccine injuries pose to our immunization social order. I term this turn to law the legalization of vaccine injury, by which I mean its placement within a court setting for resolution in an adversarial process. We come to know what a vaccine injury is through the law, in other words.

Vaccine policies are formed within power struggles over individual liberties, health decision making, disease control, personal responsibility, and mothering. As Monica Casper and Laura Carpenter have pointed out, for example, the human papillomavirus (HPV) vaccine is a "gendered pharmaceutical technology" that "cannot be understood outside gender relations and attendant cultural politics" because of its initial targeting to young girls to prevent a contagion spread by sexual contact.[6] "Politics," Casper and Carpenter elaborate, "shape the ways drugs are produced, used, and so forth; but drugs may also instigate political struggles, and, potentially, social change over their lifecourses, as well as embodying extant conflicts."[7] The federal government licenses, regulates, promotes, and monitors the safety of vaccines, which are produced and developed by a web of university-based researchers, biotech firms, and large pharmaceutical companies. The federal government recommends a standard vaccine schedule for children from birth to age six that includes immunizations against fourteen diseases: chickenpox, diphtheria, Haemophilus influenzae type b (Hib), hepatitis A and B, flu, measles, mumps, pertussis (whooping cough), polio, pneumococcus, rotavirus, rubella, and tetanus.[8] State legislatures enact immunization requirements for school entry. Children cannot decide for themselves whether to get vaccines, and much of the benefit of vaccines would be lost if we vaccinated only adults capable of giving their own consent. Babies receive the same vaccine spread out over several different administrations in the first years of life because the body needs to build up immunity over time. That means parents who follow vaccine recommendations must bring babies to their pediatrician every few months to get multiple shots at once.

Both parents and children perform these acts of citizenship, but they secure the communal benefit only if enough other parents and children are doing it, too. No vaccine is completely risk-free, and some previously healthy recipients suffer painful or even rare but damaging adverse reactions to vaccines. People tend to overestimate these rare events and perceive risks from actively doing something (vaccinating a child) more keenly than risks from inaction (not vaccinating against a potential disease).[9] From an individual's perspective it might seem best to avoid vaccines while everyone else gets them, but if enough people see it that way, vaccine-preventable diseases will come back. Nationwide, very few children are fully unvaccinated, but unvaccinated children (or, more commonly, children whose vaccines have been delayed) tend to cluster in like-minded communities or particular schools, making it possible for diseases to spread in those areas.[10]

If paying taxes were voluntary and not paying carried no penalty, we might expect that many people would rather keep all their money while still enjoying the roads, schools, and public services that others fund. Similarly, securing the benefits of widespread vaccination has usually meant some form of legal compulsion to avoid too much free riding in the form of exemptions. In the United States, vaccines are required at the state level for children enrolling in school (and in some states for day care attendance). All states offer medical exemptions for children if a doctor says they should not be vaccinated, and all states except for California, Mississippi, and West Virginia offer parents the opportunity to exempt their children because of religious belief. The most controversial exemptions are those offered in eighteen states on broader philosophical grounds, which allow parents to avoid vaccinating their children but do not require them to claim a religious reason. Parents who choose not to vaccinate are still able to send their children to public schools and day care centers by using the exemption process, depending on how easy it is to navigate. Because obtaining a philosophical exemption can be as simple as completing a form in some states, our vaccine mandate system functions more like an opt-out system than a true mandate. The easier the opt-out process is in a state, the more parents use it, and rates of pertussis are higher in those areas.[11]

Confronting fears about vaccine injuries is critically important, then, and any society that maintains widespread vaccination programs should both guarantee a very high level of safety as well as respond justly to injuries when they occur. The central issue in vaccine safety is determining whether an adverse event is causally linked to a vaccine. But the question of causation can be very hard to answer. Some infants and children will develop medical problems or even die suddenly for many reasons. Because they are also receiving regular vaccinations, some of those problems will likely appear soon after the shots. Many diagnoses that parents are most worried about, such as autism, attention-deficit disorder, learning disabilities, and other neurodevelopmental problems, do not have well-understood causes, are often subtle and contested as diagnoses themselves, and may emerge years after vaccinations were administered. These conditions are perceived to be widespread and to affect a child's ability to advance socially and economically in a competitive world and thus are highly salient to parents, particularly affluent and educated ones. To make matters even more complicated, some adverse events are so rare that their rates of association with vaccines are difficult to measure. The mainstream consensus is that our stable of vaccines is extremely safe, that adverse events are quite rare, and that reactions that cause significant injury are even more rare. Yet, no government since the invention of vaccines has been able to convince everyone. Vaccines and immunization have always been controversial for some people.[12]

The vaccine injury story illustrates how we settle disputes in U.S. society at the intersections of science, medicine, politics, law, and social movement activism. The vaccine court is the centerpiece of a no-fault compensation program that removes vaccine injury claims from the tort system and places them before special masters in the U.S. Court of Federal Claims. Injuries claimed from vaccines regularly recommended for use in children are covered, and all awards, attorneys' fees, and costs are paid from a trust fund built up from a seventy-five-cent excise tax on each dose of vaccine sold.[13] The vaccine court has been in place since controversy in the 1980s over the safety of the whole-cell pertussis vaccine mobilized parents, doctors, and industry into an unusual coalition to help pass the National Childhood Vaccine Injury Act (NCVIA) of 1986. Our national systems of vaccine injury recognition and redress were born in one conflict but have weathered many others, as I will show, including the autism-vaccine controversy of recent years (in which the vaccine court roundly rejected autism as a vaccine injury).

Whether a vaccine caused an adverse event may seem like a medical or scientific question, not a legal one, and so it might seem regrettable or misguided that we had to drag down such questions into the muck of the adversarial courtroom to be batted about by nonexperts. But what if we think of vaccines as social and political from the start, and in fact already the subject of a firestorm of claims about what they are and what they do? What if we think of law as a special sphere of the political where we send disputes for resolution through legitimated processes? If vaccine injury is a political question about an individual harm in a democratic society, then a court is a perfectly reasonable place to resolve it. Then law looks more like a useful mediating process for absorbing and creating new knowledge in complex debates, all within a legal framework that tries to take seriously the context of doing justice to an injured party. Forcing an issue to become a legal question in an adversarial process can have significant consequences, however. In the case of vaccine injuries, the legalization solution forces social movement activism and injury-based rights claiming into a framework of careful reason giving and mustering of evidence before well-informed judges. Professional fees and expenses are paid no matter the outcome, and the special masters will wait as long as the petitioners want to gather the evidence to make their case.

But from critics' perspectives the court has become too stingy with compensations, issues conflicting and baseless judgments, and combines the worst features of both an adversarial court and a mind-numbing bureaucracy.[14] As Tom Tyler's influential work on citizen compliance with the law shows, people will obey the law even when a legal ruling goes against their self-interest if they feel the process treated them fairly, if they had a chance to make their case and were listened to by fair-minded judges, and if they normatively endorse the overall fairness of the law.[15] Though there is variation among critics' views, many mobilized parents believe not simply that the court is a tough hurdle, but that its requirements are part of a government plan to mislead citizens and to conceal vaccine injuries by denying claims. As vaccine critic and activist Mary Holland charges, "[The vaccine court] is stacked against families because let's face it, vaccine injuries make vaccines look bad."[16] The activists who focus on the vaccine court do not share any of Tyler's normative commitments to the immunization social order because they regard vaccines as unsafe (rooted in beliefs about autism causation principally but not entirely) and thus they see the court as an illegitimate cover organization. Compensating for vaccine injuries does indeed create tension for our immunization social order because these cases are a concession that some people will suffer for the population-level freedom from vaccine-preventable diseases that we all enjoy. The vaccine court must do justice to those people—who may still accept the value of vaccines and the immunization social order overall—while managing the confrontations of a hostile social movement eager to exploit this tension.

Our vaccine court has been successful not because it has managed to please both scientists and activists, but rather because it has compromised between a vision of scientific certainty and a duty to compensate injuries to uphold the immunization social order. As Sheila Jasanoff reminds us, "The grand question for the law is not how judges can best do justice to science; the more critical concern is how courts can better render justice under conditions of endemic uncertainty and ignorance."[17] The vaccine court has forged this compromise through its rules and practices (for instance, its openness to all kinds of evidence and expert testimony and its flexible and often lengthy decision process), through the labor of the people who work there (especially the special masters, who are nonexperts but who hear the same issues over and over again), and through their judgments about a wide array of evidence held to a legal standard of causation, which is lower than what constitutes certainty for most scientists but requires petitioners to prove that it is more likely than not that the vaccine caused the injury. Compromises often please no one, yet judges and lawyers are very good at negotiating them.

Sometimes it is not possible to know if a vaccine "really" caused an injury. But as Annelise Riles explains, sometimes legal knowledge can be generative when it is not working simply in the service of another field's knowledge claims: "Law is out of touch with reality, as the critics routinely tell us, and that is precisely, if counterintuitively, its promise."[18] In many cases, especially the high-profile autism claims, the vaccine court has more or less reflected and amplified the scientific consensus, but sometimes it muddles along. It can never win over critics who reason from a different interpretation of the evidence or based on incommensurable first principles. But I argue it has managed uncertainty to do justice.

Our vaccine court stands as the exclusive forum for trials of vaccines for causing injuries. It draws on scientific expertise but has an explicit policy mission to dwell in uncertainties and to use a wide range of epistemic resources. Its flexibility and epistemic openness are its hallmark traits, yet its rulings ultimately promote accountability to sound reasoning and good evidence (as the special masters understand those boundaries). The vaccine court serves several critical purposes in contemporary American society. First, its rulings regularly affirm the mainstream consensus that our vaccines are safe while acknowledging some agreed-upon injuries. It has fulfilled its original mission of protecting our national vaccine supply from the unpredictability of the tort system. Second, the court is an audience for evidence of vaccine safety, but also an engine for producing it. The vaccine court in the United States was also notably the only public venue in the world for the debate over autism and vaccines to become formalized and legalized, and for the arguments to be fully heard, discussed, and reviewed. Third, it serves as the site for the meeting of the individual, the knowledge products of the scientific establishment, and the state. Most other areas of vaccine safety research are focused on the population, and activists, who often focus on the individual, do not otherwise get a chance to present an individual injured child before the state. What happened to this person? Fourth, the vaccine court channels dissatisfaction with vaccines into compensation rather than social movement activity, at least for some people. When the special masters deny compensation, as in the case of autism, they provide something for losing claimants to mobilize against in particular structured ways. Finally, those structures require reason giving that promotes accountability. That accountability flows in multiple directions: activists can haul health bureaucrats before congressional committees to testify about vaccine safety, but their experts will also be mercilessly cross-examined in vaccine court. Of course none of these features of the vaccine court guarantee perfect knowledge, and it would be naïve to hope for that. But its imperfections and contested settlements should not keep us from acknowledging its profound public service to our immunization social order.

Many critical social scientists and feminist scholars would not celebrate the law's power over bodies and injuries as much as I do in this book. Anthropologist Sarah Lochlann Jain points out in her study of American personal injury law that law's recognition of injury seeks to frame it as exceptional within an otherwise well-functioning capitalist, consumerist culture.[19] The interactions between bodies and products that cause injuries are inflected with inequalities, she emphasizes. Indeed, vaccines are understood to injure only in exceptional circumstances and to keep us healthy and working. I argue that robust vaccine safety requires a strong central state with surveillance powers to detect and investigate possible adverse events within de-identified medical records, yet Rachel Dubrofsky and Shoshana Amielle Magnet present the emerging field of feminist surveillance studies as identifying the nearly always oppressive and hierarchy-reinforcing nature of surveillance.[20] Critically, nearly all of the cases of surveillance they analyze as problematic involve "real people being watched, often unknowingly, doing real things."[21] Vaccines, I argue, challenge us to be more nuanced and affirming of the power of the state to produce health and to recognize injury even as we accept the overwhelming scientific consensus that they are safe and effective for the vast majority of people. More privileged people are represented in the medical records being surveilled because they have employer-provided health coverage, for example, and so reducing inequality would mean adding better surveillance for adverse events among people using government programs such as Medicaid or health departments for immunizations, or for people who are uninsured. Vaccines certainly keep us showing up to work, but they also prevent pain and discomfort, remove the need for caregiving labor with high costs, such as the burden on single working mothers with sick children, and shield vulnerable people who cannot be vaccinated themselves, such as those with suppressed immune systems from cancer treatments. Bringing an injury claim before the state legitimizes its often vast and subtle power arrangements, as Wendy Brown has compellingly argued.[22] It matters quite a bit, however, what the forum for the claim is, what kinds of evidentiary mobilizations that forum invites and produces, and the worth of the underlying social order being defended. The case of the vaccine court, in the details of its daily work, should give critical scholars some reason for a bit more optimism.

Mobilization around Autism as Vaccine Injury

Fears that vaccines cause autism have framed the terms in which we have discussed vaccine safety for the past fifteen years, and thus the autism issue necessarily plays a large role in this book. And yet, I am convinced that many of the most interesting challenges of our vaccine safety regime have little do with autism, predated it as a hot topic, and will be with us for many years to come. For instance, how will we manage an ever-crowded childhood vaccine schedule as new vaccines are invented and at the same time as a large subset of parents seem to be at their limit in terms of the number of doctor visits and the number of shots they will tolerate? So while I acknowledge the predominant position of autism in the vaccine debates, I pull the frame of this book back to bring in a wider perspective. Nonetheless, it is hard to overstate the importance of the autism issue in vaccine politics. It has forced advocates to reveal whether they will adapt to new information or double down on conspiracy theories, framed every government intervention and court ruling through the high-stakes suspicion of parents mobilized around autism, and deepened mistrust between government officials and vaccine activists. No scientist can be credible and assert that vaccines cause autism; no vaccine critic has backed down and said they were wrong. Every assertion, every report, every press release is bathed in the harsh, unflattering brightness of clearly drawn sides.

Do we know enough or too much about vaccine injury? Claims on all sides almost always come down to assertions about how much we know about vaccine injury and what policies flow from a correct assessment of the state of knowledge. Autism is very well studied as a possible vaccine injury and wholly rejected in the mainstream, despite critics' attempts to muster alternative accounts and to insist there is still uncertainty, or what Claire Decoteau and Kelly Underman call "non-knowledge" about autism and vaccines.[23] For many adverse events that families and individuals have brought to the vaccine court, there is simply not enough published research about a possible connection and no population-level evidence of a problem, so it is very difficult to determine in a particular case whether the vaccine caused the problem or if it was coincidence. Activists mobilize for more research and emphasize all the studies that could be done but have not been done. Mainstream scientists and regulators, however, are reluctant to fund studies into pathways for vaccine injury that they do not think are biologically plausible and have not set off any official alarms in previous studies or ongoing safety surveillance.

Use of the law played a critical role in the emergence of what we know today as the vaccine-autism controversy. There are many places one could begin, but one critical point is the mid-1990s United Kingdom, where Dr. Andrew Wakefield's research into autism, gut disorders, and the measles component of the MMR was supported by funding from the U.K. Legal Services Commission (LSC; formerly the Legal Aid Board, now the Legal Aid Agency) with the aim of marshaling evidence to bring a suit against pharmaceutical companies.[24] In 1998, Dr. Wakefield and collaborators published a paper in the British medical journal *The Lancet* that presented an uncontrolled study of twelve children with autism and gastrointestinal symptoms, noting that the onset of both was associated with their MMR vaccination.[25] The litigation-driven funding of the research significantly damaged its credibility when it became widely known, but at the start the effort was part of a general commitment by the British government to support claimants who might have a blockbuster case but just needed some support to build it. The Legal Services Commission ceased funding the litigation in 2003 after reviewing about sixty expert reports and concluding the claim was not sufficiently meritorious. The press release announcing the decision to withdraw funding noted that the MMR case was the first in which Legal Aid had funded new research to uncover scientific evidence to bolster a legal claim, and "[i]n retrospect, it was not effective or appropriate for the LSC to fund research." "The Court," the organization said, "is not the place to prove new medical truths."[26] As I describe in Chapter 6, our own vaccine court would go on to be the public trial of vaccines for causing autism after the British case litigation collapsed.

Ten of Wakefield's co-authors distanced themselves from the paper in 2004 after it surfaced that Wakefield had not disclosed that the research was litigation-driven,[27] and in 2010 *The Lancet* formally retracted the paper.[28] The U.K. General Medical Council found in February 2010 that he had committed professional misconduct in his work with the twelve children from the 1998 study (subjecting them to unwarranted interventions to search for the measles virus in their guts and spines, among other things) and subsequently removed him from the registry of physicians licensed to practice. Wakefield has now been widely labeled a fraud in the mainstream,[29] but enjoys pockets of strong devotion from supporters.[30]

There was another path to critical mobilization around autism as a vaccine injury in the United States: mercury in vaccines.[31] A preservative called thimerosal, about half ethyl mercury by weight, had been added to vaccines since the 1930s to prevent harmful bacteria from growing in multidose vials.[32] U.S. mercury activists were initially mobilized by some unfavorable publicity about thimerosal in vaccines, capitalizing on and amplifying uncertainty about its possible effects. The hepatitis B vaccine, the DTaP (diphtheria, tetanus, and acellular pertussis) vaccine, and the Hib (Haemophilus influenzae type b) vaccine contained thimerosal, which could have delivered up to 187.5 µg (micrograms, 1/1,000,000 or a gram or 1/1,000th of a milligram) of ethyl mercury to an infant in the first six months of life (if she received an assortment of vaccines with the highest possible levels, that is; many combinations would have delivered less ethyl mercury).

After complying with a 1997 law requiring the Food and Drug Administration (FDA) to survey mercury additives in products, federal regulators realized in 1999 that an infant could potentially be exposed to more ethyl mercury (as thimerosal) through the recommended vaccine schedule than the Environmental Protection Agency (EPA) limit for methyl mercury, a different type of mercury that is a known environmental contaminant in fish. Methyl mercury was well studied at the time, but ethyl mercury was not, and it did not have its own safety standard. The American Academy of Pediatrics and the U.S. Public Health Service then recommended the removal of thimerosal from vaccines as a precaution.[33] This decision happened very quickly with heated debate about whether it was a reasonable precaution or a rush to judgment that would only arm critics and scare parents.[34] If thimerosal was not harmful, why rush to remove it? The mercury-autism controversy emerged in a context of missteps and uncertainty, and worried parents quickly stepped up to try to fill the knowledge gaps.

The theory that autism is caused by mercury toxicity was first spelled out by lay advocate, mother, and marketing consultant Sallie Bernard and others in a 2001 article called "Autism: A Novel Form of Mercury Poisoning," published in a journal called *Medical Hypotheses*,[35] a venue for publishing "radical, speculative and non-mainstream scientific ideas provided they are coherently expressed."[36] One government expert witness would testify in the Omnibus Autism Proceeding at the vaccine court that Bernard's article was "the only reason all of us are here today" (and go on to dispute its conjectures).[37] Bernard and other mobilized parents founded the group SafeMinds in 2000, which has continued to push links between mercury and autism and has given nearly $1.5 million in research funds to promote the hypothesis.[38] A 2001 Institute of Medicine (IOM) report on thimerosal-containing vaccines held it was "biologically plausible" that thimerosal could be related to autism and that the evidence was inadequate to accept or reject a causal relationship due to insufficient research.[39] By 2002, there were sixty-eight lawsuits pending in sixteen states alleging damage from mercury in vaccines or requesting health monitoring after receipt of a mercury-containing vaccine, eleven of which were putative (uncertified) class actions potentially covering more than 175 million people. As I discuss in Chapter 2, the thimerosal lawsuits posed a significant threat to the ability of the vaccine court to absorb and adjudicate vaccine injury claims. Ultimately, these lawsuits did not progress nationwide because they had to move into the vaccine court and could not be brought as regular civil actions.

A couple of years of uncertainty combined with the energy and resources of the mobilized parents created a powerful second burst of energy for vaccine critics after the 1998 Wakefield paper, though both the MMR and the thimerosal hypothesis would not withstand scrutiny for long. The Bernard paper's allegations that autism is similar to mercury poisoning were quickly debunked in the scientific mainstream.[40] By 2004 enough new studies had been published that an IOM review committee rejected hypotheses connecting either the MMR vaccine or thimerosal in vaccines to autism.[41] A World Health Organization (WHO) vaccine safety committee also monitored the thiomersal (an alternative spelling used in WHO documents) research beginning in 2000, reaffirming in multiple reviews that "there is no evidence of toxicity in infants, children or adults exposed to thiomersal in vaccines."[42] Activists have remained mobilized, but they have not been able to maintain enough credibility behind the thimerosal hypothesis to change policies,[43] and as I explain in Chapter 6, they would go on to lose their court claims. Furthermore, thimerosal's usefulness in keeping vaccines free of harmful pathogens endures, both in the manufacturing process and particularly in a global vaccine program in which use of single vials is not always practical.

Polite Company: A New View of the Vaccine Wars

In October 2010, I attended a reception in Washington, D.C. in honor of the retirement of former vaccine court Chief Special Master Gary Golkiewicz. Special Master Golkiewicz had led the federal no-fault vaccine injury compensation court for twenty years and enjoyed broad rapport with the many different people who argued before him. I was there to observe a conference of vaccine court practitioners, which also drew social movement activists interested in the ongoing Omnibus Autism Proceeding, a set of trials about whether autism would be compensated as a vaccine injury. There were toasts to the former chief from Department of Justice attorneys (who represent the government) and from members of the vaccine petitioners' bar. I recognized prominent activists who had gained national prominence criticizing the vaccine court and its rulings, such as Becky Estepp from Talk About Curing Autism, who was widely quoted a few months before deriding the vaccine court as a place "where government attorneys defend a government program using government-funded science before government judges."[44]

We all stood around together, sharing drinks and hors d'oeuvres, politely chatting and clapping for the retirement occasion. Department of Justice attorneys mingled with petitioners' attorneys, other special masters, Court of Federal Claims judges, the activists, and me. There were perhaps forty people in the room. At another one of the same yearly conferences I attended later, the lead attorney who had just litigated (and lost) the autism claims and the special master who had penned a particularly strong rejection of the case's merits joked about their karaoke duet the night before. After the government advisory meetings I observed, the representatives of parents of vaccine-injured children, the vaccine industry lawyers, the petitioners' lawyers, the pediatricians, and the government administrators of the program would go off to dinner together. Now, my point is not that these polite and even warm gatherings reveal some unseemly entanglements. It is perfectly natural to make the best of being stuck at an event with one's adversaries. Might as well have a drink and join in the toast.

These moments illustrate the ordinary and surprisingly close connections between the people who encounter each other over and over again as they manage and debate our vaccine injury compensation system in the contemporary United States. We hear so much about the "vaccine wars" and the unbridgeable gulfs between mistrusting parents and health officials and doctors. But there is another perspective in which it is not a war at all. To borrow Francesca Polletta's phrase, the vaccine debates at the level of government policy are an endless meeting.[45] Or, better yet, an endless series of sparsely attended, earnest, and sometimes tedious government meetings. If we think of the vaccine debates as a war, it all seems quite exasperating. If we think of them as a meeting or court hearing, they are an example of thoughtful yet adversarial exchange.

I gather together here the public officials, judges, lawyers, and activists who determine what counts as a vaccine injury. My methodological approach centers the institution and their work within it rather than the legal doctrine or even the individual stories behind the cases. This decision sacrifices some humanizing detail and makes this book into a story about how elite professionals decide what is a vaccine injury, which is the critical question for justice and politics and should be important to us all. I have spent the past six years systematically gathering and analyzing the records of their work and their debates with each other. I attended events at the vaccine court (in the U.S. Court of Federal Claims in Washington, D.C.), the advisory committees within the Department of Health and Human Services that oversee the Vaccine Injury Compensation Program (the National Vaccine Advisory Committee and the Advisory Commission on Childhood Vaccines), and a national public conference organized by the National Vaccine Information Center (NVIC), the oldest vaccine-critical organization in the United States whose current leadership helped pass the original legislation that created our vaccine injury compensation and safety system. A more classically legal approach to the vaccine court would prioritize its rules and cases, assuming that the key to understanding how the special masters judge causation can be found in the case law about its causation standard.[46] Instead, I approach the court and its actors more sociologically and politically, investigating how they do their work, what points of contestation have been critical moments for creating knowledge about vaccine injuries, and what policy outcomes their conclusions of justice uphold. This approach goes well beyond a conception of law as a fulcrum that can push public health up or down. Law does not function so simply and thus an account of its role in our immunization social order must begin from a broad interdisciplinary perspective about where law appears and what it does.

Because my focus is on the public wrangling over vaccine injuries, my method prioritizes public testimony, documents, and events over personal interviews. There is a vast documentary record at the vaccine court and on government and activist web sites, and much available through Freedom of Information Act requests.[47] For example, I obtained and analyzed over five thousand pages of hearing transcripts from the autism litigation at the vaccine court and twenty-seven years of meeting minutes from the government advisory committee that oversees the compensation program. There was an office policy against granting on-the-record interviews at the Office of Special Masters, but I was able to speak with some people in the Vaccine Injury Compensation Program off the record. This book is greatly enriched by their perspectives, but I cannot quote from them or identify them here. Leaders in the vaccine-critical movement declined my interview requests, and so I rely on their speeches, publications, blogs, and press conferences instead.[48] I gathered interviews with a few leading petitioners' attorneys and observed a closed meeting of the petitioners' bar association.

Notably, this book does not focus on ordinary parents' views about vaccine injuries. Privacy protections and legal rules prohibited me from reaching out directly to the parents who bring cases to the vaccine court. Luckily, Jennifer Reich's detailed study of Colorado mothers who choose not to vaccinate and Chloe Silverman's account of parents of children with autism in the vaccine court process have provided compelling accounts of these stories.[49] Feminist approaches to science studies have often adopted a methodology that permits a close examination of ordinary people's disease experiences, such as Janet Shim's study of the politics of race and gender in heart disease and Ruha Benjamin's work on patients' and activists' responses to the call for stem cell research, for example.[50] Law and society approaches also highly value the layperson's ideas and experiences with the law, exemplified in works such as Laura Beth Nielsen's study of people's experiences with street harassment and David Engel and Frank Munger's long-term inquiry into the meanings of disability rights law in the life experiences of people with visible and invisible disabilities.[51] My own work on the civil rights consciousness of fat rights activists took such a path as well.[52] By contrast, this project became much more about the vaccine court as an institution and therefore required a more synthetic, higher-up approach to considering the politics of courts.[53] The project evolved away from personal experiences and toward the politics of the vaccine court because of the unique methodological challenges here, but most of all because, in spite of all the attention to vaccines in recent years, the story of the vaccine court itself has yet to be told.

I approach the topic of vaccine injuries, as we all do, from a situated position that both extends and limits my understanding of the question. My mother was a subject in the early polio vaccine trials as a young girl growing up in New York, and she remembers my grandmother crying with joy and relief at the news that the vaccine worked. My father is a family physician, and my siblings and I received our vaccines in his solo practice office, sometimes from him and more often from his nurse colleague whom I have known my whole life. I even volunteered to be in a herpes vaccine clinical trial as a cash-strapped graduate student at the University of Virginia in 1996. Someone I knew had just contracted genital herpes, and I hoped I could be part of securing a vaccine against this really unpleasant experience. As it turns out, an effective herpes vaccine still eludes vaccine developers. My mother tells a sad story from a trip she made in the late 1990s as a nurse midwife to Uganda, where she bought a coffin for a thirteen-year-old girl who had died of measles. Perhaps these family memories about vaccines are unusual; it is probably unusual to volunteer for a vaccine trial, let alone to have two generations of vaccine trial participation, or to know someone who knew someone who died of measles thirty years after U.S. access to the measles vaccine. More than simply giving me a positive posture toward vaccines, my perspective on the research and development reminds me that creating a vaccine is a long and uncertain process and that the benefits of our immunization social order do not extend to people in many poor countries. My accounts and arguments here are admittedly partial and situated, though that does not distinguish them from anyone else's.

Terms and Labels

One challenge in writing about the vaccine controversy is characterizing the people and groups who compose it. I refer to the medical and scientific establishment as the "mainstream," "pro-vaccine," or "immunization supporters." The contentious label is for the other side: anti-vaccine or merely advocates for improved vaccine safety? Scholars generally refer to the people they study by the names the subjects choose for themselves. The argument for avoiding the anti-vaccine label is that in nearly all cases, the people and groups most associated with vaccine criticism insist repeatedly that they are not anti-vaccine. David Kirby, whose 2005 book argued that mercury in vaccines is responsible for the autism epidemic, made a point to say in a 2008 Capital Hill briefing that "I'm certainly not anti-vaccine, and this is not an anti-vaccine briefing."[54] "[P]lease know," he continued, "that if people speak about vaccine safety, about making the vaccine program better, that doesn't make us anti-vaccine." Barbara Loe Fisher of NVIC has repeatedly said she is not anti-vaccine. Her position is that vaccines should be like any other good in an open market, with people free to use them, but not compelled in any way. She refers to herself as a vaccine safety advocate or a consumer watchdog.

The argument for disregarding this self-labeling is that it is disingenuous. On this view, critics cannot openly call for banning or boycotting vaccines because it is not politically feasible to do so and retain much legitimacy, so they claim to be simply concerned about safety (which no one is against). At one point at the NVIC public conference I describe in Chapter 3, NVIC President Barbara Loe Fisher, holding the microphone, reassured the audience she was not anti-vaccine, but this framing was clearly part of image management in the face of a more radical member-ship. A woman's voice could clearly be heard shouting back at her, "*I'm anti-vaccine!*" Red plastic bracelets distributed in every conference reg-istration packet read simply "No vaccine for me." As I will discuss in de-tail in this book, the movement is deeply interdependent with those who are avowedly anti-vaccine and whose commitments are incompatible with any support for vaccines. There is not another wing of the vaccine-critical movement that disputes these avowedly anti-vaccine elements.

Well-known pediatrician, author, vaccine inventor, and immuni-zation advocate Paul Offit points out that Fisher and NVIC have not contributed to efforts to make the vaccines we have any safer (such as the move to the killed-virus polio vaccine, which is incapable of caus-ing vaccine-associated polio).[55] Pro-vaccine advocates in government and mainstream medicine also argue that without levels of vaccination coverage approaching 85 to 90 percent and sometimes higher, vaccine-preventable diseases will return.[56] Vaccine critics clearly mean to con-vince people to resist vaccination by telling them it is unsafe. Content review of websites critical of vaccines has shown that they promote inac-curate information,[57] and one German study found that viewing an anti-vaccine website for only five to ten minutes increased perceptions of vaccine risk and decreased intentions to vaccinate.[58] To call the groups and individuals behind such websites anti-vaccine is thus to associate them with the end result of their policy agenda, which from a public health perspective would be the widespread loss of herd immunity—that is, the loss of the primary goal of immunization programs—and the return of disease.

I agree that the activists I discuss throughout this book are not merely vaccine safety advocates (though some of them occasionally function as such). Though they have been highly mobilized to engage with the vaccine safety system, the basic underpinnings of their beliefs are not compatible with acceptance of mainstream medicine or the legitimacy of government regulation, and so it has been very difficult to construct a well-functioning partnership over safety issues. Federal government of-fices are filled with scientists and bureaucrats whose entire job is vaccine safety, but the activists I discuss here frame them as their adversaries and regularly accuse them of covering up the widespread poisoning of American children. But since activists resist the anti-vaccine label and at the very least do not argue that vaccines should be banned or criminalized, I settle on the more neutral terms "vaccine critics" and "vaccine-critical movement" to describe them.

Another choice to make is whether to use the term "vaccine injury," as many vaccine critics do, or to use the term more common in the public health and medical literature, "vaccine-related adverse event." Vaccine-related adverse events are distinguished from "adverse events after vaccination" by their causal connection. "Related" adverse events mean that there is reason to think the vaccine *caused* the adverse event, but an adverse event that happened *after* a vaccine may be only a coincidence and not causally related. This distinction is critical in mainstream science. The medical terminology has the benefit of this extra precision, but I have elected to call the harms that are claimed to result from vaccines by the term "vaccine injury" even though I embrace the distinction throughout this book between causally proven adverse events and those that seem to be linked but turn out not to be. Indeed, most of this book is about how we as a society figure out the difference between something that *seems* to be vaccine-related and something that *really* is. I prefer to use a term from ordinary language, however, and in addition, the legal claims that are at the core of this book are fundamentally about injuries as understood by the people bringing the cases. The law that created the vaccine court was clearly labeled as the National Childhood Vaccine Injury Act. Vaccine critics argue that vaccines are widely injurious, but I do not believe that is true. Nonetheless, vaccine injuries are what everyone is arguing about.

Science, Social Movements, and American Law

Understanding how the vaccine court does its job informs broader scholarly debates about how well courts handle social problems generally and scientific or medical problems with controversial social aspects specifically. I also approach vaccine critics as leaders of an energetic health social movement whose arguments resonate deeply within many groups in our society, although ultimately I do not accept their arguments. My acceptance of the mainstream evidence about vaccines—that they work, that they carry some risks but severe reactions are rare, and that they should be credited with saving millions of lives and considerable resources—necessarily informs my framing here, particularly its normative bent. Writing about vaccines for me is like writing about climate change or evolution, in which it makes little sense to pretend that the evidence for the mainstream view is anything other than overwhelmingly strong. Mobilization and attention are important for democratic engagement with science and expertise regardless of the merits of the underlying arguments, however. I weave the activists' contributions through the whole story, but I do not spare them my critiques.

I begin with the assumption that law, society, and science are dynamically interconnected rather than separate. Scholars of law and society have long argued that law does not stand separately and over the rest of our lives, but rather creates and is created by our values, politics, imaginations, popular cultural representations, ideological projections, and institutions.[59] Legal controversies over scientific, medical, or technical questions give us the opportunity to see how law and science interact to, as Sheila Jasanoff puts it, "co-produce the social order."[60] This co-production is not only inevitable but, as I will argue, often desirable. Some commentators, however, note these interconnections between law and science only to lament them because they infringe on scientific expertise.[61] As one doctor writing in the *Washington Times* as the autism test cases headed to trial put it, "I find it unsettling that the safety of vaccines must be put on trial before three 'special masters' in a vaccine court. . . . [T]he truth about scientific and medical facts is not, ultimately, something that can be decided either by the whims of judges or the will of the masses," he wrote, noting with disapproval that the "three judges are not experts in medicine or science."[62] Lawyers, on this view, make strategic, one-sided arguments while scientists objectively seek the truth. Law is political, social, and adversarial, while science is disinterested and collaborative.

Assuming a mutually constitutive relationship between science and law, however, points to the social aspects of both while leaving plenty of room for their significant differences. As Jasanoff explains in her classic work on science and courts, *Science at the Bar*, "A core project of science and technology studies has been to display the fluidity of the divisions among the social, material, and natural worlds, showing that much of what we know through science or use as technology is produced and given solidity through socially accredited systems of rhetoric and practice."[63] What we understand as reputable medical opinion about vaccinations emerges through structures such as research laboratories and their teams, competitive funding, peer review, and public presentation of conclusions in language meant to persuade. Credibility, for example, is something that must be built up and maintained, and scientific controversies often put these struggles on display as outsiders compete to establish credibility for their views that challenge the mainstream.[64] We must rely on expert knowledge to guide law and policy, but we cannot simply hand over power to scientific experts, who are also our fellow interested citizens in our democratic society. This is an ongoing puzzle: how to manage expertise in democracy, where it should be both cultivated and controversial.[65] The vaccine court is the focus of both expertise as well as social movement attention (and where precisely the expertise is found is part of the argument), letting us see how they might be fruitfully managed together.

The approach to the connectedness of law, science, and society I employ in this book combines Jasanoff's approach to the knowledge-making projects of law and science with philosopher Elizabeth Anderson's insights about how to evaluate knowledge claims in a democratic society. Jasanoff urges us to take note of the congruence between law and science: both are formal spaces with great power and legitimacy in which people try to discover the truth through entertaining assertions about reality, hold those assertions to standards, test them, and weed out liars and incompetents.[66] They are both "situated and purposive" ways of developing knowledge, but differ significantly as well. "[T]he law," she elaborates, "takes the case as its theater of operation . . . and finds facts in order to settle disputes, whereas science makes claims to extend previous lines of inquiry and enable new ones to take shape."[67] Jasanoff cautions us to keep law's powers to do justice in mind and not simply transcribe scientific conclusions into law. By focusing on a court that has been explicitly tasked with upholding scientific credibility but also with doing justice to particular injured people, I show how the vaccine court crafts a balance beyond transcribing the scientific consensus. Anderson's work on the epistemology of democracy proposes that there are some readily identifiable criteria that ordinary people can employ to see whether we are getting legitimate knowledge out of our social institutions.[68] Are there enough paths for dissenting views to be taken up within the institution—here, the vaccine court—and can ordinary people make reliable second-order assessments about whether their rulings represent a trustworthy consensus? Reflecting on how the vaccine court attempts to satisfy Anderson's criteria helps us understand how it produces science for justice in Jasanoff's terms.

I accept that most often law operates to justify and sustain hierarchies of knowledge and power. Therefore, any sociolegal analysis must include a frank acknowledgment of those hierarchies. As Michael McCann notes, "virtually all scholars agree" that "law often significantly supports prevailing social relations as well as provides limited resources for challenging those relationships."[69] Feminist legal scholars have long pointed out, for example, that abortion as a privacy right means being left alone without resources,[70] and that a police- and prosecution-focused response to domestic violence best assists those who can trust the criminal justice system not to exploit them further.[71] Putting a dispute in legal terms also transforms it, often narrowing it and permitting only a limited view of the harms, rights, duties, and relationships involved.[72] A central challenge for any social order, then, is to maintain compliance and the faith of the citizenry even in the face of legal requirements that put them in the losing position: getting a traffic ticket, losing a civil suit, having one's vaccine injury claim denied, having to pay taxes, and so on. As psychologist and legal scholar Tom Tyler has shown, people will obey a legal decision even if it counters their interests if they feel they were treated fairly in the process and if they feel committed to the legitimacy of the legal authority generally.[73] Vaccine critics continue to argue against the basic legitimacy of the court's rulings against them, but I show how overall the vaccine court has been an important part of the legitimation of the immunization social order.[74]

In spite of the hegemonic power of the law to defend the status quo, social movements can sometimes mobilize litigation and the language of rights to accomplish their goals.[75] This book examines in detail how vaccine critics have worked both to produce and to challenge our immunization social order and the legalization of vaccine injuries. Organized vaccine critics were, after all, a primary mover behind all the vaccine safety law and compensation that we have today in the United States, starting with the NCVIA of 1986. They achieved a dramatic national success that has eluded many other social movements. Vaccine activists managed to break what Shobita Parthasarathy terms the expertise barrier to their participation in elite policy making by reading up on journal articles, introducing new facts about vaccine injury through their claims making, reframing vaccine policy as everything from an infringement on parental rights to an environmental harm, and attacking the vaccine court as illegitimate as it evolved to be more hostile to their claims.[76] Many of these parents became professional activists and continued to work at the state and national levels to organize testimony, elect sympathetic legislators, write and introduce legislation, lobby and fund-raise, produce and sponsor their own research, and operate sophisticated grassroots and social media organizations that continue to influence the vaccine views of millions of parents. They run blogs, produce documentaries, write books and articles, hold press conferences, and purchase billboard advertising in Times Square. Leaders have also been a part of every appointed government advisory committee that has monitored vaccine safety in the contemporary era, where they have had a vote and a voice as well as a chance to monitor and amplify what happens in government for their constituents nationwide.

Throughout the book, I show how vaccine critics have led a sustained health social movement for decades, forcing our laws, institutions, and politics to respond in ways that have ultimately strengthened our immunization social order (much to critics' chagrin). It is often a politically conservative movement (if one looks at the leadership, especially), and although there has been some study of movement conservatives and legal strategies, most scholars have studied social movements from the left of the political spectrum, such as the civil rights and feminist movements.[77] I argue that approaching vaccine critics as a legally focused health social movement helps us to see how libertarianism, individualistic mothering, and attention to personal health have come together ideologically, letting us trace the roots and effects of these ideologies and legal strategies. In a twist on the usual resources story, these are relatively elite biopolitical citizens who want *not* to consume the proffered technoproducts. Their activism, along with the uptake of some of their initial arguments within the U.S. health bureaucracy and courts, has "made rights real" in critical ways that have improved our vaccine safety system and probably would not have occurred otherwise.[78] Vaccine critics have also succeeded in attracting many ordinary people to their views at the same time (and introduced popular social practices such as delaying childhood vaccines on an alternative schedule), but overall immunization rates remain high and the movement has had few political or legal victories in recent years.[79]

Broader Contexts: Anxious Mothering and Feminist Health Activism

Scholars have long realized that controversies over scientific knowledge reveal important fissures in society over fundamentally political questions about access to power or the value of different ways of living or groups of people.[80] These are deep tensions over basic values, and they can only be managed rather than fully resolved. Mark Largent argues that we must understand how parents feel pushed along and overwhelmed by our extensive childhood vaccine schedule and that their concerns must be respected, particularly once we situate those fears in historical context and recognize that sometimes vaccines do cause adverse reactions.[81] Many people mistrust pharmaceutical companies and resent the political advantages and great wealth these corporations enjoy. Vaccine controversies implicate the meanings and duties of motherhood, the power of citizens to control environmental risks they perceive as dangerous,[82] the legitimacy of legal institutions that attempt to remedy these harms, and the trustworthiness of the government regulators and researchers who regulate them. Understanding the wide range of broader contexts to vaccine injury debates will disabuse us of the notion that there is a simple informational correction to parents' concerns, for example.

Contemporary debates about vaccine injuries take place within a much longer history of concerns about vaccines, situated within broader shifts in ideas about health and illness and the status of the mainstream and the alternative health professions. Historians have documented the history of vaccine controversies in the United States and Europe, highlighting how our societies have weighed public health imperatives against the problem of coercing resistant citizens.[83] Many vaccine critics today embrace alternative healing traditions that have a long tension with mainstream professionalized medicine in the United States, and pushing back against the dominance of the germ theory of disease as an account of health has been part of vaccine opposition since its beginning. Rejection of a germ-based account of disease also connects to many larger conversations about health and disease prevention in contemporary American society, in which healthy living, exercise, and high-quality food are widely accepted solutions for chronic health problems. Vaccine critics uniformly maintain that healthy living makes vaccination unnecessary, extending the dominant lifestyle view of health one step over into the realm of infectious disease.

This concept of lifestyle control over one's health merges easily with contemporary understandings of intensive motherhood, individual responsibility, and the middle- and upper-class focus on maximizing the life chances of one's children.[84] Medical anthropologist Sharon Kaufman situates parental concerns within the terrifying freedom and responsibility that parents, mostly mothers, now have for children in a world in which every decision seems fraught but must still be made.[85] Critiquing a "one-size-fits-all" vaccine schedule binds nicely to the idea that health care should be highly individualized and that each child is unique, and perhaps uniquely vulnerable. I situate organized vaccine critics within their often-unseen gender, race, and class politics, guided by these feminist social science perspectives on mothering work and especially by Jennifer Reich's observations that contemporary mothers' vaccine resistance is often enabled by white middle-class privilege and the anxiety of mothering.[86] The desire to maximize children's life chances combines with the responsibility to become one's own expert, do one's own research, and micromanage the family's risks of harm, assisted by patterns of labor force pullback and financial resources. These priorities crowd out the benefits of herd immunity when enough parents with these views cluster together geographically, as they tend to do.[87]

So while one might think that maternalism could promote a sense of duty to protect all children, in this context it is more easily mustered as part of a broader picture of feminized self-care and privatized motherhood. It is easy to see under this ideology how a mom who just goes along with the recommended vaccine schedule looks like she is failing to personalize it, to fully inform herself, and to take control over her family's health. Feminist scholars of the women's health movement have greeted this turn to personal responsibility with careful criticism, and I argue that this concept of privatized motherhood is a linchpin of what I term the health libertarianism that unites the left and the right over vaccine resistance.[88] Health libertarianism often has a champion in mainstream public health discourses on other topics, however, as public health officials instruct us that we should all be making lifestyle changes to avoid cancer, to weigh the right amount, to make sure our children weigh the right amount, and to take responsibility for being healthy and not costing too much.[89]

Vaccines and vaccine mandates contravene nearly every aspect of this very popular health libertarianism and intensive mothering. They are highly technical products used on us by experts and manufactured by powerful global pharmaceutical corporations. They are for everyone, and they work on the children of both supermoms and slacker moms. The fact that vaccines create an immune response in nearly every-one means that they cannot constitute individual health achievement through doing the right things, which I argue is the dominant view of health.[90] There is one recommended schedule for all children, and al-though authorities support some deviations for unusual medical con-ditions, vaccine recommendations are overwhelmingly unitary and communal rather than individual and variable.

The contemporary political and legal context for claims of vaccine injury, therefore, would not be possible without the feminist health ac-tivism of the past fifty years.[91] While vaccine critics are often mater-nalist rather than feminist (that is, invoking motherhood as grounds of legitimacy and knowledge but not criticizing gendered power relations in structural ways), their achievements have been greatly assisted by the success of earlier feminist arguments that, for example, powerful male doctors should not dismiss women's knowledge and observations as ir-rational. The feminist health movement that began in the late 1960s and early 1970s has been enormously influential in shifting social attitudes about who should have power in medical care and in matters of personal health. Feminist health activists were pivotal in producing both much-needed social change as well as theoretical innovation as they showed how the body is political and health is gendered.[92] They offered detailed and much-needed critiques of an overbearing medical profession and a device and drug industry with a record of damaging mistakes.[93] These feminist health activists touted their achievements in "requiring future meetings of the U.S. FDA to be made open to the public and to have consumers as well as industry representatives and scientist/practitioners on the expert panels" and "us[ing] publicity to catch drug companies or device manufacturers in their lies and over-zealous medicalising, as well as to provide critical information to the public."[94] The women's health movement was a knowledge movement that was successful in altering the boundaries of expertise and the power relations in health care.[95] Feminist scholars celebrate it because we think the activists were right on the facts as well as energetic participants in democracy. Vaccine critics have modeled their activism after these successes and benefited from the pathways for participation laid by women's health activists, but they have not been able to make their alternative knowledge claims credible in the same way.

The ways that vaccines and vaccine injury debates are racialized are not quite as obvious as their gendered dimensions but no less important. First, the movement of vaccine critics is overwhelmingly white in both membership and perspective. Practically every activist I have observed (save one, an Asian woman) has been white, and the various constituencies served by the broader movement are also overwhelmingly white (especially the libertarian wing, but also the holistic moms). Either movement leaders are very wealthy themselves or their organizations are supported by a small number of very wealthy donors. Parents of children in the United States who have received no vaccines at all tend to be over thirty (for the mother), white, married, and college-educated, with a household income of more than $75,000 per year (in 2001 dollars, over $100,000 in 2015).[96] Families who have refused at least one vaccine for any reason for a child are also wealthier and more educated than nonrefusing families.[97]

Second, the critics' rhetoric displays an awareness of the power of minority rights language in U.S. society, but they appropriate it to defend the privileges of the white middle and upper classes. This strange obliviousness stands in stark contrast to public health efforts at vaccine promotion, which figure racial and ethnic minority groups as the focus of targeted outreach (but also sanction welfare recipients in some states if they do not fully vaccinate their children). Children who are behind on vaccines tend to have multiple siblings and African American mothers with less than a high school education, without a child-rearing partner, and with incomes below 50 percent of the federal poverty level.[98]

As Reich points out, privileged white nonvaccinating mothers' practices show little regard for the possibility that other children may need the protection of herd immunity, but instead describe how they are able to keep their own children away from disease (such as in day care) and to properly care for them so that vaccines are not necessary.[99]

The people arguing about vaccine injuries are a small and elite group, and this national conversation entirely excludes poor people and non-white communities. On one view, this exclusion is a benefit if one sees the debates through the lens of the debunked, distracting, and wasteful search for an autism-vaccine link because there is no need to draw diverse communities into a debate characterized by misinformation. Another perspective, however, is that debates over vaccine injury are really about evaluating whether our immunization social order is worth upholding. Vaccine coverage for children is one of the few bright spots in an otherwise grim national picture of unequal access to health care by race and class, with no racial or ethnic disparities at all in MMR or polio vaccination rates since 2005, for example.[100] We have achieved this level of equality through a combination of legal pressure, federal funding, and public health outreach to underserved communities,[101] but we do not have the data to know whether poor people or other vulnerable groups experience vaccine reactions at the same rates as the insured population because our safety surveillance systems draw on health care records in managed care organizations to which these groups may not belong. We do not know whether there are racial disparities in vaccine injury claims in the compensation program. The claims database does not track petitioners by race. Even if we understand our immunization social order to have achieved a level of economic and racial justice not seen elsewhere in our society—and I argue that the safety and efficacy of vaccines give us good reasons for seeing it that way—then we must hold back our self-congratulation until we know more about the perspectives of poor people and members of racial and ethnic minority groups within this social order, especially their abilities to be compensated for vaccine injuries when they occur.

This book addresses the immunization social order and the legalization of vaccine injury in the contemporary United States, a country that leads the world in vaccine development and in the reach of its legal mandates. Vaccines are also a global product, however, and as WHO puts it, "vaccine pharmacovigilance is an international responsibility."[102] Vaccine safety debates appear transnationally as well, often intertwined with legacies of colonialism and confronting the wide disparities between the wealthy vaccine-producing countries and the poor countries with worrisome rates of diseases but little money to buy vaccines.[103] Promoting immunization in poor countries has such a high rate of return on investment that it has become a top priority of philanthropist and Microsoft founder Bill Gates. Vaccines in the transnational order emerge as tools of wealthy private individuals and global public-private partnerships that cannot create stable democracies but can immunize large numbers of people. Millions of lives can be saved and improved through these programs, but they also reveal what they cannot touch: the underresourced state of the formerly colonized societies of the global South. A transnational perspective on vaccine injuries would have much to offer, but it is beyond the scope of this book.

The Plan of the Book

In Chapter 1, "How Are Vaccines Political?," I show how to think of vaccines as thoroughly social and political, that is, created through law, regulation, political will, and ideologies as well as through scientific development. This chapter explains how vaccines are approved and recommended, what the current recommended vaccine schedule for children in the United States looks like and how it has changed over time, and the state-level politics of school entry immunization requirements. I also detail the structure of our federal vaccine safety monitoring system, underscoring how federalism and our lack of a comprehensive national health care system create difficulties in detecting vaccine injuries. All these political features are crucial for understanding the struggles at the vaccine court over recognizing vaccine injuries.

Chapter 2, "The Solution of the Vaccine Court," tells the story of the founding and shifts in the vaccine court over time, placing it in a rich context of parental protest against the diphtheria-tetanus-pertussis vaccine in the 1980s and showing how the scientific and legal conflicts that have riven it over time have shaped its responses to vaccine injury claims. In particular, I present the challenge that the potentially massive lawsuits claiming that thimerosal in vaccine caused autism posed and note the court's flexibility over time and its shrewd balancing of science and policy in the face of panic and uncertainty.

Chapter 3, "Health and Rights in the Vaccine-Critical Movement," introduces the leaders, organizations, and underpinning ideologies of the social movement mobilized around the vaccine court. Activists understand fundamental concepts like risk, harm, health, and parental duty in ways that are incompatible with the mainstream, and these divergences in turn help explain why they do not see vaccine court evidence in the same way. They perceive themselves as fighting for individual health freedom at the same time as they muster an aggrieved and vulnerable minority status to protest vaccination and to criticize the vaccine court.

Chapter 4, "Knowing Vaccine Injury through Law," asks how it matters that we have legalized vaccine injury in the ways that we have and describes our institution in detail. I dwell here on the contemporary, ordinary business of the vaccine court, describing the kinds of professionals who work there and how they do their jobs. I focus on what I call the middle-ground cases, in which there is some reputable story of how a vaccine might have caused the injury and no studies accepted as definitive that rule it out, and so the court has adapted a way of compensating these people but without full agreement that vaccines are really the cause. Our vaccine court design is part of a globally shared understanding that some kind of vaccine injury compensation is appropriate, but I explain how ours stands out among the nineteen other systems set up across the industrialized world. Finally, I argue that comparing the vaccine court to other kinds of domestic alternative compensation schemes confirms the status of vaccination requirements as a national call to service in our immunization social order.

Chapter 5, "What Counts as Evidence?," returns to the problem of why activists and scientists cannot see vaccine injuries in the same way even after they have argued over the evidence in courtrooms and meeting rooms for years. I recount the full range of contested evidence the special masters draw upon to decide cases and show how incommensurate the competing views of that evidence often are. This chapter also sets out how activists tried to use the legal process and the vaccine court itself as a way of exposing what they see as conspiracy and misconduct. In turn, government scientists and bureaucrats also mobilized their story of vaccine safety through the vaccine court.

The autism cases are the court's biggest recent challenge, and the story of how the court found that autism is not a vaccine injury is the topic of Chapter 6, "The Autism Showdown." These cases were a showdown because the court had previously compensated for vaccine injuries without much population-level evidence but with a reasonably credible causal story of how they could have happened to individuals, and thus it seemed at the start that the claims could go either way. Instead the vaccine court strongly repudiated a vaccine-autism link in ways that delegitimized vaccine critics, who nonetheless argued that the vaccine court was hopelessly stacked against them.

The concluding chapter, "The Epistemic Politics of the Vaccine Court," offers reflections on what the vaccine court helps us know. Our knowledge is imperfect but perfection cannot be the standard. The vaccine court has helped to uphold an immunization social order in a legalized way that deeply reflects American political and cultural values and strategies for problem solving.

1

How Are Vaccines Political?

Vaccines in an Ecology of Science and Politics

Science and politics are ineluctably intertwined in vaccine policy debates. There has been controversy as long as there have been vaccines.[1] What does it mean to say that vaccines are political? First, what they are depends significantly upon the state and its laws and regulations; second, the nature of this relationship is the subject of contested power relationships between individuals and groups. Vaccines simply would not exist as we know them without law and politics. Like many other technoscientific objects, they could not be developed, tested, marketed, sold, distributed, regulated, and administered into our bodies without the complex networks of investment, research, and regulation available in the modern capitalist state. Vaccination has historically been supported with explicit calls to maintain a healthy fighting force for our national defense.[2] More broadly, getting vaccinated is a form of civic duty or national service to the community and to vulnerable people. Vaccines need the state; the state needs vaccines.

Vaccine politics in the contemporary United States are very specific to our American state and its political organization. The way we maintain our American immunization social order is politically and economically different from how it is done in other similarly modern capitalist European states, for example, and differences in our political and economic policies explain some of that variation. The American state is a federal system with limited national power, particularly over health matters, atop fifty states with their own legal powers. It is a neoliberal capitalist state with a grudging social welfare and national health care infrastructure. National identification cards linked to health information are unthinkable, for instance. American vaccine politics have transnational reverberations, however, and whether needed vaccines will be available in the developing world may depend on economic and regulatory decisions we make here in the United States. Finally, as I argue throughout the rest of the book, the vaccine court itself is a policy-making institution and is political in the ways that courts are often political: engaged as an arm of the state in the allocation of resources, in the legitimation or rejection of grievances, and in processes of social change and social control.

Thus while scientific knowledge plays an important role in vaccine law and politics, it does not simply stand outside it as a resource for getting policy right. This view represents science as a black box with information in it: there is stuff called science in a black box that most of us cannot understand, but the goal is to retrieve what we need from it and transcribe it directly into politics and policy so that we can make the best choice. This "myth of transcription," as Sheila Jasanoff terms it, also undergirds the hope that judges can adopt rules such as the *Daubert* criteria for judging expert testimony that simply validate good science and write it into the law.[3] Under this view of science and politics we would be primarily concerned with increasing the amount and quality of science in the black box (more funding, more science majors), increasing politicians' and laypeople's understanding of what experts tell us, and keeping politics (understood as dirty or irrelevant concerns) from distorting the science (understood as value-free and untainted by power struggles). But this view overly romanticizes science and medicine and does not give enough credit to the legitimacy of our political and social institutions—regulatory bodies, courts, or the media, for example—which must be acknowledged as rightful partners in governance. Taking a politicized view of science, medicine, and technology does not commit me to degrading expertise; rather, it directs attention to the contested social, material, economic, and political decisions that make vaccines what they are.

Vaccines working in our bodies produce political and social realities. When the law both brings about an outcome (approval of a vaccine, for example) and is changed and remade by that outcome (as additional laws are passed to secure the herd immunity created by widespread use), sociolegal scholars say that law and society are *mutually constitutive* of each other.[4] Science and technology studies scholars have a similar term to describe this interaction between science and politics. "Increasingly," as Jasanoff observes, "the realities of human experience emerge as the joint achievements of scientific, technical and social enterprise: science and society, in a word, are *co-produced*, each underwriting the other's existence."[5] Thinking about vaccines as political objects therefore means thinking about their constitutive relationships and their co-production with laws, policies, and social practices.

That vaccines are political as a practical matter is one thing; whether it is good that they are is another question. On one view, vaccines and their safety are medical and scientific questions properly in the realm of experts, and to politicize them is to give them over to ignorant politicians, trouble-making lawyers, and an easily misled public. Many scholars have roundly criticized the tendency of science to become overly politicized or given over to lawyers and incompetent witnesses.[6] As Scott Frickel puts it, when science becomes part of social movement activism, both scientists and activists may think "mixing science and politics amounts to a form of epistemological miscegenation that is best avoided."[7] But on another view, even highly technical questions are quite rightly political because the answers determine the basic social order in which we all live. Vaccines and the herd immunity they confer would not exist without academic research institutions, government grants, corporate pharmaceutical innovation and regulation, intellectual property and patent protections, state public health laws, local government involvement, computer registries and medical records, and systems of distribution and storage and the infrastructure those require. All these things in turn are the products of power struggles and collective decision making within institutions (that is, politics). Put another way, we can say vaccines are political because ridding our society of diseases is a common benefit secured by individual acts (vaccination), the force of law (state mandates), public investment (federal regulations and spending at all levels), and interlocked information systems (pharmacovigilance and surveillance). Making sure these individual acts take place regularly and on a massive scale is a significant feat of governmental power that requires a blend of democratic legitimacy and scientific expertise.

Understandably, we want more scientific research, firmer knowledge, and uncorrupted evidence to use in policy making. These concerns will remain central to relations between science and politics. But if we understand science as also itself social and political, then we will see the context of vaccine politics quite differently. There is no black box of science; instead, there are numerous communities of expertise contributing to the politics of vaccination. Government and the state are involved at all stages, and individuals normally outside science such as parents and advocates also offer observations and forms of expertise that are different but also important. A better way to conceptualize the politics of vaccines is as an ecology of science and politics: a lush and tangled garden with many sources of growth and stunting that can yield both weeds and flowers (and which is which will also depend on one's perspective). Understanding science and politics as properly entangled rather than as regrettably distorting each other will make our study of childhood vaccination richer and more complex. In this chapter I explain a few key ways that vaccines are political creations as well as medical and technical objects.

For example, federalism in the United States means that the states and the federal government share public health powers, and in the case of vaccines, federalism often promotes confusion and ignorance, muddled incompatibility in systems of information gathering and sharing, and policy variation. We lack a national database of every person that could link vaccines received with health outcomes, for example. By contrast, in Denmark every person living in the country (not just every citizen, but every resident) has an identification number and a national medical record, so it is much easier to conduct a statistical analysis of hundreds of thousands of children to see if any associations emerge between vaccines and certain conditions. In the United States, a national identification card or number has always been a political nonstarter because of concerns about too much federal power and monitoring of individuals.

When states build immunization registries, they do not have to coordinate with other state health departments on what kind of information system they use and the systems may be incompatible across states or vary widely in how complete they are. National single-payer, government-run health care has also been politically untenable in the United States. The fact that we have a health care system rooted in private insurance coverage and a bricolage of public and private health care delivery sites means that vaccine records are often the property of private companies. In addition, American pharmaceutical companies dominate the world market for vaccines and other drugs (followed closely by European companies), and two-thirds of the world's vaccines were developed in the United States (although production now commonly happens abroad). About 90 percent of the world's market share of vaccines comes from GlaxoSmithKline (United Kingdom), Merck, Novartis, Pfizer (United States), and Sanofi (France). The Serum Institute of India now makes the largest share of measles, rubella, and DTP vaccines, and their products are used in 140 nations. China is the world's largest manufacturer, mostly for its own annual birth cohort of about seventeen million babies. The Brazilian vaccine industry is also growing and will soon fulfill its own domestic needs.[8] Vaccines have flourished in the prosperous U.S. economic system with its heavy support for basic research in our excellent universities, a base of investors and large corporations, and strong patent laws that protect intellectual property in new vaccines. But our federal system and distaste for national unification of health systems mean that federal oversight of such a robust industry is not as well organized as it could be.

Left and Right in the Vaccine Debates

It might seem like I am leading up to a political story of how Republicans support the big business of vaccines while Democrats want more regulation that could slow the development of new vaccines. But then the public health system, particularly gaining access for all people, has traditionally been a focus of the Democratic Party, while the libertarian wing of the Republican Party would resist nationalization, tracking registries, and coercion to vaccination. From that perspective, Democrats would be expected to support strong immunization policies such as school entry mandates while Republicans would favor voluntary participation only. Indeed, President Obama publicly supported vaccination in the middle of a measles outbreak, while prominent Republicans such as Chris Christie and Rand Paul issued statements supporting vaccine choice (the favored term for repudiating immunization mandates). It turns out that vaccines are ideologically cross-cutting, however, and vaccine policies attract supporters and detractors from both parties in shifting coalitions. Moreover, Yale law professor and psychologist Dan Kahan's empirical research into ordinary Americans' attitudes toward vaccines shows that a supermajority of adults support childhood vaccination and that those who oppose it are outliers and do not cohere along other recognizable cleavages such as religiosity or denial of human-driven global warming.[9] Large majorities across all demographic groups see vaccines as high-benefit and low-risk, that is, and no political ideology predicts one's views about vaccines.

While there is no neat political division between those who doubt vaccines and those who support them, it is nonetheless true that there are highly mobilized subgroups with very clear ideas about health, healing, and the role of the state, and that they are opposed to our current vaccination practices. Leaders and activists are also very different from the ordinary people who fill out large polls about vaccine trust. Antivaccine activism often comes from libertarians (doctors opposed to federal intervention in the practice of medicine, for example), alternative health adherents (such as homeopaths and chiropractors as well as so-called holistic moms), supplement and herbal remedy manufacturers, and some religious groups (such as Christian Scientists). These are the types of people who would compose Kahan's outliers and who would likely answer a survey saying they oppose current childhood vaccine policy or do not think vaccines offer a benefit worth the risks. I have termed this group "health libertarians" because ideas about health offer an overarching structure to unify their mistrust of government and support their conviction that individual free choices are the primary way to properly pursue health.[10] This term better fits the right-leaning members of this group since libertarians generally support corporate freedom (particularly supplement and herbal manufacturers' freedom from regulation of the purity and efficacy of their products). The left-leaning health libertarians mistrust pharmaceutical companies, Big Food, and other business interests that they regard as unhealthy, but they share the notion that individual responsibility and choice—avoiding toxins, going organic, refusing vaccines—is the best way to maintain health.

Recent outbreaks in religious communities are related not to explicit theological rules, but rather to secular doubts about vaccines flourishing within a close-knit community with global movement of its members. The fundamentalist megachurch in Texas that was the locus of a measles outbreak in 2013 is an interesting example, in which religious practices such as mission trips combine with secular vaccine doubts about autism and "too many, too soon" to result in a pocket of unvaccinated children who contracted measles. Measles cases in the United States originate from foreign travel, and Christian religious missions (such as the one to

Indonesia in the Texas church case) are often to places where measles is endemic.[11] A Brooklyn measles outbreak in 2013 among orthodox Jews was traced to a deliberately unvaccinated adolescent returning from Great Britain into an extended family with objections to the measles-mumps-rubella (MMR) vaccine.[12] Most orthodox Jews in the community were vaccinated, however, which helped to limit the outbreak. Similarly, a 2011 measles outbreak in Minnesota was traceable to an American-born toddler of Somali descent who had contracted the virus on a trip to Kenya and returned to spread measles within that community, where uptake of the MMR vaccine had dropped dramatically because of fears that it causes autism.[13] Disease outbreaks in wealthy California enclaves tend to get the most media attention, likely because of the prominence of Hollywood stars like Jenny McCarthy in promoting vaccine fears as well as the ways these communities stand in for white liberal privilege and self-centeredness. Measles outbreaks highlight the existence of undervaccinated populations as long as there is a conduit into the community from a place where measles is more common, however, and expensive leisure travel has not been the most frequent route of exposure; rather, the origins have been from within these communities' global religious and ethnic ties as well as from Disneyland (mingling international guests as well as unvaccinated people).

So is there no political organization to vaccine criticism, or are there identifiable political ideologies driving it? Both of these observations can be true if we consider the researchers' differing perspective. A scholar looking at the results of a properly designed public opinion survey will not see significant political patterns in responses to questions about vaccines. A scholar studying the arguments of organized political movements, however, will see both forms of argument as well as material support coming from both the ideological right and the left, but with a predominance of support for anti-vaccine positions coming from the place where libertarian lifestyle and health politics unite Democrats, Republicans, and independents.

The Unique Political Features of Vaccines

Vaccines are unique as medical and technological interventions. They are administered to healthy people to prevent disease, not as a treatment that a sick person receives for illness. Certain new kinds of therapeutic vaccines are being studied in the hopes that they can muster a person's own immune system to fight cancer cells,[14] for example, but the focus in this book is on the widely used and approved preventative vaccines for diseases like measles and meningitis. Administration to healthy people makes safety even more important and risks more salient than in the case of a treatment for a person whose pain level or quality and duration of life were already impaired by disease. Vaccines vary in their properties such as how long immunity lasts, but there are some common features that make them politically and socially significant.

The first significant feature of vaccines is obvious but critical in the contemporary U.S. context: we vaccinate very young infants and children, and legal mandates to vaccinate focus almost entirely on this special population. Vaccine recommendations begin with the birth dose of hepatitis B vaccine, though public school entry is often the first legal pressure point. There are no other pharmaceutical products whose use is mandated by law. Bike helmets and car seats are distant analogies, but no other product or drug approaches vaccines in their promotion through legal coercion. Because infectious disease can be controlled only if a very large percentage of people in the population are vaccinated (termed "herd immunity" or "community immunity") and because babies are often most vulnerable to those diseases, pediatricians and public health officials aim at maximum vaccine coverage at the earliest age at which a vaccine is effective.[15]

We vaccinate young children to protect them from the diseases, but also because they are a population that receives a lot of regular medical care in the early years of life, and thus are an easily reachable population from which to begin to wipe out disease burdens that impact other groups. So for example, while hepatitis B can be transmitted to newborns through mothers' bodily fluids, most infections and the chronic liver disease they can cause occur in a hard-to-reach adult population through sex or IV drug use. The hepatitis B vaccine was available in 1982, but public health officials found it difficult to target the adult at-risk population for immunization. After it was added to the routine childhood schedule in 1991, however, new infections have dropped approximately 82 percent.[16] So not only are vaccines legally mandated for children's protection, but the benefits of vaccination are explicitly for the broader society, even other harder-to-reach groups.

A second significant feature is that vaccination programs have two major phases: an initial phase in which a common disease may be wiped out or reduced dramatically by the introduction of a vaccine, and then a maintenance phase in which vaccination continues to prevent the disease from coming back but the disease itself is quite rare. This second state, which we are in and have been in for decades for many once-common diseases, requires vaccination as everyday citizenship to maintain our immunization social order. Unless the disease can be totally eradicated (and smallpox is the only example), this maintenance phase goes on indefinitely. Memories of the diseases quickly fade, but parents must continue to vaccinate their children against them. Fear of adverse reactions becomes much more salient than fear of the disease, and unvaccinated children are protected by the high levels of herd immunity all around them. Mobilizing political and legal backing for a vaccination program in the middle of an outbreak is much easier than the long slog of maintaining vaccination rates without much disease threat (though history teaches us that there has always been vaccine resistance even during outbreaks). Vaccination as everyday citizenship requires high levels of government credibility as well as legal responsiveness to adverse events and ordinary citizen buy-in to the idea of the community as a bulwark against the return of disease. As I will discuss in detail throughout this book, all these elements are contested in contemporary American society, but overall we have created a fairly stable social order that has withstood attacks on its legitimacy.

A third observation about the politicized nature of vaccination in the contemporary United States is that thirteen to eighteen vaccines (depending on how one counts, as I explain below) are bundled together in a recommended immunization schedule for children rather than differentiated by, say, how dangerous the disease prevented is, how likely one is to contract it, or how comparatively efficacious the vaccine is. Sometimes the argument for the benefit of a vaccine is that parents do not need to stay home from work for a child with chickenpox anymore, while other diseases such as polio are much more frightening (even though there has not been a case of wild-virus polio in the United States since 1979). In other words, vaccination as everyday citizenship asks us to squish vaccines together in one conceptual category rather than to differentiate or contest them, even though they have different properties, were invented and added to recommendations and laws separately, and have different cultural meanings.[17] The aggregation into a schedule consolidates compliance, but because the schedule is fairly crowded and complex, makes it relatively easy to violate it by asking for an exemption from even one of its requirements. Surveys estimate that fewer than 1 percent of American children receive no vaccines at all; noncompliance is much more likely to be delay in completing the schedule or opting out of a subset of vaccines.[18]

If scientists were able to develop a vaccine that everyone could receive only once to protect against all diseases, then getting vaccinated would be a very different experience. But because of the current state of the science of childhood immunization, vaccines require repeated acts of citizenship that promise significant protections for self and society but also provoke anxiety and pain. No vaccine is wholly risk-free, and some previously healthy recipients suffer a painful or even damaging adverse reaction. Both parents and babies perform these acts of citizenship in the case of mandated childhood immunizations, but they secure the communal benefit only if enough other parents and babies are doing it, too. From an individual's perspective it might seem best to avoid vaccines while everyone else gets them, but if enough people see it that way, vaccine-preventable diseases come back. This calculation is a source of conflict between individual vaccine resisters and the state, and how much pressure to exert on parents who wish to opt out of vaccination is a political decision made by state legislatures and health department officials.

There are other unique features of vaccines that shape political debates about them. Vaccines work well in vast numbers of people with only a brief intervention. These remarkable features also make them fleeting, depersonalized, and easy to decouple from broader structural factors that influence a person or a community's health. Both critics and supporters invoke these qualities and spin them differently. These features have been part of their high status, as in the vanquishing of polio in what we now think of as the high point of American medicine's prestige, but can also make them seem like a lazy alternative to reducing poverty, promoting health infrastructures in poor nations, cleaning up waste, and providing clean water and adequate nutrition. Making sure every woman gets proper cervical cancer screenings and treatment would prevent cancer deaths from the human papillomavirus (HPV), for instance, though it is easier if the HPV vaccine can simply prevent it from starting in the first place. It is much easier to run a vaccination program in a poor area for a few months and then depart without helping build long-lasting health care infrastructures than to build those infrastructures. In this framing, widespread use of vaccines can be portrayed as an acknowledgment that these social provisions of health care are unrealistically difficult.

Vaccine Approval and Recommendation

Vaccines are biological products manufactured by multinational pharmaceutical companies and regulated at the FDA by the Center for Biologics Evaluation and Research.[19] Vaccines go through the same approval steps at the FDA as other drugs and devices. Before the approval process begins, a vaccine has been studied in smaller biotech companies, larger pharmaceutical companies, or academic centers for several years. Much of this basic scientific research is supported with federal funds (when done by government scientists or professors with federal research grants) or, in the case of biotech firms, with private venture capital funding. Once a vaccine looks promising, smaller companies or academic researchers sell their intellectual property in the vaccine to a bigger company capable of managing the extensive and costly route to approval and marketing.

To begin the FDA approval process, a company submits an Investigational New Drug application explaining what the vaccine is and how it is manufactured, along with any information about its safety and efficacy from animal studies already completed. The second step is clinical trials in humans, beginning with a few dozen people to see if the vaccine produces an adequate immune response and to detect any safety problems and expanding to include thousands of people to hone the right dosage and to monitor adverse reactions.[20] Testing proceeds in three phases: Phase I trials test immunogenicity and safety in a small number of people, perhaps only a few dozen; Phase II trials explore the dose range needed to get the right immune response and continue safety monitoring in hundreds of people; and Phase III trials enroll thousands of people to finalize evidence of efficacy and to show more safety evidence. A prelicensure Phase III trial with thirty thousand subjects (those given the vaccine) and thirty thousand controls (given a placebo and watched and compared to the treated subjects) will detect adverse reactions that happen to one in ten thousand vaccinated people.[21] That is, the adverse event will be able to be causally connected because it will be mathematically possible to see that having had the vaccine meaningfully increased the risk of the adverse event's happening in the vaccinated group as compared to the unvaccinated control group. An adverse event rate of one in ten thousand would be considered problematic, and if the event were serious the vaccine would not be marketable. Serious adverse events are those that require hospitalization or result in lasting impairment or death. Mild reactions such as soreness at the injection site would be considered tolerable at that rate.

Each vaccine package insert describes all the phases of testing in detail, including the exact numbers of people included in each studied cohort. If the vaccine works well (meaning it provokes a sufficient immune response in nearly everyone who receives it) and does not induce worrisome reactions, the company makes a Biologics License Application to an interdisciplinary team of FDA reviewers, who examine all the study results so far to see if the vaccine is worth approving and licensing under a risk/benefit calculation. Inspectors also visit the manufacturing site at this point. The twelve-member Vaccines and Related Biological Products Advisory Committee, housed in the FDA but composed of academic experts in relevant fields from institutions around the country as well as a consumer representative and an industry representative, also evaluates and votes on recommendations for the new vaccine. Once a vaccine is licensed and approved, it is available for use just like any other drug or device.[22]

The bigger the clinical trial, the finer the ability to detect ever-rarer adverse events. But if an adverse event is very rare, it is not feasible to hold a clinical trial with enough human subjects to detect statistical likelihood that the vaccine caused the adverse event. This means that all vaccines will be approved and mandated even though some yet-undetected rare adverse event could exist. We could spend many years and many millions of dollars enlarging clinical trials to look more closely before approving vaccines. There is a trade-off between spending resources this way (as opposed to all the other ways research dollars could be invested

to promote health and cure disease) as well as the cost of delay in bringing the vaccine to market. Children will continue to get the disease while
the vaccine is being held back for more testing, and their parents will
want to know why it was not brought to market sooner. The current approach balances the need to test vaccines enough to rule out intolerable
risks with the need to distribute vaccines that appear safe after the FDA
approval process and thus prevent the targeted disease.

Vaccine supporters acknowledge that there will still be some risks to
vaccines: widely known and small risks that are fairly likely to happen,
such as a sore arm, and the tiny possibility of some greater risks. Adverse
events that appear in early trials are flagged as possibilities for genuine
causally linked adverse reactions (and listed on the package insert), but
the official pose toward these events is curious neutrality, not knowledge. Vaccine critics do not generally argue for bigger clinical trials before licensure to detect rarer events, however. That critique would be
well within the normal conversation that federal regulators and health
bureaucrats have about all candidate vaccines. Critics' arguments that
vaccines are unsafe usually rest on much broader claims that vaccines
cause a whole host of common problems such as asthma, ADHD, what
they call immune dysfunction, and allergies, for example. The debate is
over whether they are plausibly related to vaccines at all. Critics argue
that if vaccines trigger a wide range of chronic health problems in children, the model of detection—the prelicensure clinical study that goes
on for a few months, no matter how big—will fail to detect them if they
emerge a few years later.

For a newly licensed and approved vaccine to become part of broad
public health recommendations for children, it must go through review
at the Advisory Committee on Immunization Practices (ACIP) at the
Centers for Disease Control and Prevention (CDC). ACIP is fifteen-
member body composed of professional health experts and a consumer
representative that meets three times a year to vote on recommended
vaccine schedules for adults, children, and international travelers. ACIP
members and their immediate family members cannot work for vaccine
manufacturers or serve on their board of directors, and they cannot hold
a patent on a vaccine or a related product.[23] The committee uses a decision guide introduced in 2010 called Grading of Recommendations, Assessment, Development and Evaluation, which directs them to specific

factors—the balance of benefits and harms, the type of evidence available, the values and preferences of the people affected, and economic analyses—and presents them in evidence tables.[24] The most important factors are the burden of disease—how many infections and how serious they are—and the proposed vaccine's efficacy and safety. There is no particular dollar amount that defines when a vaccine is too expensive to be worth broadly recommending, but it is part of the calculation. Now ACIP also considers the problem of a crowded vaccine schedule and the risk that parents may opt out even more if new vaccines are added.

ACIP also votes to make vaccines eligible for federal funding under the Vaccines for Children (VFC) program, which provides immunizations for free to low-income children (under nineteen) whose health insurance does not cover them and to Native American and Alaskan native children.[25] The federal government buys 55 percent of childhood vaccine doses to supply to state health departments and private physicians.[26] The VFC program was a response to the 1989 to 1991 measles outbreaks, and grew dramatically from its start in 1993 under President Clinton as six vaccines were approved and added to the children's schedule (1991: hepatitis B; 1996: varicella or chickenpox; 1998: rotavirus; 2001: pneumococcal; 2002: flu, added as a broadening of the adult recommendation; 2006: hepatitis A). After the passage of the Affordable Care Act, more families will have insurance that includes vaccines for no charge as preventive care, but the VFC program will still provide vaccines to any children who are still not fully covered.

From an industry perspective, it is of course crucial to get FDA licensing and approval for a vaccine that has likely spent years in development, but to secure an ACIP recommendation and a place on the CDC children's vaccine schedule means that the vaccine will likely be mandated for use in the states as well as supplied through the VFC. Vaccines are not as profitable as many other pharmaceutical products, but a company can count on very steady sales once its vaccine has been FDA approved, ACIP recommended, and mandated by the states as a prerequisite to attend public schools. Initial research, development, and factory building can cost millions or even a billion dollars, but it is hard for other companies to develop a later competing vaccine, and demand is always replenished with a new birth cohort. Merck's MMR vaccine, for instance, has no U.S. competitor and has been in use for decades.[27]

It is possible that if ACIP were to decline to add a new vaccine to the schedule, it could be FDA approved but not widely available since it might not be worth manufacturing from the company's perspective. For example, GlaxoSmithKline stopped making its Lyme disease vaccine in 2002 after a fairly limited 1999 ACIP recommendation that did not include administration to children under age fifteen, even though five- to nine-year-olds are at the highest risk of contracting Lyme disease from tick bites.[28] We already have the vaccines that were the easiest to develop and that prevent the most common diseases. Industry has been working for decades on other vaccines that would command a large market share, such as a herpes vaccine, but without success. Therapeutic vaccines to treat cancers are considered promising, but they would not be part of the preventative recommendations for healthy people.

For now, ACIP routinely recommends FDA-approved vaccines to be added to the vaccine schedule. As new vaccines target ever-rarer diseases, however, we may reach the point where ACIP stops recommending even FDA-approved vaccines because the benefits at a population level get too small and the costs too high. Even with FDA approval, a vaccine may not be worth manufacturing from the company's perspective if it is not part of the required schedule. ACIP has failed to recommend an FDA-approved vaccine only once, and it was because of these concerns about cost relative to the number of infections the vaccine would prevent if given to every child. The FDA approved the meningococcal conjugate vaccine, or MCV4, for use in babies starting at nine months of age to prevent meningitis, but it is part of the routine vaccine schedule for children only starting at age eleven or twelve. Meningitis is a rare but very serious disease that can kill or disable previously healthy young people in a matter of days. We often hear about it when a college student dies from it, and indeed, since 2005 ACIP has recommended that all first-year college students living in residence halls receive a meningitis vaccine.[29]

ACIP chose not to add MCV4 to the schedule for infants quite deliberately in 2012, however, because the burden of cases is very small and the vaccine would not prevent a significant share of them because it does not protect against all versions of the meningitis bacteria.[30] There are six different serogroups of the meningitis bacteria that cause the disease in humans and no vaccine that protects against all of them. Serogroups C and Y cause most of the disease in the United States, but serogroup B also causes disease and was not included in any U.S.-licensed vaccines until 2014 (now there are two FDA-approved serogroup B meningococcal vaccines).[31] As Dr. Amanda Cohn, the CDC's pediatric meningitis expert, explained at a community engagement event in Chicago I attended prior to the ACIP vote, out of about twenty million children in the United States under age five, there would be about two hundred fifty cases of meningococcal disease, seventy-five of which could be prevented if the twenty million children received MCV4. Thirty-five of those infected would survive with disabilities, and twelve of those would be preventable with MCV4. Thirty children would likely die of the infection, and ten of those deaths could be prevented with the vaccine. MCV4 presented several different reasons not to extend the recommendation to infants because it is both expensive (per life saved, easily over $13 million), would not prevent a large share of infections, and would add another shot to the schedule that is already under pressure from parents for being too crowded.

Meningitis Angels, a nonprofit organized around bacterial meningitis awareness and promotion of the meningococcal vaccines founded by Frankie Milley after the death of her eighteen-year-old son Ryan from meningitis, criticized the federal government for not recommending the meningitis vaccines widely enough. As Milley wrote on the Angels blog, "As I sat through the October 23 CDC/ACIP hearings and listened to the committee discuss and vote to only recommend the life saving vaccine for use in high risk infants, my heart along with other parents broke. What determines high risk, we all had to ask ourselves? None of us had what was deemed high risk children, yet we all suffer. I sat there and in my mind, in my heart, I watch my only child Ryan die a grueling death all over again." Addressing the cost-benefit calculation, she writes, "We have to be that voice of science, reason, care, love, and most of all protection of healthy life. One child, my child, your child lost, is one too many. We must protect our ALL our children from deadly vaccine preventable disease. It is NOT cost effective to let even one child suffer or die from a preventable disease."[32]

Although they are on opposite sides of the vaccine issue, the parent-founded organizations National Vaccine Information Center (NVIC) and Meningitis Angels have a few prominent features in common. They both use the language of mothers' grief and loss to personalize vaccine experiences, featuring stories and photos of children in their organizing. They also both amplify the horrors of disability as the cost of inaction—for the vaccine critics at NVIC, promoting the burdens of children's conditions such as autism, and for Meningitis Angels, highlighting the disfigurement and amputations that child meningitis survivors often have. Both organizations present the loss of the once-perfect child as the cost of the wrong vaccine policy.

The Current Childhood Vaccine Schedule in the United States

Describing the current recommended childhood vaccine schedule in the United States is rhetorically contested, with vaccine critics preferring to count in ways that add up to the biggest numbers of jabs to emphasize its excessive reach and public health promoters preferring to emphasize the diseases that the vaccines prevent. For example, NVIC's promotional documents ask incredulously, "49 doses of 14 vaccines before age 6? 69 doses of 16 vaccines by age 18?"[33] One can come up with quite different numbers by expanding or contracting the age (count children only up to age five, when they have to show a vaccine record for school, or up to eighteen, the official end of childhood) or by including the flu vaccine each year. Combination vaccines cover multiple diseases in one jab, but nearly all require two to five doses to obtain the desired immune response. Most vaccines are administered with a needle injection, though the flu vaccine comes in a nasal spray and the rotavirus vaccine given to infants is a clear liquid delivered in drops to the mouth. Different vaccines also have very different properties as well as different cultural scripts that go with them and different levels of public awareness and name recognition. Some diseases like polio loom large in the public imagination, while others such as Hib disease have had little popular prominence.

A child who gets every recommended vaccine through age eighteen would get thirteen vaccines in fifty-two doses to prevent sixteen diseases: hepatitis B (HepB, three doses), rotavirus (RV, two or three doses depending on the formulation); diphtheria, tetanus, and acellular pertussis (DTaP, for children under seven, five doses); tetanus, diphtheria, and acellular pertussis (Tdap, the booster for children over seven and adults, one dose); Haemophilus influenzae type b (Hib, two or three doses depending on the formulation); pneumococcal conjugate (PCV13, four doses); inactivated poliovirus (IPV, four doses); influenza (one or two doses); measles-mumps-rubella (MMR, two doses); varicella (VAR, two doses); hepatitis A (HepA, two doses); human papillomavirus (HPV2 for girls only; HPV4 for both girls and boys, both three doses); and meningococcal (one dose in the tween years plus a booster before college).[34] For the overall dose total, I counted the flu vaccine eighteen times since there is a new formulation each year, typically a single-dose administration (without the flu, there would be thirty-five doses). It is not uncommon to get four or five shots in one visit, and it would take about nine pediatrician visits to complete the schedule for a child up to age five.

Though we have stopped using a few vaccines or certain formulations, the trend has been overwhelmingly toward multiplicity and increasing complexity in vaccine recommendations. Edward Jenner developed his smallpox arm-to-arm inoculation method in 1796, and by 1971 the modern smallpox vaccine was no longer generally recommended because of near-total (now total) elimination of the virus from the globe.[35] Diseases caused by viruses that have no nonhuman host and for which a vaccine is available that confers lifelong or near-lifelong protection are considered candidates for global eradication; so far smallpox is the only victory. Measles would be a potential candidate, though it is still endemic around the world. Polio is currently the subject of a Bill & Melinda Gates Foundation–funded global eradication effort that has been thwarted by murder, poverty, terrorism, mistrust, conspiracy theories, and war.[36]

The next round of vaccines developed—against pertussis in 1914, diphtheria in 1926, and tetanus in 1938—were combined in 1948 as the DTP (diphtheria-tetanus-whole-cell pertussis) vaccine. At perhaps the most triumphal moment in the golden age of medicine in the United States, the Salk polio vaccine was licensed in 1955. The measles vaccine dates to 1963, and in 1971 new vaccines against mumps and rubella were combined with it to create today's MMR vaccine. The hepatitis B vaccine was available in 1982 but not added to the children's immunization schedule until 1991 after a disappointing campaign to vaccinate high-risk adults such as IV drug users. The Hib vaccine was licensed in 1985 and added to the schedule in 1989. The FDA licensed a new diphtheria-tetanus-pertussis vaccine known as DTaP in 1991 and by 1997 it had replaced all the doses of the older DTP vaccine. (The lowercase "a" stands for "acellular," meaning there are only parts of the pertussis bacteria rather than the whole cell.) The chickenpox, or varicella, vaccine came in 1996, followed by the rotavirus vaccine in 1998 (which was removed within a year and replaced with new versions in 2006 and 2008), hepatitis A in 2000, and pneumococcal in 2001. In 2000, we switched to an inactivated polio vaccine (IPV) from the oral polio vaccine (OPV) to eliminate the risk of getting polio from the vaccine. In 2002, the recommendation to receive the flu vaccine was also extended to children.

The vaccine schedule has thus changed considerably over the years.[37] A parent today who was born in 1983, for example, would compare the current schedule to her experience of getting only the MMR, DTP, and polio vaccines. The polio vaccine was oral, not a shot, and the others were combined so that there were only five shots over two years and not more than one per visit. Moreover, practically everyone contracted chickenpox as an ordinary episode of childhood (except for those few who experienced a more severe form, carried lasting scars, or even died). It is not hard to see how the vaccine critics' slogan "too many, too soon" would be salient to the cohort of today's parents encountering what would look like a large number of shots for their children that they did not receive themselves.

Vaccine Mandates and Exemptions in the States

State legislatures are a critical location for policy contestation over vaccines, as vaccine mandates are matters of state law.[38] Legislatures can directly set vaccine policy, grant discretion to the state public health department to do so, or both. All U.S. states require a set of immunizations before admission to public schools (and in some states, to day care), and these mandates may include all ACIP-recommended vaccines, or there may be lags or gaps in what a state has mandated and what ACIP recommends. States may grant exemptions from mandated vaccines for medical, religious, or philosophical reasons, and in many states the policy is really more of an easy opt-out request than a true mandate with real consequences. In eighteen states, philosophical or personal belief exemptions to childhood vaccine requirements for school or day care entry permit parents to opt out of immunizations without claiming a religious reason or a medical contraindication for nonvaccination.[39] Most parents seek an exemption due to vaccine safety concerns, making the philosophical exemption the best-fitting justification. Christian Scientists may claim the religious exemption to vaccination, but none of the major religious groups in the United States have a doctrinal ban on vaccination.[40] When exemptions are easy to obtain (just signing a form), parental opting out increases and occurs more than in states that either have no philosophical exemption or have some informational or administrative requirements making exemptions somewhat more difficult to secure.[41]

Some states have facially ambiguous statutory language about what their exemptions are and who can use them, and because each state's legal regime is shared among the legislature, health administrators, and courts, it may not be obvious from the statutes alone how exemptions actually work in practice. For example, a state may not explicitly list a religious exemption, but religious belief can be considered a subset of its personal belief exemption. Adding to the complexity, a state can have a religious exemption and no philosophical exemption, but administrators or judges can order that there be no interrogation of the basis behind religious exemptions so that they function as de facto philosophical exemptions. The questions in these disputes are whether a state must accommodate religion by permitting a religious exemption under the free exercise clause of the First Amendment, how stringently the state may define what qualifies as religious belief or membership, and whether the differential treatment of religious people as opposed to anyone else seeking an exemption is permissible. Lawsuits by parents have tested religious exemptions in many jurisdictions, generating different court opinions on whether the state can require a certain level of demonstrated sincerity of religious belief or membership in a recognized religious order. New York courts and federal courts applying New York law have permitted inquiry into sincerity and religious membership, holding that scientific doubts about vaccines,[42] chiropractic ethical objections,[43] and fears that vaccines cause autism[44] do not count as valid reasons for invoking the religious exemption; however, litigation in New York also established that membership in a religious organization is not required.[45] Litigation struck down Arkansas's requirement that petitioners for exemptions belong to a recognized religious group with a doctrinal opposition to vaccination,[46] and the next year the legislature enacted a broader philosophical exemption. In New Jersey, administrative directives prohibit examining the content of religious belief or membership,[47] and in Florida[48] and Wyoming,[49] judicial opinions have forbidden any administrative inquiry into the details of the religious belief. These states have a de facto philosophical exemption in the form of their religious exemption (but for the purposes of counting here I do not include them in the list of states with formal philosophical exemptions).

At the last high point of vaccine-critical political activism in the states, three states added new philosophical exemptions (Arizona in 2002 by regulation and Texas and Arkansas in 2003 through legislation). The account by Texas activist Dawn Richardson of the fight for the 2003 exemption showcases a politically savvy side of vaccine-critical politics, as seven years of instilling credibility, trust, and moderation, cultivating relationships in the legislature, avoiding partisan divides, and creating an appealing personal image ultimately paid off.[50] Richardson advises advocates to emphasize the risks of vaccines by pulling out the manufacturer's own package insert and reading off the list of possible adverse effects, which must be listed regardless of whether a causal relationship has been established. Vaccine critics share personal stories of vaccine damage at legislative hearings, emphasizing the risks in highly emotional terms. They blame the pharmaceutical companies and the government for insufficient attention to safety and present themselves as a sympathetic target group in need of legislation to protect their parental rights. Together, these themes were persuasive in conservative legislatures in 2003, but advocates have not been able to repeat those successes. Notably, however, between 2002 and 2010, a time when exemption rates were rising in some communities across the United States, no states were able to tighten exemptions in any way, although immunization supporters introduced nine bills to do so.[51]

Vaccine critics have attempted to broaden or add vaccine exemptions, but they have also innovated other political responses to contemporary vaccine debates. Vaccine-critical activists have made much of the facts that vaccines contain formaldehyde or mercury and that they may have been developed with cell lines originally obtained from aborted human fetuses.[52] The first legislation to ban mercury in vaccines appeared in

2001, and by 2012 eight bans had been enacted even though the federal government had acted to remove thimerosal already. Bills requiring doctors to give parents a list of vaccine ingredients appeared sporadically, starting in 2002. Highlighting vaccine ingredients is part of a strategy to heighten perceptions that vaccines are dangerous and to draw support from Catholics and other pro-life groups. A focus on vaccine ingredients also rhetorically links the vaccine-critical cause with health movements against environmental contaminants and with natural food movements. As the popular food author Michael Pollan warns, "Avoid food products containing ingredients that a third-grader cannot pronounce."[53]

None of the vaccine ingredient bills introduced between 1998 and 2012 passed in any state, however. Activists have not advanced their anti-thimerosal agenda very far in Congress or internationally, either. The Mercury-Free Vaccines Act has been introduced four times in Congress (2004, 2005, 2007, and 2009) by both Republicans and Democrats, but none of these bills advanced out of committee.[54] In January 2013, the United Nations finalized language on the Minamata Convention on Mercury, which exempts mercury use in vaccines from its global efforts to reduce exposure to mercury.[55] Advocates for immunization globally want to use thimerosal-preserved vaccines because it thwarts the growth harmful bacteria in multidose vials, which are easier to use, transport, and store and are less expensive that individual doses packaged separately, and because they do not think the levels of thimerosal in vaccines are harmful. Vaccine ingredients such as thimerosal and formaldehyde that sound alarming in the context of consumer demand for purity in food have so far managed to preserve their scientific legitimacy as life-saving complexities that do not need to be "greened" (as Jenny McCarthy urged in her "Green Our Vaccines" rally in 2008).

The tide has turned against vaccine critics at the state level, too. Between 2011 and 2013, Oregon and Washington increased the stringency of their philosophical exemptions by requiring parents to obtain information from a health care provider about the benefits and risks of vaccination in order for their child to qualify for an exemption. There were numerous reasons for the bills' final success, including the high salience of pertussis outbreaks in those states then; a persistent, scientifically credible, and well-led coalition in support of the bills; a loss of anti-vaccine credibility, specifically around the debunking of the autism-vaccine hypothesis and the retraction of Dr. Andrew Wakefield's work; the separation of the Christian Scientist community and its concerns from the concerns of parents opposed to vaccines for nonreligious reasons; and the successful framing of the bills as increasing information rather than persecuting parents or restricting choices. One particularly notable force behind the tightening of exemptions was the CDC's ranking of states by rates of unvaccinated kindergarteners. Washington had the country's highest rate of unvaccinated schoolchildren in 2011 according to the CDC, and being at the top of that list was publicly embarrassing and galvanizing to state legislators. When Washington's exemption rate dropped after its new law went into effect, the unflattering spotlight came to rest on Oregon, which then passed its own education mandate for parents seeking an exemption. Most dramatically, in 2015 California withdrew its philosophical and religious exemptions to school vaccine requirements entirely, joining Mississippi and West Virginia as the three states in which only medical exemptions are available. Vermont withdrew its philosophical but not its religious exemption in 2015.

Federal Vaccine Safety Surveillance: Looking for "Signals" in Large Databases

I have so far presented the political features of vaccines in our social order, telling the story of how they come to be created, endorsed, and mandated. Affirming and testing their safety is a critical part of this process, but it does not end with a vaccine recommendation. To maintain this state of ongoing vigilance in which diseases are controlled but vaccination continues, we must have a legitimate and responsive system in place to detect, prevent, and compensate for vaccine injuries. How can we gather adequate knowledge about whether a medical problem really is a vaccine injury? Who decides when we know enough, and upon what basis? What is the difference between detecting a relationship at the population level through epidemiological studies and big data surveillance and judging that a particular child has been harmed, and how can we blend both of these inquiries together? The health bureaucracies of the federal government monitor the safety of vaccines after they are on the market. Their observations and questions frame the possibilities for official recognition of when a vaccine may have caused harm.

After a vaccine is licensed and approved for use on the pediatric vaccine schedule, millions of children receive it. Once the vaccine has been administered to these large numbers, the goal of postmarket surveillance is to find any adverse reactions that could not have been detected earlier and to act quickly enough to prevent as much injury as possible. There are federal-level monitoring systems in place after licensure for vaccine safety at the FDA and CDC. These surveillance systems rely on several forms of knowledge-gathering and information pathways to detect what government officials call "signals" of a possible problem.

What is a signal, and how do officials know when they see one? A signal is information coming from various governmental and international databases that could be an indication that a vaccine has caused a serious adverse event. The primary way that a signal shows itself is through a higher-than-expected number of adverse events, perhaps in a temporal or geographic cluster. Seeing a signal thus requires an extensive background apparatus of equipment, communication, regulation, and prior knowledge about what a predictable background rate of a condition would be. Our federal-level vaccine safety surveillance systems have different histories, capabilities, limitations, and uses. Many of them are far removed from public view and used by only a small group of expert researchers, but the two most important and visible ones are somewhat accessible to laypeople and have become salient points of controversy in debates over knowledge of vaccine injury.

The first surveillance program is a reporting tool called the Vaccine Adverse Event Reporting System (VAERS, pronounced like "bears"). VAERS is an open, passive reporting system operated by the CDC and the FDA that anyone can use to report a suspected adverse event through the online portal (vaers.hhs.gov), by mail, or by fax. To submit a VAERS report, one must fill in a form with as much information as possible about the vaccine (when and where administered, by whom, lot number, manufacturer, which dose of a series, and so on) and the adverse event. Passive surveillance is like setting up a trap and then standing back to watch if anything appears in it. The passive design of VAERS is both its strength and its weakness: the system is likely both underused (when possible adverse events are not reported) and overused (by advocates hoping to gain official recognition of a condition as a vaccine injury), but it is open to filing from anyone. Mandatory reporting requirements strengthen its reach. The National Childhood Vaccine Injury Act (NCVIA) requires health care providers to report certain adverse events to VAERS, and manufacturers are also required by additional regulation to submit any adverse event they observe. VAERS is exceptional as a source of knowledge of vaccine injury because of its deliberately open design, and as I explain in detail in Chapter 5, both vaccine critics and government regulators invoke it as evidence in different ways.

VAERS has been used to detect vaccine safety problems that first appeared as signals for syncope (fainting), Guillain-Barré syndrome (GBS), febrile seizures, and intussusception after vaccination.[56] Wyeth Laboratories' now-discontinued rotavirus vaccine RotaShield and its link to intussusception is the most-cited story of vaccine safety monitoring success for vaccine supporters, and it showcases the pivotal role of VAERS in signal detection.[57] Rotavirus gastroenteritis causes severe diarrhea, and before rotavirus vaccines, it killed twenty to forty American children per year and hospitalized more than fifty thousand. There had been a few more cases of intussusception, a potentially life-threatening bowel problem caused by part of the intestine telescoping down into itself and getting stuck, in the treatment group of the prelicensure studies, but not at statistically significant levels. (With greater sample sizes in the original clinical trials, perhaps the association could have been detected, and follow-up studies of rotavirus vaccines subsequently utilized much larger numbers of people.[58]) Intussusception would be expected in one in every two thousand to three thousand babies per year in the United States without the vaccine.[59] Wyeth listed intussusception in the package insert for RotaShield based on its appearance in the clinical trials, and it was then on the list of flagged events for health care reports to VAERS.

RotaShield was approved for use in the United States in August 1998. Soon after this new rotavirus vaccine began to be widely used, safety monitors saw fifteen VAERS reports of intussusception in babies who had recently gotten that vaccine.[60] These reports were a recognizable signal because they hinted at a jump in intussusceptions right after vaccine administration and because intussusception was already noted as a plausible problem after the prelicensure trials. The CDC suspended use of RotaShield on July 13, 1999.[61] Researchers at the CDC then performed a broader statistical analysis that showed there was indeed a twenty to thirty times greater risk of developing intussusception for babies under twelve months of age within two weeks of the first dose of RotaShield.[62] The manufacturer pulled the vaccine from the market just as the CDC was withdrawing its recommendation.[63] The whole process from detection to withdrawal took place between June and October 1999 (a very fast pace, considering many studies take a year or more and vaccine approval can easily take a decade). RotaShield was used in the U.S. market for nine months.

Jason Schwartz's analysis of the social and political implications of the RotaShield story shows how it has been held up repeatedly as the classic story of how our vaccine safety surveillance system works well but actually reveals far more.[64] The summer of 1999 was a high pressure moment for vaccine safety because Andrew Wakefield's paper promoting the MMR vaccine's purported link to autism had been published the year before and because the government was preparing to require removal of thimerosal from vaccines as a precaution in light of the revelation that children receiving vaccines on the recommended schedule could be exposed to thimerosal levels exceeding the EPA's limit. With unflattering publicity about vaccine safety building, government officials were especially eager to respond quickly and transparently to the RotaShield problems. Officials did not have a broader discussion about vaccine safety, risk, and public perceptions, however, nor did they define what threshold of elevated risk would justify pulling a vaccine. RotaShield was the only approved rotavirus vaccine available, so a decision not to use it was also a decision to allow more children to get the disease. Once officials knew their statistical analysis tied RotaShield to a rare but serious condition, it was simply not feasible to maintain that its overall benefits made it worth keeping on the recommended schedule.[65] As Dr. Paul Offit (an ACIP member at the time and a co-developer of a later rotavirus vaccine) explained, "We said this is unsafe for American children, period, without ever defining safety. What we meant by doing it the way we did was absolute safety, which isn't a reasonable definition. It's a lawyer's definition. It's not a doctor or scientist's definition."[66]

Pulling RotaShield in the United States had global repercussions that were more ethically complex. Wyeth had counted on the profitable U.S. market as a springboard for selling RotaShield globally, particularly in developing countries where profits would be lower. Vaccine safety determinations are based on a cost-benefit calculation, and in a context in which many more children die of the disease, such analysis would lead to using the vaccine—even with the relatively rare intussusception risk—because the overall benefit is so great. But as Schwartz recounts, it was unappealing to say that American children should not bear the risk of RotaShield-caused intussusception while children in Africa and Asia should, and so even though U.S. regulators were very aware that their actions would impact children's health everywhere, they acted for the highly politicized and risk-averse U.S. context. Once RotaShield was deemed unsafe for American children, it was "politically nonviable to the health ministers of [developing] nations" to use it for their children even though rotavirus-caused diarrhea kills over half a million children in developing countries every year.[67]

Wyeth did not proceed with international testing and development of RotaShield without the profit base of the U.S. market. The next generation of rotavirus vaccines would not be available until 2006, and in those years hundreds of thousands of children in developing countries died from the disease. The two rotavirus vaccines in use now, RotaTeq and Rotarix, are more expensive than other vaccines because of additional safety testing. GlaxoSmithKline and Merck have agreed to sell them at reduced prices to developing nations, and the Global Alliance for Vaccines and Immunization (now called the GAVI Alliance) has pledged to pay for them, but they remain out of reach for many poor countries.[68] Placing a new vaccine on the U.S. list of recommended and then mandated childhood immunization is a global economic, political, and social calculation with ripple effects far beyond U.S. disease rates.

VAERS reports can signal possible safety problems, but to perform studies of a possible causal link, a second type of monitoring system is necessary. For regulators, a VAERS report simply conveys that someone thinks a health problem could be an adverse event related to vaccination. An active monitoring system, by contrast, is one that does not depend on external reports filtering in, but provides a snapshot of the U.S. population in real time matched with health information about what vaccines people have received and what the health outcomes have been; researchers can conduct hypothesis testing whenever questions arise. This information source is the Vaccine Safety Datalink (VSD), a system that draws on health information databases (stripped of personal identifiers) containing over nine million people from nine managed care organizations around the United States, with an annual birth cohort of about ninety-five thousand children.[69] The VSD includes Kaiser Permanente in Oakland, Portland, Atlanta, and Seattle, as well as Harvard Pilgrim in Massachusetts and the Marshfield Clinic in Wisconsin.[70] The system is considered the best source of knowledge to confirm vaccine injuries because it contains full electronic medical records with verifiable information about health outcomes for a very large number of people. It is still unrepresentative of people who do not have health insurance through these types of group plans, however.

A team of researchers receives weekly updates from the VSD about any possible signals. This process, called Rapid Cycle Analysis,[71] compares the background rate of certain adverse events in people who had not had a certain vaccine to the reported rates coming in from the VSD in people who have had that vaccine. An increase above the background rate in the vaccinated cohort would count as a signal, and an epidemiological study in the broader VSD population would provide the answer. A vaccine is considered to have caused an adverse reaction if the risk of experiencing that adverse event is several times higher in the vaccine-exposed group than in the nonexposed group, assuming the study population was representative, well drawn, and large enough to be statistically powerful. Often there are sufficient data of reliable quality in the VSD to allow investigators to draw conclusions about whether a given vaccine causes an adverse event (as in the case of intussusception and the RotaShield vaccine) or is only temporally linked to its emergence (as in the case of vaccines and autism). Still, its study population of nine million may be too small to power studies capable of detecting very rare adverse events.

Government officials monitor other large databases of medical records in addition to the VSD.[72] The Defense Medical Surveillance System includes the approximately 1.4 million active duty military personnel, and the Veterans Affairs Database adds 1.2 million veterans. The Centers for Medicare and Medicaid Services (CMS) has data on vaccinations for the 38 million seniors and low-income people covered under those services. The Indian Health Service collects health data on 1.4 million Native Americans as well. These populations are nearly all adults, and they may receive no vaccines or more unusual ones such as anthrax that are not administered to the civilian population. In addition, the ability of investigators to access medical records quickly within each database varies, and each system is run by a different office (in the Department of Health and Human Services [HHS]) or by another agency entirely (such as the Department of Defense). Medicare provides near real-time access similar to the VSD for the elderly population, a target for influenza vaccines.

The groups included in these medical surveillance databases are those brought under federal governing power through very specific and different pathways, such as through the military or the federal relationship to the sovereign Native tribes. They are nonrepresentative of the general population and may not receive the vaccines prioritized for study. If we had a national health care system in the United States, it would be much easier to have a national records system comparable to those in Denmark or other European nations. The Affordable Care Act requires the use of electronic medical records but still operates through private insurance companies rather than as a national single-payer system, and so the future of vaccine safety surveillance is likely to look more like the private-public partnerships of the VSD than the federal oversight of the Medicare population under CMS.

VAERS and the VSD arose from the urgency of the 1980s pertussis vaccine controversy, while these other federal monitoring systems arose from the preexisting governmental institutions that monitored populations such as Native peoples, the elderly, and soldiers. Another significant force behind more recent expansions of vaccine safety systems was the challenge of the 2009 H1N1 influenza pandemic and its 1976 predecessor, still called the swine flu pandemic. The 1976 swine flu vaccine had been linked to an increased risk for Guillain-Barré syndrome (GBS), and so the 2009 H1N1 flu scare combined heightened awareness of vaccine risks with an ambitious program to vaccinate 159 million people (about half the entire U.S. population) in time to quell the spread of disease. To prepare for the need to assess the safety of the monovalent H1N1 flu vaccine, HHS created a new safety surveillance system called the Post-Licensure Rapid Immunization Monitoring System (PRISM). PRISM combined claims data from the HMOs Aetna, CIGNA, Health-Core, and Humana with the immunization registries from eight states (Arizona, Florida, Georgia, Michigan, Minnesota, New York, Pennsylvania, and Wisconsin) and the city of New York, and included about thirty-eight million individuals. PRISM monitoring of over three million H1N1 doses revealed a small but statistically insignificant risk of increase in GBS cases after vaccination. It is difficult to estimate the base background rate of GBS in the population because the disease is so rare.[73] Epidemiologists calculated that this increased risk, if not due to chance, would have added 2 or 3 GBS cases per 1 million vaccinations. The 1976 swine flu vaccine, by contrast, had been linked to nearly 9 excess GBS cases per 1 million vaccinations.[74]

PRISM was the first vaccine safety surveillance effort to incorporate state immunization registry data, not just data from HMOs. To understand why, consider the signs one sees at every pharmacy from September to March: "Get your flu shot here!"[75] Many people receive a flu shot in more informal ways than through an appointment with a primary care physician, and those shots may be recorded in a state immunization registry rather than an HMO claim. State immunization registries vary widely in their coverage, however, and states often use incompatible information technology systems that do not mesh well either with federal resources or across states. Even so, more than 60 percent of the first three million doses of H1N1 vaccine monitored under PRISM would not have appeared in the dataset without the state immunization registries' contributions.[76] This dispersed system—within a federal system with separate registries for every state in a nation without a national health system—adds even more complexity to the effort to determine who has received the flu vaccine or how many doses have been used.

The FDA is expanding this type of active safety monitoring beyond vaccines to all the drugs and devices it regulates in a congressionally mandated effort called the Sentinel Initiative, which will draw on insurance claims data, electronic medical records systems, and registries (of immunizations, but also of diseases or devices) to detect safety problems with all the products and devices the FDA regulates, including vaccines.[77] A pilot version called Mini-Sentinel has been operating since late 2009,[78] and as of August 2013 had data on 150 million Americans.[79] Mini-Sentinel is funded by an HHS grant to Harvard Pilgrim Health Care, which then subcontracted out work on the project among twenty-four other health plans, university statistics departments, and research hospitals across the country.[80] The project leaders had to devise a way to collect and use health data from millions of people stored in many different health care and insurance service sites both public and private, all without violating medical privacy and ethics laws or triggering a public outcry. Crucially, Mini-Sentinel is classified as a public health effort, not as human subject research. This distinction means that institutional review boards do not oversee Mini-Sentinel, and Health Insurance Portability and Accountability Act (HIPAA) privacy rules permit health care organizations to disclose protected health information to public health entities without patient permission, although partners must abide by HIPAA's minimum necessary standard so that they share only the data the FDA needs. The health information is not linked to personal identifiers, but it reveals all health problems that become insurance claims and links them to the drugs, vaccines, and devices that the people in the database were exposed to.

There are additional sources of knowledge, however, that draw on other methodologies such as surveys. The National Immunization Survey, the Healthcare Cost and Utilization Project, and the National Hospital Discharge Survey can all provide information about immunization experiences, parents' feedback about vaccinating their children, and the kinds of medical problems that lead people to seek health care treatment (that may be vaccine-related). States run their own immunization registries that could one day become usefully linked as sources of information, but now they vary widely in how many residents have immunization records on file with the state.[81] The highly fragmented U.S. federal system, the employer-based health care system, and the lack of any nationally unified health databases or tracking systems means that it is structurally difficult to assemble a representative sample of U.S. children and to know enough reliable health information about them to enable researchers to explore these causal questions. The same libertarian wing of the vaccine-critical movement that demands more and better research studies also opposes any structural reforms such as nationalized health care or records systems that would make answering their questions much easier. In its recent report on possibilities for future vaccine safety studies of the type critics have been asking for, the Institute of Medicine (IOM) concluded that the VSD and future databases like it are the best sites for answering new vaccine safety questions.

The move to electronic medical records, the requirement to provide vaccines free of any co-pay under the Affordable Care Act, and the extension of insurance coverage to millions of people who have been going without it will nonetheless improve the ability of our vaccine safety researchers to get the kind of broad, interlinked, and nationally representative health data they need to know and recognize vaccine-related adverse events. The United Kingdom, Denmark, and Canada have similar linked databases and surveillance systems, and in Denmark in particular, insistence on providing every resident (citizen or not) with a unique health identification number that follows them through the health care system has made their vaccine safety and research system the gold standard. Vaccine safety studies using the Danish databases can easily gather half a million children with complete medical and vaccine records going back years, and some of the early and most pivotal studies vindicating vaccines in the autism debates were performed in these databases.[82]

John Gilliom and Torin Monahan point out that we have only just arrived at the age of so-called big data surveillance, and they regard it with extreme caution: "[W]are witnessing the emergence and perfection of a system of human regulation that uses identification, visibility, and surveillance as its central strategies. In that process, all significant institutions are implementing similar models of governance. Colleges and universities, banks, data aggregators, grocers, state governments, insurers, police departments, the FBI, and so on—they're committed to practices of management and control that rely on gathering and acting on detailed information about our lives."[83] Is this kind of surveillance more benevolent when it is in the service of vaccine safety rather than espionage, or even just sending us the perfectly timed Google ad for that product we searched for but did not yet purchase? If it is not possible to detect and properly evaluate whether a medical problem is a vaccine injury without this scale and type of surveillance, how can we govern these drug, vaccine, and device surveillance systems justly? Interestingly, Gilliom and Monahan do not discuss health surveillance in their book on surveillance in society, but the vaccine safety issue (and all drug and device safety questions) put surveillance in a more positive light than the examples they highlight from other spheres. Any system powerful enough to detect and analyze potential adverse events is going to have to pull records from millions of people, and we must maintain a political order capable of safeguarding private health information at the same time. Commitment to the vaccine program we have—with a large number of mandated vaccines given to healthy children—means committing to an aggressive and fine-tuned safety surveillance system.

2

The Solution of the Vaccine Court

The vaccine court is part of the social contract of our immunization social order and a solution to a problem, invented at a particular political moment. What exactly was the problem the vaccine court was established to solve, and how was it designed to solve it? Policies and institutions designed to solve one kind of problem often drift and change over time, adapt to new needs and pressures, and end up looking rather different than their designers imagined. This is the story of our vaccine court. The court itself, the social conditions to which it responded, and the state of scientific knowledge about vaccine injuries have all shifted over time, pulled by each other in a multifaceted, co-productive relationship.

The vaccine court was born out of legal mobilization and social movement pressure in the 1980s and focused on adverse reactions to the diphtheria-tetanus-pertussis (DTP) vaccine. Its original rules and practices compensated generously under conditions of uncertainty, but with increased study and review of vaccine injuries, much of that uncertainty has given way to a consensus that vaccines are not actually responsible for many of the events that initially alarmed both parents and doctors. In 1995, that new scientific consensus totally transformed the legal standards at the vaccine court, removing most of the simple administrative process and replacing it almost entirely with claims requiring a full causation hearing. This more adversarial vaccine court was then ready and waiting in the late 1990s when the autism controversy began the second recent wave of legal and social mobilization. Lawyers and activist parents tried to send a tidal wave of lawsuits over thimerosal in vaccines purportedly linked to autism to our regular state and federal civil courts, but these claims were funneled into the vaccine court instead. This chapter tells the story of how vaccine injuries came to be seen as a problem, how the vaccine court became the solution to that problem, and how the vaccine court has adapted over time to meet new scientific and legal challenges posed by evolving claims of vaccine injury.

Vaccine Injuries as a Social, Political, and Legal Problem

It is hard to overstate the influence of the whole-cell pertussis vaccine on the shape of vaccine politics and injury compensation over the past few decades. The pertussis vaccine galvanized vaccine critics in both the United States and the United Kingdom and resulted in new compensation programs in both nations. The original DTP vaccine (with the whole-cell pertussis component) was featured in *Vaccine Roulette*, a dramatic documentary about vaccine injuries shown on a Washington, D.C., NBC-affiliated television channel in 1982 that launched the anti-vaccine movement as we know it today in the United States. The show depicted children with devastating health problems after the DTP shot, and parents who viewed it organized in the United States first as Dissatisfied Parents Together and then as the National Vaccine Information Center (NVIC), still run today by the original founders. The parents' activism galvanized the push for the compensation program and vaccine safety measures, and kept the program's focus on the adverse events following DTP vaccination in the early years. Even after the vaccine compensation court was up and running, misleading television representations of DTP continued. In November 1993, a syndicated program called *The Crusaders* aired, claiming that the vaccine court records showed that two children per day were killed or injured by the DTP vaccine. In fact, the wildly exaggerated two-per-day claim acknowledges neither that the court's cases included claims as far back as 1918 nor that experts no longer believed that the vaccine was truly responsible for all the injuries that had been attributed to it.[1]

Mainstream experts and critics agree that whole-cell-pertussis-containing vaccines can be among the most reactive vaccines and can cause fever, febrile convulsions (convulsions with fever, alarming but not associated with any long-term effects), hours of inconsolable crying and screaming, irritation, and persistent nodules at the injection site.[2] Even though the organizing occurred around the DTP vaccine, it was the whole-cell pertussis component of the combination vaccine that was the real focus of attention. The parent-activists of the 1980s claimed that the DTP vaccine caused a wide range of serious neurological conditions including permanent brain damage, convulsions, seizures, learning disabilities, hyperactivity, allergies, epilepsy, diabetes, thrombocytopenia (a blood disease characterized by reduced platelets), hemolytic anemia (a condition in which red blood cells die too soon and cannot be replaced by bone marrow quickly enough), and sudden infant death syndrome (SIDS).[3] As I describe later in this chapter, those claims would not survive scientific scrutiny over time, but the institutional structures formed in response to those claims live on. Parents became organized politically and began to file lawsuits against the vaccine manufacturers, claiming that the DTP vaccine was too dangerous and that manufacturers should have brought a safer acellular version to market. Although my story is focused on the United States and our vaccine court solution, it is important to note that the pertussis vaccine controversy was a transnational phenomenon that also sparked the British vaccine injury compensation system through the passage of their Vaccine Damage Payments Act in 1976.[4]

As political scientist Tom Burke recounts, the vaccine court was developed as an alternative to regular civil court litigation over both the DTP vaccine as well as the polio vaccine.[5] As Burke explains, a strange coalition—doctors, drug makers, parents of injured children, and politicians from both parties—who otherwise distrusted each other assembled in support, some much more grudgingly than others. Supporters of the idea of a compensation program had to overcome strong antipathy in American politics and social activism for consolidating claims within a national-level government program rather than in a court-based strategy, which movement activists often prefer because it keeps policy making out of the hands of politicians and bureaucrats and does not require raising revenue from legislatures. Most importantly, as Burke explains, promoters of the vaccine court "had to convince all concerned that vaccine injuries should be handled as a social problem, an unavoidable cost of vaccination for which all should pay, rather than a product of the sins of pharmaceutical companies."[6] Moving away from finding fault and placing blame is the essence of any no-fault alternative litigation scheme, after all. Movement activists who were involved in the creation of the vaccine court now decry it and this social problem frame, and try to substitute frames of pharmaceutical corporate misdeeds, government conspiracy, and violated rights. How then did this odd coalition manage to create the solution of the vaccine court?

Designing a political and legal response to the DTP controversy meant confronting many tough decisions. The first decision was whether to move vaccine compensation into some kind of no-fault scheme or keep it within the tort system, perhaps with a few tweaks such as damage caps. The Reagan administration preferred the latter solution, suggesting that instead of a new no-fault scheme, bans on punitive damages and a hundred-thousand-dollar cap on pain and suffering damages in the tort system would control manufacturers' costs while avoiding creation of a new government program.[7] Even after it became clear that the consensus clearly favored a move away from the tort system to a no-fault scheme, there was significant disagreement over who would administer the program. Would it be a fully bureaucratic system, administered by civil servants within the Department of Health and Human Services (HHS)? Or would it be placed in the judicial system, perhaps in a new court or within the existing federal court system? The organized parents did not trust HHS to administer a compensation program because there would be a conflict between promoting vaccines as a public health effort and acknowledging the reality of vaccine injuries.

There was also the thorny question of whether, when, and how easily families could withdraw from the no-fault system if they did not like the judgment they received, and bring a tort suit against the vaccine manufacturers. Would there simply be two options from the start, and families could select a no-fault option with a quicker process and a greater chance at compensation? Or would they have to complete the no-fault option, and be able to sue only if they were unsatisfied with the compensation court's offering? The manufacturers and organized pediatricians favored an exclusive remedy in a new compensation court, with no way to have a second bite at the apple in regular civil court. And finally, who would pay for damage awards? Other no-fault schemes in the United States, such as no-fault insurance for car accidents and workers' compensation, are funded through private insurance. New Zealand, by contrast, has replaced tort litigation with a government-funded compensation system that pays for injuries out of general tax revenue and an employer levy.[8] It does not have a specific vaccine injury program because such injuries are simply covered under this comprehensive system.

Passage of the National Childhood Vaccine Injury Act of 1986

Several factors prompted the initial creation of the vaccine court. First, the usual operation of civil litigation came to be seen as imposing unsustainable costs to public health. It seemed reasonably likely that litigation might undermine vaccine manufacturing so much that herd immunity would collapse, or at least vaccine manufacturers were able to make that case convincingly enough to put the issue on the congressional agenda. Two high-profile jury verdicts in the early 1980s awarded large sums to families based on, first, the theory that Lederle, a DTP vaccine manufacturer, could have developed a safer acellular version of the vaccine but chose not to, and second, that the Sabin polio vaccine continued to be used even though the Salk polio vaccine was known to be safer (because it is not capable of causing polio).[9] In 1984, one of the three vaccine manufacturers of DTP announced it would stop producing it, leaving only two suppliers, one of which was also considering leaving the market because of the escalating costs of liability insurance. Manufacturers responded to these litigation threats by drastically raising prices, so that by 1986 the price of a DTP shot had gone from eleven cents to over eleven dollars. The vaccine makers argued that their business could soon become impossible to insure at any price and that they would all have to stop making DTP vaccine.

Even though vaccine manufacturers may have overstated their vulnerability to gain leverage in the final design of any compensation program, it was undeniable that vaccine manufacturers had left the market and that some recommended vaccines had only one supplier. This sense of precariousness was sufficient to help propel the National Childhood Vaccine Injury Act to passage in 1986. Manufacturers got what they wanted in a final formulation of the bill, in which parents would first have to go all the way through the vaccine court and receive a final judgment before they could opt out and file a tort lawsuit. They also received additional protections in any eventual tort lawsuit, such that they could not be held liable for unavoidable injuries when the vaccine had been properly prepared and accompanied by proper warnings, or for any strict or absolute liability theory, nor would they pay any punitive damages if the vaccine complied with FDA standards. Merck endorsed the final version of the bill, though Lederle did not.

Second, the parents' options in civil lawsuits were unpredictable and precarious for everyone. Scholars of American adversarial legalism have long noted the uncertainty of litigation,[10] and the likelihood that some people bringing lawsuits may reap large awards while the vast majority of similar plaintiffs may get nothing. Prior to the establishment of the vaccine court in 1986, parents of children who became disabled or died after getting vaccines brought suits over so-called bad batches or negligent administration by doctors (vaccinating a child at the wrong age or after previous adverse reactions, for example), but it had generally been very difficult to bring successful suits alleging that manufacturers should have been able to prevent these injuries.[11] Vaccines (along with prescription drugs) in American law fall into the category of "unavoidably unsafe" products, which means even before the establishment of the vaccine court, manufacturers were protected from liability from injuries if the vaccine was properly prepared, appropriately marketed, useful for its stated purpose, and the only way to accomplish that purpose.[12] In other words, legal doctrine already recognized the notion that vaccines could cause some adverse events that could not reasonably be prevented. The only way to prevent them would be not to manufacture the vaccine at all. This legal doctrine had given manufacturers long-standing protections that had begun to be undercut in litigation. For example, failing to warn of vaccine risks could make a manufacturer liable again under the usual doctrine of strict liability for defective products, and families won a few cases arguing that they were not warned of the risks.[13] It was unclear how far courts and juries might go to protect vaccine-injured children, and which families would prevail and which would not.

And third, the vaccine court owed its founding to the political skills of Congressman Henry Waxman and the alignment of interests he assembled within Congress and the Reagan administration. The final bill that contained the vaccine program was packaged for an up-or-down vote with several other health-related bills, including a bill to allow American pharmaceutical companies to sell abroad products that were not FDA approved (something the pro-business, anti-regulation Reagan administration wanted very much), an Alzheimer's disease initiative (the pet project of a senator who opposed the pharmaceutical export bill), a bill to make reporting doctors' record of medical malpractice lawsuits easier (something the American Medical Association wanted), and a repeal of a federal health planning law (something the Reagan administration and congressional Republicans wanted).[14]

Tom Burke's study of an archive of memos in the Ronald Reagan National Library reveals the competing concerns surrounding the vaccine program. Some endured and grew into real problems over time; other difficulties never materialized, as I shall explain. The Reagan administration, particularly the Justice Department, opposed the Vaccine Injury Compensation Program because they were afraid of creating another costly entitlement program that would be hard for the president to control because it would be placed in the courts, not in an administrative agency. Assistant Attorney General John Bolton (later President George W. Bush's United Nations ambassador) argued that judges would be so sympathetic to disabled children that they would overcompensate for injuries like epilepsy and cerebral palsy that were not really vaccine-related and that keeping an option for parents to sue in regular courts would mean double liability for vaccine companies. Even after the omnibus health bill passed both houses, he urged President Reagan not to sign it.[15] White House counsel Peter Wallison countered in support of the bill that vaccine injuries were a special, rare case because vaccination is mandated and because injured children were so worthy of sympathy in the courts that the protective legal doctrines could no longer hold back large jury verdicts. He emphasized the program's protection for manufacturers, which was in line with the Reagan administration's broader tort reform goals.[16] HHS Secretary Otis Bowen worried that the vaccine program would combine the worst elements of both bureaucracy and tort law, but ultimately wanted most to stabilize vaccine prices and supplies and supported the bill.[17]

President Reagan reluctantly signed the bill containing the vaccine compensation program on November 13, 1986. The enacted law was understandably a collage of compromises. Because time was beginning to run out to get a bill signed that year, Congressman Waxman had agreed to strip out the start-up funding for the court. Awards were to be funded from an initial sum from general revenue appropriated by Congress, and thereafter from a surtax on vaccines. The funding to begin making awards did not come until a 1988 budget reconciliation bill passed with $80 million for each of the first four years. The parents retained the right to sue vaccine manufacturers, but only after going through the compensation program and rejecting a final judgment. The program was not set up within HHS, but neither was it placed in the Article III federal courts. As a compromise, Congressman Waxman located it in the Court of Federal Claims, which is a legislatively created court under Congress's Article I powers handling claims against the federal government such as tax refund suits or disputes over government contracts. Unlike Article III judges, Article I judges are not lifetime appointees. There is no Seventh Amendment right to a jury trial in an Article I court, either. When an earlier draft of the bill set the court within Article III federal district courts, HHS was required to act as the respondent to ensure that each case presented a justiciable controversy. When the court was relocated within the Court of Federal Claims, the constitutional requirement for a justiciable controversy with adversarial parties no longer applied, but HHS was still named in the final bill as the respondent to push back against claims that lacked merit. In the end, the parents got a route to compensation and an open if not unimpeded path to a tort suit, the manufacturers got stability and protection from litigation, and pediatricians were reassured that the nation would have an uninterrupted supply of childhood vaccines.

Confronting the Early Realities of Vaccine Court Processing

Criticism of the vaccine court frequently opens with an account of a lost promise of nonadversarial generosity followed by a decline into hostility and penny-pinching, all a departure from congressional intent.[18] As Barbara Loe Fisher recounts, "The young parents of vaccine injured children, who came to the table in the early 1980s at the request of congressional staff to fight for the rights of vaccine consumers and the vaccine injured, agreed to work on the Act because of promises made by Congress and the American Academy of Pediatrics (AAP) that the proposed legislation would provide a fair, expedited, nonadversarial, less traumatic, less expensive no-fault compensation alternative to civil litigation."[19] As Barnes and Burke tell it, the creation of the vaccine court was first a bureaucratic solution to adversarial legalism, which then lurched back over time toward adversarialism.[20] After observing the program's first year of operation, however, one early evaluator noted that although it was clearly an "innovation in federal benefit systems," combining "elements of Social Security disability-type determinations and administrative tribunal proceedings," its "very structure encourages, if not dictates, fact-finding and decision-making processes that resemble litigation."[21] When confronted with claims based on the good old days, it is always good to ask whether those good old days really ever existed and whether they were as good as they are made out to be.[22]

I show here that the court was always more complicated than politicians and advocates made it out to be and that in fact the central problem it was tasked with—recognizing vaccine injuries with reasonable accuracy and credibility—was always destined to be contentious. That it is complicated to figure out vaccine injury causation is not a fault of the court, and indeed many critics of the court either sidestep the problem of compensating for injuries that are not at all likely to be vaccine-related,[23] or already embrace marginal ideas about widespread vaccine injuries and thus would not agree that it is important for the special masters to avoid compensation decisions that lack mainstream scientific credibility.[24] Looking closely at original documents detailing the conflicts in the court's early days, I argue that its adversarialism and formality have been long-standing and that the essential dispute—whether vaccines really cause particular injuries or not—was covered over for a few years only because the original Vaccine Injury Table was written generously.[25] The original law created a legal fiction in place of a scientific consensus that did not yet exist (and would not ever form)—that a wide range of permanent disabilities and deaths could be causally linked to the whole-cell pertussis vaccine—and this legal fiction helped the vaccine court work relatively quickly and easily to compensate a lot of families in its first years. But the law also required scientific review of the evidence for vaccine injuries, and thus it directed the undoing of its own legal fiction. In other words, the good old days of nonadversarialism are at least quite overstated if not illusory, and it is not actually such a bad thing to balk at quickly compensating for vaccine injuries when the whole contentious question is whether there is enough evidence to do so.

Even though a generously defined Vaccine Injury Table governed the court, the early days are a lesson for anyone who thinks setting up a special court is a neat and simple policy solution. It is widely accepted that courts are "swamped" with heavy caseloads, though sociolegal researchers observing some American courts in which very few actual trials are held have shown that sometimes these claims are overstated.[26] (The vast majority of criminal charges end in plea bargaining; civil suits largely result in settlements.) After its first year of operation, the vaccine court really was swamped with cases, many of which were poorly documented and thus difficult to judge on causation.[27] Initially, the court took claims going back in time without any restriction, with the oldest pre-program claim dating from 1918.[28] The bolus of pre–October 1, 1988, retrospective claims would eventually grow to 4,264, and the last one would not be finally resolved until 2002.[29]

Against a backdrop of this huge backlog of claims, the vaccine court and its administrative partners had to establish rules, practices, and re-source allocations to create and run itself, and in a context in which congressional interest and urgency had subsided. Parents and pediatricians had supported an informal compensation process, and the parent advocates had opposed to giving the same agency that promoted vaccines (HHS) control over adjudicating claims in an in-house administrative procedure. Placing the adjudications within the federal judiciary kept them out of HHS, but created the conditions for a more traditional court format. The eight attorneys hired as special masters began wearing judicial robes, swearing witnesses, and allowing cross-examination of witnesses. After hearing some complaints about the formality imposed by the black robes, the special masters stopped wearing them.[30] Both Department of Justice (DOJ) and HHS wrote memos to the claims court asking for informal procedures, but the court produced thirty-five pages of procedural rules that other stakeholders thought were much too complex.[31] The vaccine court's rules have devolved into a simpler set of procedures (far less complex than federal rules of evidence and procedure), but they remain complex enough that petitioners are strongly discouraged from representing themselves.[32]

From the very start, disputes over how formal and adversarial the proceedings would be were bound up with resource allocation problems. Whether the trust funds should be spent on costs other than paying compensation to those injured by vaccines has been a long-running controversy. Should the Justice Department get access to the trust fund to pay for its attorneys to represent the HHS secretary in an adversarial proceeding in which they may oppose the families? The special masters and petitioners' attorneys had been funded from the vaccine act trust fund but the DOJ side had not. The work was overwhelming for the two assigned attorneys, one of whom resigned.[33] The DOJ tried to get the program suspended for ninety days to discuss restructuring it, and when that was not successful, it took the extraordinary step of filing a motion of withdrawal of counsel, leaving the secretary without representation from April 1989 until late that year.[34] It was the first time in history that that DOJ had withdrawn from representing a federal agency in a whole program.[35]

Meanwhile, HHS had hired a medical officer to review the incoming claims, but the court refused to accept her written reports as evidence and HHS declined to make her available for cross-examination. According to the HHS general counsel, the medical officers had hoped to be "an adviser on the medical issues," but "the court's rules and the actions of the special masters cast [HHS medical officers] in the role of adversary party, responsible for litigating in a formal sense the range of issues before the Court."[36] Parent advocates objected to the level of adversarialism in the program, too, but also wanted parents' attorneys to be able to cross-examine the HHS medical officer in person.[37] Citing resource constraints, HHS ultimately negotiated for a more expert advisory role in which their medical officers would file reports but not testify in person. This role allowed HHS to blend a posture of expertise with protection from the quickly escalating adversarialism within the program.

In December 1989, Congress passed a set of amendments to the vaccine program that attempted to address the adversarialism and resource allocation problems that were causing so much friction between the court, HHS, and the DOJ. Each of the three sites for the program received a $1.5 million appropriation from the trust fund to run their operations (and these three partners continue to be funded by the trust fund today). Congress explicitly directed the court to use a less adversarial and more expeditious and informal process, and the court responded by adopting rules limiting discovery and cross-examination and allowing summary judgment. The special masters were also empowered to make decisions rather than to simply advise the judges of the Court of Federal Claims, with an option for petitioners to seek review using an arbitrary and capricious standard. The bill included public accountability measures as well, requiring the program to make reasonable efforts to publicize its existence and to submit itself for a full program evaluation by

1992.[38] The DOJ attorneys agreed to represent the secretary fully in the cases handled under the amended format.[39]

The vaccine court was cobbled together to solve an immediately pressing problem without much consideration of its long-term operation. When its founding moment passed, it would prove to be much more difficult to get congressional attention for fixing the more everyday problems, even though they were quite fundamental to what the court was supposed to be doing and for whom. The Vaccine Injury Compensation Program (VICP) had been set up to cover injuries or death in children from the DTP, MMR, and polio vaccines, but had no criteria for adding new vaccines to the program. This omission meant that the orderly scientific rationality imagined for the process was riven continually by political contestations over what I call coverage and corralling. Coverage is the question of what people, vaccines, and injuries are included in the program's jurisdiction; corralling is the process of attaching the right amounts of money to each vaccine being included (through a surtax) as well as making sure that claims go into the vaccine court and stay out of regular civil courts. An alternative justice scheme is useful only if it can include the right people and gather their claims in the right place, after all, and these were critical problems.

Surely a covered vaccine should be FDA approved, but how much should be known about its potential for adverse events before including it? A list of possible adverse events could be both under- and overinclusive. The FDA approval process might uncover some adverse events, but rare problems (such as a one in a million occurrence) can be detected only after a vaccine has been given to very large numbers of people (and if it is even more rare, perhaps not even then). Waiting to establish enough data to have any degree of certainty about adverse events could take years, but covering a vaccine without any linkage to adverse events would leave attorneys and special masters with little guidance for adjudication when petitioners brought novel theories of harm. Administrators at HHS opted to cover new vaccines without any linked Vaccine Injury Table conditions, preferring to wait the years it would take until experts could validate any causal links.

Would vaccines for people of all ages be included, or only those subject to mandated use by the states for school-aged children? This dilemma raised the issue of the basis of the social contract: was it linked to vaccines and their status as a biological product with the potential to react in harmful ways not well understood, or was the compensation scheme needed because of the compulsion the state puts behind vaccination for children in particular? The program remained focused on children, and even today only vaccines that are universally recommended for children are covered.[40] Another question about the social compact was whether it gave special priority to children with DTP claims. When resources were tight, the founding parents would have preferred to keep the focus on a narrower range of vaccines, even as new vaccines such as Hib were in the pipeline. When it was clear the pre-1988 funds for compensating many of the older DTP claims would run out, the parents who had organized around DTP resisted adding more vaccines to the program until funding for those claims could be resolved.[41] On their view, the social compact should remain focused on children and the DTP vaccine. They had organized around the DTP vaccine, after all, and the court was sitting on thousands of claims from their constituents with a dwindling supply of money to compensate them. But new vaccines being given but not covered by the no-fault program meant that the old dangers to the vaccine supply from civil suits threatened once more. Manufacturers and physicians' groups got their way, and new vaccines were included without much delay after being recommended by the ACIP for universal use in children.

Should the excise tax on each vaccine reflect its risk? If so, how would that be determined? This question reflects the larger question of how much differentiation by vaccine is best for public policy. Initially there was not a uniform amount of excise tax for every vaccine; instead, the tax varied by the level of risk associated with each vaccine so that those responsible for more claims would bring in more revenue. It was difficult to gather enough evidence to calculate a risk price before adding a vaccine to the program, however, and by 1997 Congress had shifted to a flat tax of seventy-five cents on all covered vaccines. (The tax applies per disease prevented, so combination vaccines such as the measles-mumps-rubella vaccine get an excise tax of $2.25, for example.) This level of taxation keeps the trust fund well funded and has provided a simple and secure funding mechanism (and also prevents some vaccines from gaining worse public reputations than others); however, it lacks a clear theoretical justification. Everyone benefits from childhood vaccination by either being protected from disease oneself or by living in a society that is free of vaccine-preventable diseases (and likely both), but the burden and awareness of paying for compensations are extremely attenuated. Insurance companies and the federal government pay for vaccines, and so the tax is spread out through insurance payments or through an indirect government self-tax (taxing the vaccines but then paying most of the tax through vaccine purchases). The main benefits of this funding scheme are not its ability to promote vaccination as a public duty and shared risk, but rather its simplicity, its largesse, and the fact that its cost is quite painless and invisible and thus politically protected.

"Science versus Policy": Conflicts over the Vaccine Injury Table

By far the most formative and insoluble tension of the vaccine compensation court is what court insiders call "science versus policy." Court insiders all agreed that this issue is the foundational challenge of the vaccine court. By "science" they mean the firm knowledge that a vaccine can and does indeed cause a specific adverse event. Court actors understand "science" as offering various ways to show causation, some more firmly than others, but nonetheless held it out as an objective source of information that ideally should guide all compensation decisions. The problem, as I will explain, turns out that there is just not enough science out there to be used in this way. "Policy" means the political, legal, and conflict management goals of the vaccine court, set out to the court actors by the original vaccine act. Policy goals include compensating enough people for a wide enough range of health problems so that the program fulfills its mission to safeguard the nation's vaccine supply by keeping those people from wanting to file civil suits or join anti-vaccine movements. Both science and policy have been highly contested and shifting concepts at the vaccine court, and changes in understandings of both have altered the power relations at the court significantly over time.

The simplest solution to the science versus policy question in the compensation program is simply to gather enough causal evidence to link an adverse event with a vaccine, put it on the Vaccine Injury Table, and fast-track it to compensation. The Table is supposed to represent the best state of scientific knowledge about vaccine adverse events, and thus questions about what is on it, what is left off, how it is derived, how it should be interpreted, and how, whether, and when to change it are the most fundamental of the science versus policy debate. The Table is quite literally a record of officially recognized vaccine injuries. Back when the problem was the DTP vaccine and its attendant lawsuits and parent activism, the solution of the vaccine court was designed primarily to compensate for neurological damage that occurred close in time to receipt of the whole-cell pertussis component (mostly encephalopathy, broadly defined as brain disease, malfunction, or damage), and the court was set up to do so generously even without much knowledge of how the vaccine actually caused these injuries. That era of broad and generous compensations came to an abrupt end, however, after scientific review of those purported vaccine injuries. Now there is simply not enough of the right kinds of scientific knowledge to justify making a lot of claimed vaccine injuries into official Table injuries.

Many studies around the world attempted to determine what long-term, serious problems were actually causally linked to the whole-cell pertussis vaccine component of the DTP vaccine.[42] Most of the important, large-scale studies of this question took place in the 1970s and 1980s, around the same time the United States and other countries founded their vaccine injury compensation programs. By the early 1990s, however, the mainstream medical view was that the whole-cell pertussis vaccine caused reactions that were unpleasant but not dangerous and that "major risks . . . occur so infrequently that their precise rates are unmeasurable."[43] Vaccine expert Dr. Paul Offit has documented how the scrutiny of litigation undid confidence in some early findings of the National Childhood Encephalopathy Study (NCES), whose early indications had provided much of the basis for scientific suspicion that DTP caused brain damage.[44] A British judge had held a sixty-one-day trial in 1988 featuring nineteen experts and held that he was not satisfied, on the balance of probability, that the pertussis vaccine component caused permanent brain damage in children.[45] The judge found, for example, that many of the initially alarming reports of children's reactions in the NCES study (such as for neurological damage) were later determined to be febrile seizures with no lasting effects.[46] The British counterpart to our VICP soon halted compensations for permanent damage from the whole-cell pertussis vaccine based on this scientific consensus.[47] Experts now suspect that these early associations can be explained by the coincident appearance of symptoms (as with epilepsy) with the timing of the vaccine's administration. A recent study of our own vaccine compensations for DTP damage between 1995 and 2005 found that many compensated children had developed chronic epilepsy and had a clinical history or genetic indications suggesting their epilepsy would have occurred inevitably.[48]

How would the fledgling American vaccine court respond to this shift in scientific consensus? Just as the compensation program was finally working its way out of its initial growing pains, the administrators in charge fundamentally changed its terms. The vaccine act had charged the secretary and the IOM with investigating the science of injuries from both pertussis and rubella vaccines right away, and the IOM published its findings in 1991 and 1994.[49] The IOM review panels examined all types of evidence from epidemiological studies to unpublished case reports, adopting a neutral starting point on the question of injury causation. Controlled observational studies and controlled clinical trials could lead them to reject a causal link, but compelling case series evidence or individual case reports could sway them in favor of accepting causation.[50] The 1991 report on pertussis vaccine safety found no evidence that the DTP shot caused autism, but found evidence consistent with a causal link to acute encephalopathy (between zero and 10.5 per million children vaccinated) and a shock-like state, and a clearer link to anaphylaxis and protracted crying. There was not enough evidence to say anything about a causal relationship between DTP and outcomes such as chronic neurological damage. There was no evidence for links to infantile spasms or SIDS.[51]

The most important changes in the governance of the VICP came in 1995, when the secretary changed the original Vaccine Injury Table to more narrowly construe the meanings of encephalopathy and seizures as presumptive vaccine injuries (but added chronic arthritis as a presumptively compensable injury after receipt of the rubella vaccine).[52] Specifically, the definition of encephalopathy narrowed from a very broad concept of "any significant acquired abnormality of, or injury to, or impairment of function of the brain"[53] in the original statute to specific definitions of either acute or chronic encephalopathy.[54] To qualify as "acute," the new encephalopathy had to involve a significantly decreased level of consciousness lasting at least twenty-four hours. It had to be

sufficiently severe so as to require hospitalization, though actual hospitalization need not have occurred. To qualify as "chronic" under the
new definition, the petitioner would have to show a change in mental
or neurologic status lasting at least six months from the receipt of the
vaccine. The changes also specified that anyone who regained normal
neurological functioning after an acute encephalopathy would not be
presumed to have suffered ongoing brain damage.

These changes narrowed the grounds for Vaccine Injury Table claims
considerably. Nearly all claims become contested off-Table claims that
needed some kind of convincing science to prove causation by the preponderance standard. In this off-Table period, children with a wide range
of brain injuries and seizure conditions could no longer qualify as claimants. Their claimed encephalopathies could fail by being neither acute
enough (dramatic in the short term) or chronic enough (sufficiently
damaging over the long term). As Kevin Conway explained it, "[HHS]
effectively said there's no more injuries caused by DTP vaccine. So there's
no more Table. It's just gone."[55] "I can't think of one [encephalopathy]
case that has ever met the definition since 1995," he said (and his firm is
one of the largest handling these cases for petitioners). From the perspective of HHS and the medical community, if vaccine injury claims became
harder to win because the Vaccine Injury Table was more consistent with
scientific knowledge and vaccines were safer, that was hardly a problem.
The addition of nine more vaccines to the VICP starting in the 1990s,
often without accompanying injuries, also meant that petitioners had to
make causation-in-fact arguments in the vast majority of cases.

Curtis Webb is a petitioner's attorney who began his career at the
founding of the vaccine court and tried many of the original DTP cases
with the broadly defined injuries. Webb is also critical of the post-1995
off-Table era: "The Table wasn't supposed to be like this. But now they
only put the things on the Table if [HHS] were to choose to defend them,
they would overwhelmingly lose them. The Table was supposed to be a
generous list of things that *might* have been caused by the vaccine. And
now, it has been converted to a stingy list of those things that are un-
equivocally caused by vaccines."[56] "We always win if they're the right
illnesses," he said, chuckling, but after 1995, the list of winnable illnesses
was considerably shorter. "Congress intended generosity to be provided
mostly through the Table. But they were stupid enough to give HHS the

opportunity to change the Table, so it is no longer generous. And how do you provide generosity without a generous Table?," Webb asks. In his view, demyelinating nervous system injuries and autoimmune rheumatologic diseases should be on the Table as linked to the HepB vaccine, for example, and encephalitis, encephalopathy, thrombocytopenic purpura, and shingles as linked to the varicella vaccine.

Longtime petitioners' attorney Clifford Shoemaker points out not only that vaccine court proceedings have become just as adversarial as complex civil litigation, but also that there are multiple discrete issues to fight about. "The Program has now become a situation where you can have four separate litigations within one case," he explained. The first dispute is what he terms an "onset hearing" about whether the petition is timely (filed within thirty-six months of the onset of symptoms). Next is a "full-blown hearing on causation" with experts, medical records, and parental testimony. Shoemaker recounts one dispute over experts within a causation hearing in which the "petitioner offered an immunologist and the respondent offered a rheumatologist and counsel was instructed *by the special master* to get a rheumatologist to counter the testimony of the Respondent's experts." Then there is a damages phase, "at which point another full blown hearing may occur" over such questions as what therapies are appropriate or over competing calculations of two life care planners hired by the opposing sides. Finally, Shoemaker says, "I file my application for attorney's [sic] fees and costs and in nearly every case is [sic] met with opposition from [the DOJ]."[57] From the special masters' perspectives, however, it looks as if a case alleging a rheumatologic injury requires a rheumatologist, not an immunologist, as the expert witness, and the petitioner's attorney can either try to find one or face losing the case. The special masters regularly and informally tell the attorneys their views on the strengths of each case, and often rounds of delays are due to the petitioners' attorneys trying to find a suitable expert to keep a case alive. Once the adversarialism over resources subsided, disputes about off-Table claims took over.

The Challenge of Thimerosal Litigation

The path of two lawsuits filed in Multnomah County, Oregon, in 2002 reveals the winding story of the thimerosal lawsuits from state courts to the vaccine court. A Portland firm specializing in personal injuries from medical products, Williams Dailey O'Leary Craine & Love (now Williams O'Leary), filed *King v. Aventis Pasteur* and *Mead v. Aventis Pasteur* in state court claiming that Jordan King and William Mead became autistic because of thimerosal in their childhood vaccines.[58] The complaints alleged negligence, fraud, unjust enrichment, and strict products liability under Oregon common law against vaccine manufacturers and local doctors and were planned as a class action covering over thirty million people. As I will explain below, lawsuits like this one were designed to evade the vaccine court's jurisdiction and to play out in regular civil courts with access to hometown juries and full discovery into vaccine manufacturers' records. Attorneys from Williams O'Leary would go on to try the King and Mead families' cases as two of the six test cases in the Omnibus Autism Proceeding (OAP) at the vaccine court after this strategy failed. The law firm's website still contains a section devoted to vaccine litigation, claiming that thimerosal caused "severe neurological damage, including autism" to children. There is, however, almost no chance that such a claim would have any traction in any court in the United States now.[59] But in 2002, the picture was very different, and these civil suits were much more threatening to the vaccine court and its legacy.

By June 2002, there were sixty-eight thimerosal lawsuits pending, which observers characterized as "staggering" in their proportions.[60] Lawyers representing parents of children with autism wanted to bring their cases in state courts to get discovery and thereby access to vaccine manufacturers' records (which they guessed might be incriminating or embarrassing), and to proceed perhaps even all the way to a jury with the claim that thimerosal caused autism or other developmental disorders. State tort laws also had other significant benefits. Many families had missed the vaccine court's relatively short statute of limitations, which requires that claims be brought within thirty-six months of the first appearance of a symptom of the alleged vaccine injury. Attorneys had to find some way around this limitation, and the options were either to file in the VICP and wait to be dismissed and then file in state court or to fit claims under a more generous state law from the start. One Houston attorney, clearly planning on the first strategy, filed 167 thimerosal claims in vaccine court (a 92 percent increase in claims for the first eight months of fiscal year 2002), only 7 of which were timely.[61] State law is often much more generous, tolling the statute of limitations for tort claims based on minors' injuries until they reach the age of majority. Vaccine manufacturers wanted all claims to go first through the vaccine court and to conduct any disputes about that question in federal rather than state court.

Eleven were putative class actions (that is, filed as class actions but not certified by a judge to proceed as such). The *King* and *Mead* class actions filed in Oregon aimed to enfold an estimated 30 million members in two classes. A Florida case claimed 175 million potential plaintiffs. Cases had been brought in fifteen states: Oregon, California, Washington, Mississippi, New York, Florida, Texas, Georgia, Arizona, Massachusetts, New Hampshire, Pennsylvania, Ohio, Illinois, and Maryland. The lawsuits drew upon different state laws, but generally included claims such as negligence, fraud, failure to warn, consumer protection, and conspiracy and named subclasses of (1) children alleging injury, (2) children exposed and seeking medical monitoring for possible future illnesses, and (3) parents filing on behalf of children. Parents filed claims for medical costs, loss of consortium, and loss of services from their children's illnesses. By September 2002, the number of pending lawsuits had risen to one hundred with twelve class actions.[62] Normally sparse Advisory Commission on Childhood Vaccines (ACCV) meetings were attended by dozens of private attorneys, pharmaceutical representatives, and representatives of organizations, and Randy Moss, a prominent D.C. attorney who reported regularly to the committee during this time (and not counsel of record for these suits), characterized the flood of outside lawsuits as the most significant occurrence in vaccine litigation since the 1986 DTP crisis that prompted the court's founding. He noted that the thimerosal lawsuits re-created the same danger as before: vaccine manufacturers could be financially overwhelmed by verdicts in favor of children and parents and driven out of business.[63]

The vaccine court's existence presented a barrier to these thimerosal lawsuits' path through regular civil courts, however. The vaccine act explicitly states, "No person may bring a civil action for damages in an amount greater than $1,000 or in an unspecified amount against a vaccine administrator or manufacturer in a State or Federal court for damages arising from a vaccine-related injury or death associated with the administration of a vaccine after October 1, 1988, and no such court may award damages in an amount greater than $1,000 in a civil action for damages for such a vaccine-related injury or death, unless a petition has been filed . . . for compensation under the Program."[64] Were these vaccine injury claims that had to proceed through final judgment at the vaccine court first, in which case they would be dismissed elsewhere, or would plaintiffs' attorneys find ways of framing their claims so that they did not fall under the VICP (what I call loophole lawsuits)? Attorneys filed loophole lawsuits for damages of only $1,000 or based on thimerosal exposure from products other than vaccines, namely RhoGAM shots (the shots given to pregnant women with an Rh-negative blood type to prevent harmful interaction with the fetus's blood) and nasal spray.[65] The loophole strategy reveals the purposes behind the litigation beyond the normal business of individual recovery and attorney compensation, which was to expose the manufacturers and the federal government as complicit in a cover-up of thimerosal's toxicity, perhaps through the discovery process.

The plaintiffs wanted to step around the vaccine court entirely, however, not just get a few loophole lawsuits to move forward. The first argument for total evasion was that thimerosal was not itself a vaccine, and thus claims based solely on it were not vaccine-related. Instead, plaintiffs argued, thimerosal was an adulterant or contaminant.[66] The second total evasion argument was that including thimerosal in vaccines was a design defect that could have been avoided by use of a safer preservative or by preparing only individual doses. The language of the statute protects companies from liability only if a vaccine-related injury "resulted from side effects that were unavoidable."[67] If either of these legal arguments succeeded, the pharmaceutical companies would have no cover from the 1986 vaccine act and the cases would remain in regular civil courts.

Plaintiffs also narrowed or reframed vaccine injury claims in smaller ways designed to keep their claims in state courts. Parents filed derivative claims only for themselves, arguing they were claiming not a vaccine injury but rather that they suffered harms and losses from their children's illnesses. There was some precedent for family members to bring claims in state court. The husband and child of a mother who contracted polio as a result of the child's live oral polio vaccination (because in this older formulation of the vaccine, it was possible for the virus to shed in the child's feces and transmit vaccine-induced polio) had won the right to bring a state tort claim for their own loss of companionship and consortium in 1994, even after the mother had collected a $750,000 award from the vaccine court.[68] The medical monitoring claims were also claims not about vaccine injuries but rather about concern that harms might appear in the future. And in an attempt to defeat diversity jurisdiction and removals of the lawsuits to federal court, plaintiffs' attorneys named in-state doctors as defendants alongside the national pharmaceutical manufacturers because federal diversity jurisdiction requires that plaintiffs and all defendants reside in different states.[69] Mr. Moss cautioned that if these more narrowly framed suits could evade the no-fault court's jurisdiction, their continuation would seriously threaten the efficacy of the VICP. He also cautioned that a lot of money would be spent monitoring healthy people and the public would be needlessly alarmed.

Attorneys were ultimately unable to move thimerosal claims far enough along in the civil litigation process to get the leverage, exposure, information, or damages they hoped for. The cases were unsuccessful in different ways, however: they failed in civil court on their own terms, or became untenable after being stayed for vaccine court processing on the thimerosal issue, which ultimately concluded in the OAP with strongly worded decisions against a thimerosal-autism connection. Some cases were dismissed early on as judges found the plaintiff's attempts to get around the vaccine court jurisprudentially unconvincing given the clear congressional intent to preempt state law and to make the vaccine court the first stop for vaccine-related claims.[70] Although some judges had ruled that thimerosal claims were not tantamount to vaccine claims and could proceed, by 2005 one judge cited "overwhelming federal authority" for the conclusion that thimerosal claims were vaccine-related and must be filed in vaccine court, not in state or federal courts.[71] (Autism petitions at the vaccine court peaked in 2003 with 2,437 filings, suggesting that by that year it was fairly clear that these claims would have to be heard there.) As one judge noted, thimerosal is the "antithesis" of a contaminant or adulterant because its purpose is to prevent contamination of the vaccine in multidose vials, and moreover, federal law requires preservatives in multidose vials.[72]

Even if they could keep their cases in civil court, plaintiffs also had a hard time getting their experts past the credibility hurdles in the

Daubert or *Frye-Reed* standards for permissible expert testimony in federal or state civil proceedings. A Maryland state judge held a ten-day *Frye-Reed* hearing in 2008 over the admissibility of expert testimony on the thimerosal-autism question, and subsequently found that none of the family's experts were qualified to testify (although the five experts included a doctor and a researcher who would feature prominently in the OAP thimerosal hearings held that same year). Wyeth, the manufacturer-defendant, then won summary judgment because there was no case without experts.[73] Perhaps families were hoping to return to civil courts after rejecting a vaccine court judgment or having their case dismissed, but decisions such as these coupled with the drubbing the vaccine-autism hypothesis received in the OAP rulings would have made it nearly impossible to sustain or resuscitate a thimerosal-autism claim by this time. Even though the vaccine court had been created to address the DTP crisis—now not considered to have caused the injuries once thought—it was in place to absorb the autism claims.

Congressional Mobilization amid High Drama of Autism Claims

Political, legal, and social movement pressure on the vaccine injury compensation system was incredibly intense during the 1999 to 2003 period. Normally small ACCV meetings were filled with attorneys, pharmaceutical lobbyists, and social movement activists. Representative Dan Burton, an Indiana Republican who was convinced his grandson's autism was caused by vaccines, held highly publicized hearings in his Committee on Government Reform in 1999, 2000, and 2001 designed to expose what he and his supporters saw as government culpability and cover-up of a vaccine-autism crisis.[74] Dr. Roger Bernier, associate director for science at the National Immunization Program, launched an agenda designed to increase public trust in vaccines, trying to get ahead of what he could see was a major crisis in public perceptions.[75] There was, as I have explained, a full-scale litigation crisis over the thimerosal civil suits, which if permitted to go on outside the vaccine court would undercut its reason for existence. The presence of thimerosal in vaccines at levels that exceeded the EPA's safety limit had become a salient policy problem in 1999, but government scientists and academics were still scrambling to do the necessary research to understand what the implications might be. Recall that the RotaShield vaccine was pulled from the market in what experts agreed was a genuine vaccine safety problem in 1999, too. Vaccine court reforms that all stakeholders supported in 1998 now appeared within a highly volatile context in which the federal government and court were being accused of poisoning a generation of American children and covering it up.

Social movement activists and petitioners' attorneys have long complained that the vaccine court is hostile to petitioners because the burden of proving an injury is too high, it is too hard to make a living bringing cases there, and the window for bringing a claim is too short.[76] The burden of proof is the big struggle I address throughout the book, but nearly all the other proposals can be separated from that question and could be solved by simply amending the statute. There is long-standing wide agreement among the government advisory committee members, health bureaucrats administering the program, special masters, and advocates watching the court that Congress should amend the statute to fix some of these persistent problems. By 1998, the committee had assembled a list of legislative suggestions that were widely supported across the court's constituencies.

Some issues were fairly mundane but problematic for the daily working life of petitioners' attorneys. For example, legal fees were paid in a check that had to be co-signed by the petitioner before the attorney could cash it because the statute said money should be paid to the petitioner. The ACCV recommended that the check be issued jointly so the attorney did not have to work with a faraway client to get a signature.[77] A bigger issue for attorneys was waiting until the end of a case, perhaps years, to collect their costs; the proposed fix was to pay them on an interim basis. Other proposed changes were quite significant, such as the oft-proposed extension of the statute of limitations on claims from three years to six. Many families' find their claims time-barred by the time they discover their child's disabilities and link them to a vaccine (at least a third of his potential clients, Curtis Webb estimated).[78] Additional recommendations were that limitations on administrative spending be lifted; that the ACCV committee charter be amended to allow a person who has had a vaccine injury to serve in addition to a parent of a child injured by a vaccine; that additional family expenses such as counseling and guardianship setup costs be compensated; that the requirement that the ACCV meet four times per year be removed; that the requirement to have at least $1,000 in unreimbursable expenses be eliminated; and that the comment period be shortened and the public hearing be eliminated when making changes to the Vaccine Injury Table.[79]

While most of the ACCV's recommendations were unanimous, some were not. One more contentious question was whether to add newly discovered "factors unrelated" to the vaccine that had gained scientific acceptance and thus would rule out compensation if they were present. A "factor unrelated" cannot be something idiopathic, or of unknown medical cause. The statute specified already that infection, toxins, trauma, and metabolic disorders that have no known relation to vaccines would be considered factors unrelated, and if one of these factors is the actual cause of the injury, no compensation should be given. The DOJ urged inclusion of two more factors: structural lesions in the brain, some of which can be present from early development, and genetic disorders. Both brain lesions and infantile epilepsy can look like vaccine reactions, but they are not caused by vaccines. The committee voted to pursue legislation to include these as factors unrelated to vaccination by a vote of five to two with one abstention.

The secretary of HHS would have to pursue legislation to make all these changes, however, and getting even the most broadly endorsed improvements to the court through Congress has been very difficult. The secretary is not statutorily obligated to act on the ACCV's recommendations (and sometimes does not), but the 1998 suggestions did actually make it into several congressional bills. My informants within the program told me, however, that the 1998 push for legislative change was very poorly timed with the explosion of the autism and vaccines issue around the same time. Once it became clear that the vaccine court would be awash with claims for autism, doubling the time for filing from three to six years looked like opening the floodgates even more.[80] There was a flurry of legislative proposals to change the vaccine court's procedures as the autism challenge emerged between 1999 and 2002.[81] Most of the now-definitive journal articles that would convince most observes that autism was not related to vaccination had not yet been published, and the question was dangerously open. The politics of the vaccine court became tightly bound to one's view of the likelihood that childhood vaccines had launched an autism epidemic. Proposals that had secured broad support previously became controversial in this unsettled context and did not pass.

Even though there was wide agreement between activists and health bureaucrats that the program should be administered more fairly, anti-vaccine Congressman Dan Burton, who spearheaded efforts to scrutinize the federal government's vaccine program and who fully embraced a conspiratorial account of a government-sponsored autism epidemic, set quite a combative tone in Congress. Republicans most prominently pushed the vaccine-autism link in Congress, but there was support across the aisle from liberal Democrats. Representatives Dave Weldon (a Florida Republican, also known for his prominent anti-vaccine views) and Jerrold Nadler (a liberal Democrat representing Manhattan) introduced the Vaccine Injured Children's Compensation Act of 2001, a measure with enthusiastic support from NVIC and petitioners' attorneys, and the following year Burton (who held numerous hearings promoting the idea that vaccines cause autism) and Representative Henry Waxman (the original architect of the program) introduced very similar reforms again as the National Vaccine Injury Compensation Improvement Act of 2002. These bills would have lengthened the statute of limitations from three years to six, revised the lost wages calculation, compensated for counseling and guardianships, created a two-year window to refile if a previous claim had been impossible because of the shorter statute of limitations, and devised a provision for interim fee payments to petitioners' attorneys—all changes widely supported across constituencies. In 2001, the American Academy of Pediatrics drafted a proposal to shift the causation standard in the VICP to the supposedly more flexible "positive association" standard used in the Agent Orange Act of 1991 (included in the Weldon-Nadler bill).[82] These bills included the major unanimous ACCV recommendations from 1998 as well (though some of the housekeeping attempts such as removing the requirement to meet four times per year were not). The DOJ and the HHS secretary opposed the Weldon-Nadler bill that included the American Academy of Pediatrics–supported lower causation standard, even though they supported most of the other provisions.[83]

Congressional legislation soon included provisions both to improve justice at the vaccine court, but also to intervene in the thimerosal litigation crisis. Republican Senator Bill Frist, a heart and lung transplant surgeon and supporter of public health efforts as well as pharmaceutical companies, consulted with the then-director of the compensation program in March 2002 and introduced S.B. 2053, the Improved Vaccine Affordability and Availability Act. The Frist bill incorporated most of what the ACCV had long sought: the addition of structural lesions and genetics as "factors unrelated," the six-year filing deadline (but with no look-back period), the more generous lost wages calculation, the guardianship and counseling compensations, attorneys' fees paid without co-signature, and the charter changes allowing a vaccine-injured person to serve on the committee, which could meet fewer than four times per year. With some variation from the ACCV's original recommendations, the Frist bill also included interim payment of attorneys' fees, an increase in payments for a death or for pain and suffering, and shortening the comment period for new rules.

The Frist bill was notable, however, because it also added numerous new provisions that attempted to herd the thimerosal lawsuits back to the vaccine court. It allowed defendant manufacturers to remove lawsuits in non-VICP forums back into the vaccine court, defined vaccine manufacturers as manufacturers of any component (thereby bringing thimerosal-only manufacturers such as Eli Lilly firmly back into the fold), clarified that any listed ingredient could not be an adulterant or contaminant, defined vaccine to include all ingredients, prohibited equitable relief claims outside the vaccine court (so that plaintiffs in civil court would all have to have a present physical injury claim), removed liability for medical monitoring and claims of increased future risk, banned parental loss of consortium claims in civil court and created derivative claims in the vaccine court instead, and provided for the secretary to contract with the IOM to conduct ongoing, comprehensive review of new data on childhood vaccines and report within three years. Finally, it applied all these provisions to all claims pending in civil courts as of the date of enactment.[84] The Frist legislation was thus a combined effort to enact the long-awaited consensus reforms from 1998 and to preserve the powers of the vaccine court to decide all vaccine-related injury claims. It was carefully crafted to wipe out all the pending thimerosal lawsuits in civil court and force them back into the vaccine court. SafeMinds and other parent activists rallied against the Frist bill, arguing that they needed to bring the civil suits to expose drug companies' responsibility for the autism epidemic.[85]

The Republicans did not yet control the Senate, however, and Frist was a minority committee member. Committee chair Ted Kennedy stalled the bill,[86] and the consensus amendments to improve the vaccine court died yet again because of the thimerosal controversy. The only changes to make it through during this period were a lifting of the thousand-dollar unreimbursable expenses requirement and a modification to the requirement that the vaccine injury either last six months or more or result in death, permitting inpatient hospitalization and surgery to count as well.[87] This modification came after it was clear that RotaShield could increase risk for intussusception, which can be surgically fixed in a short period of time (and thus without the change, no claims for RotaShield that had been quickly resolved would be compensable).

In the November 2002 elections, the Republicans took control of the Senate. The Homeland Security Act of 2002 would create the Department of Homeland Security in the wake of the 9/11 terrorist attacks, and was sure to pass. One part of the Frist bill that would squelch the civil thimerosal lawsuits had been attached to the Homeland Security bill as a rider.[88] Recall that plaintiffs in the thimerosal-autism lawsuits generally named the major children's vaccine manufacturers as defendants—typically Abbott Laboratories, Aventis Pasteur, Merck, SmithKline Beecham (GlaxoSmithKline), and Wyeth, but also Eli Lilly, which manufactured thimerosal from the mid-1980s to 1992 but had not made childhood vaccines since the 1970s.[89] The companies that were active in the vaccine business did not have trouble convincing judges that they were vaccine manufacturers clearly covered under the vaccine act, but Eli Lilly remained vulnerable after some judges found that it was not entitled to the protection of the act because it manufactured only thimerosal. The company's potential liability was a primary path for the civil suits outside the VICP. The Homeland Security bill rider, like the original Frist bill, specified that thimerosal was a vaccine component, not an adulterant or contaminant, bringing Eli Lilly under the protection of the vaccine court.

The Homeland Security bill rider caught activists and their congressional supporters by surprise, and even Burton voted for the bill without knowing the provision was included.[90] It had been inserted at the last minute by outgoing Senate Majority Leader Dick Armey, who defended it "because we cannot let the tort lawyers define the conditions of science and medicine in America. They'll dumb it down as they've done so many other things."[91] SafeMinds activists portrayed the rider as a secret plot to protect Eli Lilly by politicians who were cozy with the pharmaceutical company. Burton told how he angrily confronted Armey, who said the insertion request had come from the White House, presumably through HHS.[92] Given the significant threat to the basic design of the vaccine court that the outside lawsuits posed, there would have been plenty of support for the rider among pro-immunization forces within the administration even without particular concern for Eli Lilly itself. The Homeland Security Act was enacted with the rider included, but SafeMinds activists and their supporters in Congress were able to sponsor a measure soon after that removed it. A statement from Eli Lilly after the January repeal of the thimerosal provision acknowledged that "the process by which this legislation was enacted was not desirable" and that the company fully understood the Senate repeal.[93] Litigants in the pending civil cases hoped the repeal would boost their claims against Eli Lilly. One judge explicitly rejected the argument that, in repealing the protection for Eli Lilly, Congress meant to expose the company to litigation as an independent thimerosal manufacturer, not a manufacturer of a vaccine component sheltered by the vaccine court.[94] In the end, all the thimerosal claims would be moved into vaccine court and would not be compensated. With the benefit of hindsight, the Frist bill looks like a big missed opportunity to have gotten much-needed, consensus reforms to the basic operations of the vaccine court from Congress. There has not been another opportunity as good since then.

The Vaccine Court as a Solution to Autism Litigation

All the thimerosal civil suits were either dismissed or stayed pending the outcome of the vaccine court trials in the OAP. Autism claims began to appear at the court in the late 1990s and exploded early in the century, with most filings occurring in 2003, 2004, and 2005. The special masters held hearings on both the MMR vaccine and thimerosal as possible triggers for autism and would ultimately determine in 2009 and 2010 that there was very little credible evidence to substantiate any link. The vaccine court adapted to an entirely new threat to the U.S. vaccine program that had its roots in civil litigation, but also in widespread public fears, bad publicity, and media-assisted misinformation. The vaccine court became the place in American society where the autism claim had its day in court (or, more accurately, its years of preparation leading to weeks of intensive expert testimony). This "autism showdown," as I call it, is the subject of Chapter 6. But before we get to this special episode in the vaccine court's history, it is necessary to explore the much more commonplace business of the court in Chapter 5.

The vaccine court was created to do what courts can do: cordon off a controversy into a formal setting that can process resolutions, weigh evidence, let people say their piece, attend to individual circumstances, and make an independent, legitimate judgment that is reasonable even though it is neither a scientific judgment nor the outcome of a democratic vote. Putting these questions in this legal institution was exactly the right thing to do. Even some of its greatest weaknesses from an expert scientist's perspective—such as compensations based on little available evidence—look like strengths from the perspective of upholding the immunization social order, which requires flexibility and willingness to accept error. Special masters can rule without waiting for the pace of scientific research, then adapt themselves later to new knowledge, or they can suggest to petitioners' attorneys that they wait for the science to ripen and perhaps become more favorable. The "policy" part of the court's job was a legitimate and important part, after all, and the special masters compensated in the founding years any child with any brain injury after the DTP shot because there had been a public, bipartisan political consensus that this was the right thing to do for many reasons. There was little need for more information in order for the court to fulfill its mission at its start.

The court could not go on that way for long. The original statute required the IOM studies that then led to the off-Table period, akin to a time bomb planted in the original program that would eventually destroy its early version. Institutionalizing disputes over vaccine injuries exerts pressure to increase the supply of scientific information to answer the questions that everyone is arguing about. The mobilized parents had won passage of the vaccine act with their compelling personal testimonies and individual medical records, but new forms of knowledge such as the epidemiological study became ascendant. The conclusions these forms of knowledge produced at the vaccine court made certain claims of rights to injury recognition untenable, but they also left open a space for stipulations without a causal concession. That is, some cases would still be compensated (despite a lack of convincing epidemiology showing a vaccine link) because witnesses would be able to stitch together a causal story about the individual, something a legal process is well suited to drawing out. This balancing act between individual stories and big data exemplifies the compromise solutions forged at the vaccine court, leaving everything the court was created to produce—conclusions about causation, the payment, the claims of rights and redress, and the range of political rhetoric possible to describe these cases for both sides—in a hedged middle ground, lumbering on.

3

Health and Rights in the Vaccine-Critical Movement

Vaccine-critical movements have a long history, and historians have well documented their appearances, arguments, and impacts in Europe and the United States.[1] Vaccines have always been controversial for reasons that have been fairly enduring: principally, fear of injury from the vaccine and mistrust of the authorities recommending or ordering the vaccination. Some contemporary vaccine-critical activists' goals are straightforwardly legal and political, such as getting state-level vaccine exemptions expanded, getting mandates removed, or doing away with the vaccine court, but others are more broadly cultural, such as moving individuals' relationships to risk and disease away from expert guardians and back into the private family and making medicine more holistic and individualized. These arguments predate the controversies of the 1980s that resulted in the passage of the National Childhood Vaccine Injury Act of 1986 (NCVIA) and the founding of the vaccine court. One public health researcher writing in 1969 noted that citizens had long expressed objections to being vaccinated based on freedom of religion, distrust of medical science, membership in an alternative health community, and resistance to state interference.[2] Researchers confirm that it is not level of education that seems to influence vaccine skepticism, but rather embrace of complementary and alternative medicine treatments and adoption of a spiritual rather than analytic approach to evaluating evidence.[3]

Vaccine resistance has often come from the middle classes, and the contemporary movement follows this pattern as well. The organized vaccine critics whom I observed were overwhelmingly educated middle- and upper-income white professionals, often white married women. These features are importantly different from the classic picture of a social movement: composed of deprived outsiders such as the poor or racial minorities and seeking policy change or inclusion first and perhaps only expressive cultural change as a secondary goal.[4] Vaccine critics are more similar to those mobilized within other middle-class movements that blend health, science, and politics such as the fat acceptance movement,[5] AIDS activism,[6] and breast cancer activism.[7] Despite their relative whiteness and privilege, vaccine critics employ rights-based rhetoric to construct themselves as a vulnerable minority group whose human rights are being abused by the state. They thus represent an interesting case of a relatively politically conservative movement (with leadership from the libertarian right, though not exclusively) that nonetheless describes itself as a vulnerable minority, in contrast to much New Right rhetoric that represents groups such as racial minorities, Native peoples, or people with disabilities seeking rights protections as claiming illegitimate "special rights."[8] Rather than being driven by a politics of resentment that undeserving others are taking more than their share, vaccine-critical movement leaders are what I call health libertarians, driven by a neoliberal understanding of health as individual responsibility. As I show here, this blend of health and politics is what makes their approach to rights intelligible.

In this chapter, I examine the origins and primary commitments of the vaccine-critical organizations active in the contemporary United States, with a focus on some of their broader political-rhetorical frames for discussing vaccine injury. Chapter 5 takes up the effects of these frames on their understandings of evidence in the vaccine court. My focus here is limited to the leaders and organizations most engaged with the vaccine court, that is, the group that helped found it and the ones that organize around law and the court today. The vaccine-critical movement has invoked law and rights in recognizable ways, such as for "explaining how existing relationships are unjust, . . . defining collective group goals, and . . . constructing a common identity among diversely situated citizens."[9] Even when social movement activists lose in court, as vaccine critics generally have at the vaccine court, litigation can nonetheless help consolidate the movement's identity and messaging.[10] I show how critics frame vaccine mandates and failed legal cases as human rights violations, analogize themselves to minority groups protected in civil right laws, and shift language around vaccines from fears of disease to individual choice and rights violations. They often invoke the language of rights in the classic American way—individualistic, pushing away the power of the state, and asking for forbearance rather than provision. They use moments of uncertainty, disagreement, or confusion or shifts in scientific consensus within government and the courts to construct narratives of illegality and impropriety. In these instances, critics describe a higher and more just form of law that is lost to the past or is being subverted by those currently administering the vaccine injury compensation system. They also appeal to elites within the government vaccine safety system to use already-existing laws and policies to conduct new research and legitimize new vaccine injuries. These demands for affirmative provision and resources from the government are hard to square with the libertarian rhetoric that more often dominates rights talk among vaccine critics, however.

Mobilizing Rights Claims for Vaccine Injury

Autism advocacy (of a certain variety) and vaccine criticism have been tightly intertwined in the past fifteen years, but it was not always this way. Neither autism nor vaccine activism is what it used to be. The contemporary American movement of vaccine critics has two versions: that which grew from the DTP vaccine controversies of the 1980s and was in place before the current autism causation controversy, and that which arose in 1999 and 2000 in response to the notion that vaccines had started an autism epidemic. The older organization is the National Vaccine Information Center (NVIC), formed in 1982 by parent-activists concerned about the reactivity of the whole-cell DTP vaccine and originally named Dissatisfied Parents Together.[11] NVIC founders helped pass NCVIA with bipartisan support (recounted in detail in Chapter 2), which established the foundation of our current vaccine safety and injury compensation system, including the vaccine court.[12] NVIC leaders describe it as "the oldest and largest consumer led organization advocating for the institution of vaccine safety and informed consent protections in the public health system."[13] NVIC is the most active vaccine-critical policy group nationwide. The organization maintains a grassroots political organization and advocacy portal that tracks legislation, dispatches volunteers, and helps volunteers contact their elected representatives.

Historian Robert D. Johnston emphasizes the "high level of respect, intellectual engagement, and at times celebration in the common culture" that NVIC and its leaders, particularly co-founder and current president Barbara Loe Fisher, enjoyed in the 1990s and at the beginning of the twenty-first century.[14] Jacob Heller also describes how the early Dissatisfied Parents Together activists were able to use authoritative scientific evidence as well as internal debates among physicians about adverse events from pertussis vaccines to join the conversation about vaccine injury in a credible way with real political leverage.[15] During this early period, mobilized parents were similar to the AIDS activists described by Steven Epstein, who were able to gain attention from federal drug policy makers not only by disrupting drug studies but also by becoming conversant in the scientific literature.[16] There was a lull in vaccine politics after the struggle over the DTP vaccine in the mid-1980s but before the autism linkage revived the issue for national and international attention around 1998, when NVIC nearly dissolved. NVIC received a donation from a group of chiropractors in 1993 that saved the organization financially and focused Fisher's attention on, in her words, "a larger fight for freedom of choice in health care" waged by alternative care providers like chiropractors and homeopaths.[17]

This alliance with alternative health providers may have saved NVIC financially but cemented it as an outsider organization to mainstream science, medicine, and public health. "Over time," as Jacob Heller explains, "opposition to vaccination came to imply a rejection of science, the progressive uses of innovation (mass vaccination consistently promises to rid everyone—irrespective of class—of disease), and modernity itself; opposing vaccines became, on its face, evidence of some kind of crackpotism."[18] Vaccine-critical leaders, armed with middle- and upper-class status, college degrees, and often considerable resources, have worked tirelessly to dispute this crackpot image. They have drawn on a wide range of credible formulations as well as mainstream legal and political strategies, with some limited success. However, they have not been able to maintain any broad credibility, and I argue throughout this book that a main route to exposure of the weaknesses of their claims has been through the legalized scrutiny of vaccine injury cases. The vaccine court was designed to be deferential to the scientific mainstream, and the early successes of the movement in founding the vaccine court would soon be undone as the scientific consensus moved further and further from their claims.

Vaccine criticism thus sprouted a second arm at the turn of the twenty-first century composed primarily of parent-activists from the autism community activated by the thimerosal scare. NVIC, solidly aligned with chiropractors and libertarian alternative medicine supporters, embraced the notion that vaccines were causing an autism epidemic, but parent-activists of the autism community organized independently and formed the next wave of social movement organizations. Parents founded all of the most prominent vaccine-critical groups of the past three decades. The majority are mothers, but there have been some important leaders who are fathers. Most have a mobilization story linked to their child's diagnosis with disabilities they attributed to vaccines.

SafeMinds, an organization dedicated to mercury-induced neurological disorders, was founded in 2000 by American parents concerned about thimerosal. Its mission is "to restore health and protect future generations by eradicating the devastation of autism and associated health disorders induced by mercury and other man made toxicants."[19] Generation Rescue, another prominent organization promoting the idea that mercury in vaccines causes autism, was founded in 2005 by businessman and parent J. B. Handley (who later handed over the named association with his group to comedienne Jenny McCarthy). This organization is much more oriented to parent service than policy. There are other lesser-known autism-vaccine organizations as well, and in February 2010 they formed the Coalition for Vaccine Safety (which includes SafeMinds, Generation Rescue, the National Autism Association, Autism One, Autism Action Network, Talk About Curing Autism, the Center for Personal Rights, the Elizabeth Birt Center for Autism Law and Advocacy, and Unlocking Autism).[20] Many activists maintain connections across multiple groups, attend conferences such as the AutismOne meeting in Chicago every spring, and appear regularly on blogs devoted to the vaccine-autism connection such as Age of Autism.

Some vaccine critics have mobilized explicitly around opposition to vaccine court decisions. In 2011, American parent-activists founded what they called the Canary Party as an explicit alternative to the political frameworks available for promoting their concerns. Named for the canary in the coal mine, the party is "a movement created to stand up for the victims of medical injury, environmental toxins and industrial foods by restoring balance to our free and civil society and empowering consumers to make health and nutrition decisions that promote wellness."[21] In their view, the progressive left was too bound to Big Government (as they call it) and immunization programs, the conservative right failed to see pharmaceutical companies as culprits, the Green Party failed to see vaccines as an environmental problem like chemical dumping, and the Tea Party, while interested in reining in Big Government, has not taken notice of medical injustices by Big Government.[22] The original founding position paper indicated that the Canary Party would function as a true political party, running candidates for office and introducing ballot initiatives, though that has not happened. The group has focused on lobbying in Congress to attract attention to its critiques of the vaccine court and the federal vaccine injury compensation system. The group produced a video voiced by comedian Rob Schneider arguing that vaccines cause autism and that the vaccine court is a rigged and unfair system that has unfairly denied claims for autism as a vaccine injury.[23]

The lawyer-activists and parent-activists (and many are both) at the Elizabeth Birt Center for Autism Law and Advocacy (EBCALA), founded in 2008, have also organized with a specifically legal bent around the conviction that autism is a vaccine injury.[24] While EBCALA offers workshops on many legal issues that families with a child with autism confront such as insurance law and public school disability accommodations, significant effort has been directed at criticizing the vaccine court for not ruling that autism is a compensable vaccine injury in the Omnibus Autism Proceeding. EBCALA advocates also mobilized against the Supreme Court's 2011 decision in *Bruesewitz v. Wyeth* that the vaccine act shields vaccine manufacturers from design defect lawsuits, which would have been the last route for claimants to bring autism claims in regular civil court.[25]

EBCALA is not a public interest law firm or a vaccine injury law practice, but an advocacy group focused on autism and legal issues with an assumption of vaccine causation. The attorneys who bring vaccine injury claims, termed the petitioners' bar, are a generally separate group. Attorney participation in social movement activities varies widely, and most are connected to the vaccine injury question only professionally and not as parents of children with autism or other putative vaccine injuries. Kevin Conway, a prominent petitioners' attorney at the vaccine court, is quick to point out that his children are fully vaccinated (though he personally draws the line at the flu shot).[26] Most do not have any social movement involvement beyond bringing vaccine injury petitions to the vaccine court, while a few have been heavily involved in litigation (including as parents seeking compensation at the VICP), lobbying, interest group activities, and research efforts to link vaccines and autism. Overall, the petitioners' attorneys are a small group of nationally dispersed professionals who are largely uninvolved in the other vaccine-critical organizations.

Vaccine critics make their arguments in the language of science, arguing for different causation and treatment theories and also pointing out the need for more research and study. Dan Kahan, Hank Jenkins-Smith, and Donald Braman note that "public debates rarely feature open resistance to science; the parties to such disputes are much more likely to advance diametrically opposed claims about what the scientific evidence *really* shows."[27] As Generation Rescue founder J. B. Handley puts it, "It's not like there's an absence of research that starts to demonstrate a clear correlation of causality on vaccines and their link to autism. If you go to our Web site, we have pages and pages of published research that people can pull up and read for themselves."[28] Barbara Loe Fisher insists, "[A]lthough I do not have a medical degree, I am quite capable, as are most high school and college graduates, of reading the medical literature, analyzing the methodology used to vaccine studies, in reading between the lines." She continues, "It is not difficult to understand why intelligent, rational, honest, responsible, loving mothers and fathers, who are smart, and capable of reading and analyzing vaccine science, are coming to the conclusion that the science is, shall we say, inadequate."[29] But even as they muster their own science, advocates frame mainstream science as uncertain and reject expertise as the proper guide to policy. Jim Moody of SafeMinds continued to insist in public comments at a 2010 Advisory Commission on Childhood Vaccines meeting that the "science [about whether vaccines cause autism] is still in its infancy." His colleague Sallie Bernard urged National Vaccine Advisory Committee (NVAC) members to replace themselves with a new monitoring structure that would be "less susceptible to expert opinion."[30]

Choice, Information, and Accountability Arguments

Vaccine critics insist that the lives and health of the small number of children who will experience an adverse reaction should not be sacrificed for the good of the majority and that these children matter just as much as those who may contract a vaccine-preventable disease. Their concerns center on three main themes: choice, information, and accountability.[31] Critics argue that in the absence of adequate assurance of safety, individuals should be able to choose freely whether to assume the risk of vaccination for themselves or their children (without consequences like exclusion from school or hoop-jumping for exemptions). For them, informed consent means the right to refuse any vaccine after hearing about its risks and benefits. As Fisher describes it, this right of informed consent is a "human right to exercise informed consent to vaccination, including the right to choose to use every vaccine, a few vaccines, or no vaccines at all."[32]

The argument based on information is that we do not know enough to be sure that vaccines are really safe. Critics point to more studies that need to be done and insist that even when broad population-based studies fail to show links, there could still be some vaccine-injury-susceptible subgroup that is too small to be identified. The study critics want is one comparing children who have had no vaccines at all to those who have had the full schedule at the recommended times. As Vicky Debold, an NVIC board member who has served on a federal advisory committee, put it, "We ask that the government begin to fund research that evaluates the effect of vaccination, against no vaccines at all, on biomarkers of immunity, biomarkers for metabolic dysfunction, neuro-developmental outcomes, including autism, immune-mediated illnesses of all sorts, autoimmunity, allergies, asthma, epilepsy, intellectual and learning disabilities, all the things that we know are epidemic in our children. We ask for all of that [applause]."[33]

Critics are correct that there has not been a U.S.-government-sponsored study that compares children who have had vaccines on the recommended schedule to those who have had none or had them in some modified way. There are many reasons, from study design challenges to the general acceptance that the current schedule is already well researched. New vaccines are tested along with the preexisting ones to see if there is any reduced efficacy or safety issues either alone or in combination. The recommended vaccine schedule has been produced over many years by a process that primarily evaluates vaccines as discrete, separate products regulated by the FDA. The main goal has been to take the vaccines that are available on the market and shown to be safe and effective in clinical trials and to fit them into the schedule based on balancing several factors: the earliest point at which a child has the proper immune response (as the mother's antibodies wear off and the infant's own immune system matures), the interaction with other vaccines that would be given in the same visit, and the convenience of timing the new doses with the pediatrician visits already required. This process means that the schedule accretes over time in a sedimentary fashion with limitations imposed by the properties of the vaccines themselves (which ones can be feasibly developed in the first place, how many doses are needed, at what age a sufficient immune response begins) as well as the patterns of our lives. It is difficult for busy parents, especially those with lower incomes, more children, and less access to health care, to bring their children to the pediatrician frequently, and indeed we see that for vaccines such as DTaP that require five different doses, lower income and minority children are more likely not to have received the last dose or two.[34]

The NVAC, responding to Debold and others, recommended that a body such as the IOM look into the feasibility of doing a comparative study of vaccinated, vaccine-delayed, and unvaccinated children.[35] The IOM took up the question of doing these new studies (of studying vaccinated versus unvaccinated children for a wide range of health outcomes) as well as the question of how to study the safety of the entire recommended vaccine schedule (as compared to an alternative schedule of some sort). The 2013 IOM report endorsed the possibilities of various approaches to studying these questions and acknowledged frankly that the topic is understudied.[36] But the IOM also firmly pushed back against the idea that expensive research should be undertaken just because vaccine critics propose a hypothesis, and the panel found that a clinical trial in which some children were randomized to receive no vaccines would be unethical and could not be done, and that observational studies comparing unvaccinated children to vaccinated children would be highly confounded and difficult to interpret.

Vaccine safety advocates also want more information about whether a subpopulation exists that is much more susceptible to vaccine injury than others, how to find them, and how to protect them. Their concerns arise in a context of shifts in fields such as environmental toxicology to asking about how individual genetic variation could explain children's differing responses to lead poisoning, for example.[37] A key to their concerns is the idea that children are highly variable, and thus a population-wide study wrongly aggregates them and erases their individuality. As Fisher puts it, "When public health officials embrace the concept of eradicating an infection from the world and achieving that goal means making sure that a certain number of children have gotten a certain number of vaccinations, it is very easy to turn children into abstractions and forget that human beings are not all the same and do not all react the same way to vaccines or infections."[38] Critics and mainstream researchers agree that some children may indeed be more susceptible to vaccine injuries, and we do not know entirely why or who. There is general agreement on the goal of finding out who may be more vulnerable to an adverse reaction, but it does not include as broad a definition of susceptible minority as advocates describe, nor is it clear how susceptibility would be determined or who would decide. For instance, critics would say that children with conditions like allergies or family members with allergies are hypersusceptible, but mainstream researchers are reassured by studies showing that there does not seem to be a link between vaccine adverse events and these types of common conditions.[39] Advocates would prefer parents decide and simply opt out if they suspect they may be in the susceptible group.

Vaccine critics also argue that our vaccine program needs more accountability. They maintain that the current vaccine system is beset with conflicts of interest since the same government agencies promote vaccine use as well as look for and adjudicate adverse events. Both SafeMinds and NVIC want Congress to hand vaccine safety monitoring over to a new independent agency, wholly separate from licensing and promoting vaccines.[40] They argue that the new agency should be modeled after the National Transportation Safety Board, and that scrutinizing vaccine injuries should be more like investigating airplane crashes. Another frequent criticism is that the vaccine manufacturing industry works too closely with government policy makers. (While the IOM does not allow its committee members or their families to have any ties to pharmaceutical companies, two of the seventeen members of the NVAC are representatives from the vaccine industry.) And finally, critics note that the vaccine injury compensation system has become more adversarial and less likely to compensate petitioners.[41] Because they see the claimed injuries as true cases of vaccine injury, critics understand the court to be subverting its intended purpose and acting hand in glove with captured federal health bureaucrats to cover up vaccine injuries.

Critics make arguments about choice, information, and accountability to form concrete policy suggestions in terms that are highly recognizable and legitimate in American political discourse. When critics use them in official forums, they are trying to speak in the same register as health bureaucrats and to shift the definitions of commonly used terms like informed consent to include opting out of vaccine requirements with no penalty, for example. But crucially, everyone in the room at the meetings I attended understood that underneath these policy suggestions and use of shared terms lay a chasm formed by divergent ideologies of health and incommensurable conclusions about the evidence behind vaccine injury claims. Critics want choices because they want a world with no vaccine requirements at all, they want information that shows that their theories of vaccine injury are true, and they want accountability to surmount health bureaucrats and regulators whose own knowledge systems assure them that vaccines are very safe. Therefore the real questions are, what understandings form and drive critics' incommensurable views of vaccination? What meanings do they mobilize to assign to vaccine injuries? In the following sections, I use the concept of collective action framing to describe how vaccine critics portray harms from vaccines.[42] When activists invoke a frame for a situation, action, or event, for example, they attempt to create a shared understanding of reality. For example, many feminist activists frame the right to abortion as a private health care decision, a fairly successful framing, while Reva Siegel and Catharine MacKinnon have pointed out that other more powerful reasons to support abortion rights have not been as widely invoked, such as framing abortion access as necessary for political equality between men and women.[43] Critics present vaccines within frames of holistic health, health freedom, environmental harm, disabled children, and vulnerable minority identity.

The Holistic Health Frame

Mobilized vaccine critics typically share a set of ideological commitments and paths to knowledge, which move underneath some more public rhetorical frames used to broaden their appeal. The first and most important is what I call the holistic health frame, a profoundly oppositional view of what vaccines do in the body and what health is. The holistic health frame has an accompanying historical narrative about how vaccines do not work and have systematically caused widespread damage since their invention. On this view, diseases of the past were actually defeated by sanitation, homeopathy, and nutrition, not vaccines. (Importantly, this assertion makes it possible to deny that diseases will really come back if vaccination rates were to drop. I have never heard any movement leader argue that the widespread recurrence of diseases would be acceptable as the price of free choice.)

Some critics want no less than to dethrone the germ theory of disease in modern medicine.[44] So when vaccine critics claim to be opposed to the germ theory of disease, what exactly does that mean? They are not denying that bacteria and viruses exist. They are part of a critique of mainstream medicine that goes back centuries, rooted in disputes over what really causes disease and where the focus and prestige in health should be. Critics of the germ theory of disease wish to reorient health toward maintaining a robust balance in the individual who will then not be susceptible to diseases, infectious or chronic. The argument is really about what causes ill health—something from the outside, like a pathogen, or imbalance on the inside—and what should be done to fix it—go to an expert and take a pill or take responsibility for maintaining balance and defenses ourselves. The key concepts in this account of health are balance, susceptibility, toxicity, and fragility. Balance and susceptibility have been foundational concepts in chiropractic approaches to disease for over a century,[45] and NVIC has strong ties to the anti-vaccine wing of the chiropractic profession.[46] Likewise, the notion that vaccines and medicines are pollutants getting in the way of achieving balance from within the body is a long-standing part of the chiropractic approach.[47]

The theory of susceptibility runs deep through the vaccine-skeptical world because it also has a long lineage in explaining why the germ theory of disease is suspect.[48] Germs cannot be the primary cause of disease, on this view, because not everyone who is exposed to a germ gets the disease. The reason why some people get sick and others do not must lie in susceptibility. To be healthy, we must fortify our susceptibility against disease using nutrition, sanitation, and other techniques to boost the body's natural immunity. As one homeopathy training manual puts it, "With the germ theory of disease, no longer did we have to take responsibility for sickness caused by our own transgressions of the laws of health. Instead, we blamed germs that invaded the body. The germ theory effectively shifted our personal responsibility for health and well-being onto the shoulders of the medical profession who supposedly knew how to kill off the offending germs. Our own personal health slipped from our control. . . . If we maintain our body in a clean, healthy state then germs are irrelevant, for susceptibility does not exist."[49] The susceptibility worldview can slide into blaming sick people for not being vigilant enough to prevent their own cancer, for example.[50] The libertarian politics of vaccine skeptics fit very well with this account of disease and illness, which stresses personal responsibility, not government-led public health campaigns.

Fragility means assessing small exposures as potentially devastating to a body that is easily overwhelmed and in need of attentive caretaking and detoxification. The focus on fragility is particularly crucial to understanding how vaccine critics view toxic dangers. The mainstream scientific approach taken by medical toxicologists is that toxicity is linked to dosage (the so-called dose theory of toxicology). On this mainstream scientific view, toxins like mercury are dangerous only at certain levels not reached in the vaccine schedule. Perhaps the alternative ontology of homeopathy in which highly diluted solutions have curative powers undergirds the vaccine critics' concept of fragility in which even a tiny amount can have power. A more mainstream cultural source might be public awareness about lead poisoning, which was found to have effects on children at much lower levels than anyone first realized.[51] As I explain in Chapter 5, one of the biggest credibility problems with the thimerosal-causes-autism cases in the vaccine court was the petitioners' rejection of the mainstream dose theory of toxicology. Coupled with an account of individual children's genetic vulnerability, these understandings provide the foundation for parental worry about vaccine injury. Not only do they tap into widespread concerns about overuse of consumer products and undetected contamination, but they have roots in professional disputes that are over a century old.

The Health Freedom Frame

Vaccine-critical leaders are also closely tied to and overlap with the libertarian health freedom movement. The health freedom movement (the activists' own term for it) is built on a political theory of government illegitimacy in all health care matters. Under this account, any structures of national health care including Medicare, tracking systems or registries of any kind, infant heel blood collection for newborn screening against treatable diseases, vaccine requirements, and even the whole edifice of national administrative agencies dating from the New Deal are illegitimate. Activists from the Citizens' Council for Health Freedom ("a free market resource for designing the future of health care") were invited to speak at a 2009 NVIC conference I attended, inveighing against health and immunization registries ("tagging and tracking") and collection of infant DNA through blood samples for genetic screenings. Most of the group's focus was on opposing "Obamacare" and any government monitoring of health records or medical information rather than on vaccines in particular. Perhaps the Citizens' Council for Health Freedom either did not notice or does not object to the rhetorical linkage their name shares with the white supremacist White Citizens' Councils formed throughout the South to oppose integration in the wake of the 1954 *Brown v. Board of Education* decision. The Citizens' Council appears to be composed of nonphysicians, while the Association of American Physicians and Surgeons is an ideologically right-wing private doctors' group that is organized to oppose government intrusion into health care in any form. The group's journal has been a mainstay of anti-vaccine research publishing.[52]

Why, if vaccines themselves are not a major policy focus, is the health freedom movement nonetheless closely linked with vaccine criticism? First, both movements share the same enemy: the public health establishment backed by the power of the state. Vaccine mandates enforce a collective good of population-level immunity and require government to enforce them. The libertarian vaccine critics also benefit from free market policies toward health care and supplement sales and do not want the FDA to regulate these products or the government to require that they accept health insurance rather than private pay. Second, the libertarian politics of vaccine skeptics fit very well with the holistic health frame because both place responsibility with the individual. The vaccine-critical movement is quintessentially neoliberal, blending holistic self-care with the elevation of the individual and the private family over collective goods. Though I willingly concede that there are political differences among vaccine critics as well as regional and economic variation, I nonetheless insist that this core of health libertarianism is critical to understanding their view of themselves as a vulnerable, oppressed minority group in need of a rights-based defense. The health libertarians would also never support structural solutions to detecting and compensating vaccine injuries more quickly, such as through expanding national health insurance, having a medical identification number for every citizen, or tracking medical outcomes through a centralized national database (as Denmark does, for example).

The Environmental Harm Frame

Despite the strong libertarian and neoliberal commitments within the organizational leadership of the vaccine-critical movement, there are nonetheless consistent rhetorical elements that draw more from the cultural left than the right. Vaccine critics also frame vaccine concerns as environmental matters, as population and child health problems, and as civil and human rights issues.[53] Concerns about environmental pollutants have been widespread for decades,[54] and SafeMinds' anti-mercury mission now grows from this source rather than from the alternative health professions. Jenny McCarthy led a 2008 rally in Washington, D.C., called "Green Our Vaccines," complete with green T-shirts to link vaccine criticism with environmentalism. Vaccine critics draw on the 1998 Wingspread statement of the precautionary principle, which states, "When an activity raises threats of harm to human health or the environment, precautionary measures should be taken even if some cause and effect relationships are not fully established scientifically. In this context the proponent of an activity, rather than the public, should bear the burden of proof."[55] The Wingspread statement was crafted by scientists, activists, and scholars in the environmental movement in recognition of the fact that the harmful consequences of releasing materials into the environment have become clear only after it is too late and after safety reassurances have been proven optimistic. The Wingspread statement of the precautionary principle explicitly moves the burden under conditions of risk and uncertainty onto anticipating harms, even if they have not been proven to exist.[56] François Ewald similarly locates the origins of the precautionary principle in environmental agreements, noting that it emerges in contexts of scientific uncertainty and the possibility of serious, irreversible damage or injury.[57] Fisher explains how her organization combines the precautionary principle with informed consent and frames both within a human rights discourse: "While the precautionary principle—'first, do no harm'—is central to prevention of vaccine injuries and deaths, the informed consent principle is central to the ethical practice of medicine. The individual's right to exercise informed consent to medical risk-taking can be defined as a human right because, without it, the will of the majority can be used to oppress a vulnerable minority."[58]

Almost all vaccine criticism uses the term "toxins" to describe vaccine ingredients and presents lists of scary-sounding long names of ingredients as part of the argument that they are clearly unnatural and dangerous. Vaccine-critical activists have made much of the fact that vaccines contain formaldehyde or may have been developed with cell lines originally obtained from aborted human fetuses (rubella, varicella, and hepatitis A vaccines, for example).[59] Introducing bills requiring that parents be informed about vaccine ingredients is part of a state legislative strategy to heighten awareness of vaccine dangers (though none had passed as of 2012).[60] The ingredient strategy connects vaccines rhetorically with health movements against environmental contaminants and with natural food movements. The complexity of vaccine ingredients does indeed sit awkwardly with cultural norms against eating food products that contain processed ingredients with long and complex chemical names, for instance.[61] Recall the Canary Party's founding as "a movement created to stand up for the victims of medical injury, environmental toxins and industrial foods by restoring balance to our free and civil society and empowering consumers to make health and nutrition decisions that promote wellness." The Canary Party addresses constituents who are not Ron Paul–supporting chiropractors, but rather progressive foodies and environmentalists who also worry about issues such as genetically modified organisms (GMOs) in food. Ordinarily more government regulation is the answer for progressives worried about toxins, but the focus on vaccines troubles that alliance because Canary Party–type activists do not trust the public health establishment or federal safety regulators.

SafeMinds has also taken on a broader, international environmental interpretation of its anti-mercury mission. The group's founding claim was that the mercury-based preservative thimerosal in vaccines causes autism, but it has now embraced the broader cause of eliminating mercury pollution from all sources, perhaps searching for a broader rationale for its anti-mercury activism. SafeMinds has adopted the goal of "eliminat[ing] coal as a fuel for energy generation" because coal-fired power plants are a major source of environmental mercury.[62] Both the Canary Party and SafeMinds are clearly reaching left while NVIC reaches more to the right, but all are united by their vaccine opposition and mistrust of government and share nearly identical goals as well as borrow liberally from each other's language.

As befits a movement leader trying to gather together a big tent of supporters, Fisher invokes lefty-sounding environmental terms alongside right-wing libertarian values. Her 2009 NVIC conference keynote address targeted vaccine mandates for being "one-size-fits-all" and failing to "acknowledge biodiversity," for example. She invoked suspicion of modernity and development and hearkened back to a time when the earth was cleaner and we were healthier: "[S]omething is wrong with the food we've been eating, the air we've been breathing, the water we've been drinking, the pharmaceutical products we have been consuming, and the way that we have been living our lives," Fisher explained. "The people know there's an epidemic of chronic illness and disability because they're living it, and they know it has not always been this way. So they are taking back control of their health, and exercising, and eating organic, and going green, and throwing away prescription drugs that don't work, and trying alternative, holistic approaches to staying well. They are acknowledging and embracing the balance and strength inherent in the natural order, rather than fearing, and seeking to alter it."[63]

The Disabled Children Frame

Vaccine critics argue that these disruptions of modernity and its damaging interventions are the cause of widespread declines in population health, particularly children's health. Vaccine critics employ the register of population health as well as individualizing and dramatizing vaccine injury. Fisher in particular regularly cites dismal statistics about the maternal and infant mortality rates in the United States along with rates of chronic disease and disability in American children to support her argument that vaccines are not improving population health. She connects these dismal numbers to knowledge about vaccine injury first by claiming that public health officials do not know why infant and children's health is so imperiled and then by arguing that over-vaccination is to blame because it weakens the immune system and provokes chronic disease. "Public health officials . . . can't figure out why so many infants and children in America are plagued with brain and immune system problems. The unprecedented, unexplained chronic disease and disability epidemic has gotten worse in the past three decades—with 1 child in 6 now learning disabled; 1 in 9 suffering with asthma; 1 in 50 developing autism; 1 in 400 becoming diabetic and millions more suffering with severe food allergies, inflammatory bowel disease and other chronic illness," says Fisher.[64] The Canary Party's anti-vaccine court video (voiced by actor and comedian Rob Schneider) also claims that over half of U.S. kids have "chronic disease and disability" (seemingly leaning heavily on children's increased weights to get to such a large number of children).[65] Fisher and other vaccine-critical leaders emphasize the costs and burdens of disabled children. They also portray the United States as uniquely unhealthy among developed countries and on a recent steep decline.

Vaccine-critical leaders understand these population health statistics as natural and direct, not socially constructed through processes such as environmental and institutionalized racism, increased diagnosis, expansion of diagnostic criteria, awareness and mobilization for resources, or pharmaceutical advertising. Interestingly, this perspective on Americans' ill health and its dramatization is one area of agreement between vaccine critics and much public health messaging, at least if the topic is not vaccines. Public health officials have promoted alarmist messages about the dangers of obesity, salt, and formula feeding, for example. Messaging about increasing burdens of disease has been a foundational component of public health education for decades and is not usually interrupted with caveats about how complex social forces may be contributing to greater knowledge, naming, and recording of diseases. While the scientific groundings for these claims of a causal link to vaccines are weak, vaccine critics nonetheless participate in the drumbeat of concern for child health that sounds very familiar. Tellingly, however, libertarian vaccine-critical leaders fail to make any connections between children's health problems and the poverty and racism in which the poorest and arguably least healthy children live, nor would they support any expansions to our health care system and welfare state to help them or their families.

The Vulnerable Minority Frame

Vaccine critics also mobilize legal concepts in their defense from vaccination, constructing themselves as a vulnerable minority population in need of rights-based protections. In her keynote address to the 2009 conference I attended, Fisher characterized the assembly as "a gathering of minorities."[66] (The room was filled with what looked to be overwhelmingly white middle-class professionals.) "America, from its beginning," she explained, "has been the land of promise for minorities around the world who have been demonized and persecuted for the genes they were born with, or for their religious beliefs, or for the value they place on freedom of thought and speech." In this account of minority identity, the minority status is a hidden vulnerability to vaccine injury handed down through family heritage and detectable by genealogical examination of relatives' ailments. "The first time I realized what it was to be a minority because of my genes," she continued, "was when my son Chris collapsed after his fourth DPT shot." Fisher blends an account of multiple white ethnicities with genetic susceptibilities to explain this minority identity. "Like most Americans I'm of mixed heritage, part Norwegian, Irish, Scottish, English, German, and Jewish, with a family history of teachers and writers, doctors and nurses, musicians and artists, builders and business owners, soldiers and historians. We have brought, with our contributions to society, a genetic susceptibility to atypical responses to inflammation, manifested by a history of severe food, environmental, and prescription drug allergies, rheumatoid arthritis, thyroid disorders, inflammatory bowel disease, diabetes, eczema, and migraine." Paradoxically, it is at this moment of invoking minority status that the critics successfully "whiten" their movement by explicitly claiming whiteness in an overwhelmingly white organization and then recasting it as genetically individualized and deserving of rights protections. Fisher's descriptions retain the prestigious invocation of biomedical science (including her family's achievements) and celebrate what Ruha Benjamin calls the "white American values of autonomy and free choice" in browsing and ultimately rejecting technoscientific products such as vaccines.[67]

Minority identity—usually associated with marked racial identities and civil rights struggles—is not a popular trope on the libertarian right (as many NVIC supporters in the audience were), so it must be carefully crafted as highly individualized and located within the genes (just as environmental language must not drift into support for government-led cleanup or regulation and only support individual health-promoting actions). As Dorothy Roberts's work details, turning to genetics has been a consistent way to evade structural inequalities and racial injustice, and so here it is not surprising to see the ease with which a nearly all-white social movement invokes minority status based on genetics.[68] Fisher describes how "our unique combination of genes . . . which give us our individual, physical, mental, and emotional strengths and weaknesses, our special talents and limitations and which play a profound role in defining who we are and what we will become . . . can also make us more or less susceptible to suffering complications from atypical manipulation of the immune system by vaccination." This genetic individuality that is the key to vaccine injury is also what she invokes as "biodiversity," which channels the language of diversity into nonracialized genetic variation. Notably lacking from anti-vaccine rhetoric about diversity is any sense that disability is a form of human diversity, a core argument from disability rights advocates and scholars.[69] On this view, human differences in learning, cognition, behavior, and vulnerabilities should be accommodated and sometimes even celebrated rather than stamped out in the hopes of being normal or succeeding in a dog-eat-dog world. Vaccine critics begin with the argument that children are damaged and diminished by vaccines, however.

Vaccine critics have worked tirelessly to direct government, judicial, and regulatory attention to their claims of vaccine injury. They have organized a social movement, founded new organizations, testified before

Congress and before countless administrative hearings, organized vaccine court cases, held press conferences, published their own articles in journals, produced videos, films, blogs, and websites, held public conferences, and made speeches. Their arguments blend rights claims and accounts of compensable harm with highly salient mainstream discourses borrowed from environmentalism, children's health, consumer protection, and civil rights. Despite a record of past successes using nearly all the strategies Parthasarathy identifies as crucial for health and science-based lay activism,[70] vaccine critics' cultural and political power has steadily diminished over the past decade or so.[71] Vaccine critics have joined the community of would-be lay reformers who are regarded as harmful cranks rather than helpful correctors of smug scientific self-satisfaction. All the vaccine-critical prominent organizations remain deeply committed to accounts of vaccine injuries that have been roundly rejected by the scientific mainstream. The underlying ideologies and libertarian political commitments within the movement fit poorly with their communitarian notes of environmentalism, children's health, consumer protection, and civil rights. These features of their rights claiming explain both the energy within the movement as well as its failure to achieve its political and legal goals.

4

Knowing Vaccine Injury through Law

As Bruno Latour explains in his ethnography of a French administrative court, science and law are both elite domains devoted to their own careful, painstaking practices, "sacrificing hundreds of rats" and "spend[ing] years on claims that could be easily resolved with a bit of common sense and a measure of good faith," respectively.[1] But as he points out, eventually a judge must decide and end the matter. If a factual matter is resolved within the process of the case (or goes un-rebutted in the legal file, Latour's focus and the material site of law's enunciations), then questioning ends. Scientists, by contrast, may publish an article describing their research conclusions but still consider the matter open for further investigation and challenge. To a scientist, a factual matter in a legal file is still good grounds for going back and asking more questions, in other words: what Latour calls "*research, not judgment*."[2] The vaccine court shows us a possible solution to the tensions between the ways science and law resolve contested, somewhat uncertain questions of fact. That solution lies in the vaccine court's management of knowledge and evidence over time, during which the special masters adjust the pace of decisions and permit some reopenings, but still maintain standards of credibility. As Annelise Riles describes it, "Legal knowledge . . . is not simply reducible to social pressures and forces, but . . . has its own epistemological and material autonomy."[3] The vaccine court process turns out to be much more reiterative and open than Latour's account suggests. In this chapter, I introduce the court in more detail and situate its recognition of vaccine injuries in a broader national and transnational context of injury recognition, both in other alternative structures such as the September 11th Victim Compensation Fund and as compared to the other vaccine injury compensation systems in industrialized countries around the world.

I introduced our vaccine court as a useful institution for handling the recognition of vaccine injuries, especially once we regard them as posing a simultaneously scientific, political, ethical, and legal problem. I show throughout that the vaccine court offers a desirable balance between openness to challenge and the stability of vetted expertise; that it encourages peaceful social movement activism that must be presented as knowledge-driven, questioning, and public-spirited; and that its design has allowed the special masters to give as much recognition as they can to petitioners while maintaining sufficient scientific credibility. The operation of our vaccine court since 1988 shows how rights claims and social movement activism are thoroughly intertwined with knowledge claims. The vaccine court is thus an essential institutional support for the immunization social order. Implicit in this argument is my conviction that this social order is worth upholding for many reasons, including the public health interest in preventing diseases and their many kinds of costs. Courts do not primarily prevent diseases, however; they provide rules and structures for processing disputes.

Legalizing vaccine injuries upholds this social order in several key ways. Vaccine court processing screens out and delegitimizes claims that are quite far outside the bounds of scientific credibility, such as that vaccines do not work, have never really worked, and only cause widespread disease and disability. But even as vaccine court processing closes down the least-supported grounds for claims making, it creates an alternative space for debates that would not be credible in mainstream science but that nonetheless meet a minimal standard for investigation in the public interest. These debates are quite literally underwritten by the compensation program trust fund in the form of attorneys' fees and expert witness fees and costs. Unconventional ideas do not have to attract grant funding to be aired in vaccine court, in other words, though they will still be held accountable to standards of what Elizabeth Anderson calls epistemic responsibility, or the duty to respond reasonably to justify one's views within a community of inquirers.[4] The court is a meeting place for many of the epistemic communities that have a stake in knowing vaccine injuries, and its legal structure produces a consequential frame for vaccine debates. Our vaccine court conducts these debates in a sufficiently well-resourced, structured, repetitive, and open way that is deliberative, reason giving, flexible, capable of self-correction, and ultimately democratically accountable.

Legalizing Vaccine Injury

I have placed the vaccine court at the center of U.S. vaccine law and politics as the place where the state formally recognizes vaccine injury. How does it matter that we legalized vaccine injury in the ways we have? What policies has this court made? What forms of legitimation of the immunization social order has it produced, and how has all the social movement activity mattered? As I recounted in detail in Chapter 2, Congress set up the no-fault Vaccine Injury Compensation Program (VICP) under the National Childhood Vaccine Injury Act (NCVIA) of 1986 in response to a particular political and public health crisis moment. A few large damage awards in civil litigation over injuries from the diphtheria-tetanus-whole-cell pertussis (DTP) vaccine had led vaccine manufacturers to retreat from the market and threatened the national vaccine supply. Rather than being able to bring tort lawsuits against manufacturers in regular federal or state courts for vaccine injuries, anyone who believes they have been injured by a vaccine must file a petition with the program.[5] In 2011, the Supreme Court held that the 1986 vaccine act preempts all vaccine design defect claims, which would have been the route for dissatisfied petitioners to leave the vaccine court and claim that a vaccine could have been designed more safely.[6]

Only vaccines recommended for universal use in children are eligible for claims. Petitioners can be any age, and now most are adults who received vaccines such as influenza, recommended for almost everyone. The Vaccine Injury Table (which I have called simply the Table) spells out a list of accepted adverse events, the vaccines with which they are linked, and an acceptable time frame for the injury to appear; compensation is automatic for claims that fit its criteria. For example, encephalitis, an inflammation of the brain, counts as a Table injury if it occurs within seventy-two hours of receiving any vaccine containing a pertussis (whooping cough) antigen.[7] Off-Table claims for conditions such as autism, by contrast, require proof that the vaccine caused the injury by the preponderance of the evidence. The original hope was that the Table would handle most disputes and the system would be nonadversarial and quick. Most cases, however, now fall outside the Table and go through a process to determine whether the vaccine in fact caused the injury.

A special unit of the Court of Federal Claims, the Office of Special Masters, adjudicates vaccine injury claims with a staff of eight special masters who hear claims sitting individually. The Court of Federal Claims was created by Congress in 1855 under Article I of the U.S. Constitution to hear private claims against the federal government. The government is the respondent at the vaccine court, with the secretary of Health and Human Services as the named defendant (represented by Department of Justice attorneys). There are no juries at the Court of Federal Claims or the vaccine court. Compensations to individuals, legal and expert witness fees, and all reasonable expenses are paid out of a trust funded by a seventy-five-cent excise tax on covered vaccines (not, as some vaccine critics claim, from taxpayer dollars)[8] regardless of the outcome of the claim.[9]

The way the founding statute subsidized the petitioners' attorneys' role is critical for understanding how it came to function so much like an adversarial court process. Congress wanted petitioners to be able to find lawyers and created the only program in which attorneys for losing litigants routinely get paid. The vaccine act's risk-free fee payment rules for both attorneys and experts, or what litigation scholar Sean Farhang terms a "private enforcement regime," act as an engine—a literal subsidy—for the production of knowledge and ideas about how vaccines might cause injuries.[10] The availability of attorneys for civil rights cases increased considerably in response to congressional action making that work more valuable, and thus it is likely that fee payments in the vaccine program are critical for maintaining a willing petitioners' bar.[11] There are several hundred petitioner-side attorneys throughout the country who regularly bring vaccine injury cases, with a few firms fully specializing in that area. Since the fee structure does not provide the usual "gatekeeping" effect that Herbert Kritzer documents with plaintiff-side legal practice paid by contingency fees, petitioners have brought a wide range of proposed adverse effects and received compensation even when mainstream medicine would not provide much support for the causal link.[12] Some disreputable experts have had their reimbursements refused or reduced and some travel expenses have been found to be unreasonable and were denied, but most are routinely paid with a provision for interim fees if the case drags on (as many do).[13]

The institutional context of the alternative court gives special masters more flexibility than other judges in the U.S. federal or state courts
enjoy to consider evidence. The vaccine court has its own procedural
rules and does not use the Federal Rules of Civil Procedure. The Vaccine Rules, as they are called, explicitly proclaim a preference for the
"informal and cooperative exchange of information" and set out no right
to discovery.[14] Special masters are not bound by any "hard and fast *per
se* scientific or medical rules" under the Vaccine Act.[15] They consider a
wider range of evidence in vaccine cases than judges hearing civil suits
would admit. Vaccine court rules direct special masters to consider "all
relevant and reliable evidence governed by principles of fundamental
fairness to both parties."[16] The vaccine act specifies that special masters
may require testimony or the consideration of evidence that is "reasonable and necessary."[17] Special masters have subpoena powers to compel
people to testify, and they can ask for discovery information by subpoena as well (though they almost never exercise these powers).

Dr. Geoffrey Evans, a pediatrician and director of the VICP for most
of the time chronicled in this book, divides the program's history into
four relatively distinct periods: the founding era of the court when it
operated with the original Table from 1988 to 1994 and handled almost
entirely claims for children, many from the DTP vaccine (75 percent
during that period); the first big shift in 1994–1995 to a stricter Table
and nearly all off-Table claims; the wave of autism claims and the Omnibus Autism Proceeding (OAP), roughly from 2001 to 2008; and the
current period, characterized by mostly adult claims, still nearly all off-
Table and many based on the annual flu vaccine.[18] Compensations for
DTP vaccine injuries were until very recently the largest single category
of payouts from the program (28 percent of the total in the life of the
program), with 1,273 compensations out of a total of 4,582 total payouts
from its founding in 1988 to April 1, 2016.[19] DTP compensations have
since been eclipsed by compensations for injuries linked to the influenza
vaccine (2,578 awards). Those two vaccines, representing quite different
eras of the vaccine program, compose 84 percent of all compensations
since 1998. The vaccine court received a total of 16,878 claims based on
over thirty vaccines or vaccine combinations and adjudicated 14,497 to a
final decision as of April 1, 2016, with over 800 new claims filed in 2015.
The compensation rate overall for all adjudications is about 32 percent.

Removing the bolus of 5,600 autism claims from the total adjudicated claims yields a compensation rate of 52 percent. Awards to the vaccine injured total over $3 billion, and attorneys have received over $138 million in fees and costs, including over $68 million (in more than 5,000 payments) for dismissed cases. The current trust fund balance is about $3.5 billion.

So what has it meant to *legalize* vaccine injury, to make it a subject of the law in the ways that we do? How does it matter that these moments of conflict, injury, and uncertainty are processed through this particular court in the way that they are? Several features stand out. First, it is important to place vaccine injury compensation claims within the precarious situations that people with injuries and disabilities and their families face in the United States. We do not have a guaranteed social support and health care system that would shield a person from financial ruin in the face of a disabling condition or the need to care for a child with long-term special needs and no employment prospects. Citizens rely on a patchwork of private health and disability insurance, government programs such as Medicaid and Social Security disability or supplemental income, and educational supports that end when a child turns twenty-one. A vaccine court judgment could mean lifelong financial support for a child with a disabling condition or replacement of lost wages for an adult, for example—resources that are not available at such levels any other way. When the vaccine court ruled against thousands of families of children with autism in the OAP because they could not meet the burden of proof that vaccines caused autism, for example, the judgment marked the exhaustion of the last possible public source of help in paying for expensive care. If health care and welfare policies provided a sufficiently robust safety net for all citizens with disabling conditions and health problems, whether the vaccine court compensates enough of the right people for the right injuries would seem much less pressing. Rights claiming in the vaccine court seems desperate and contentious in many cases because of the broader conditions of our politics and society. We have collectively chosen these, and we could choose otherwise.

Second, it may not be obvious whether this institution is really a court rather than an administrative panel. Some injury compensation schemes, such as the payouts to victims and families by the September 11th Victim Compensation Fund, are not really court-like at all. But in this case, our VICP has all the classic features of what Martin Shapiro terms the prototype of courts: a triad-based structure with opposing claimants bringing a dispute to an independent judge with the power to pick one winner and one loser according to preset rules.[20] Much of its business looks like either adversarial trials or negotiated settlements. The vaccine court displays many of the same departures from the ideal type that make it a political creature as well, however. The court was created amid a political crisis by an act of Congress, and as I show throughout the book, it operates using a wide range of formal and informal conflict resolution techniques, and its function is integrated with administrative and political authority to bolster our immunization social order.[21]

Closely linked to the question of whether the vaccine court is a real court is the question of whether the special masters are judges. They do the work of judges within an adversarial court system, and thus I argue that their role is perfectly in line with that of judges. Special masters are appointed to their four-year terms by the judges at the Court of Federal Claims, who are themselves appointed to fifteen-year terms by the president with the advice and consent of the Senate. The appointments are not directly political, and a president who wanted to influence the Court of Federal Claims judges' appointments would have a hard time remaking that court given the fifteen-year appointment term. The special masters' jobs are fairly secure, and reappointments are the norm. So while these judges do not enjoy the lifetime job security of Article III judges, they are relatively insulated nonetheless. Critics of the court decry the special masters as less than judges, however. Rolf Hazlehurst, the father of a child with autism whose compensation claim was denied, decries the special masters as illegitimate: "In vaccine court, the rule of law in the American system has been replaced by what is known as a special master. A special master is nothing more than a politically appointed government attorney."[22] Hazlehurst implicitly distinguishes them from legitimate judges, who represent the rule of law, are presumably not political, and were not formerly just "government attorneys." All the special masters are indeed former attorneys, not scientists or doctors. They come from a range of backgrounds in the private sector, from the Department of Justice (DOJ), and from previous appointments as judges.[23]

Third, the vaccine court is a specialized court, hearing only vaccine claims. As Lawrence Baum has shown, specialized courts are more widespread in the contemporary United States than many scholars recognize: there are drug courts, domestic violence courts, a surveillance court, bankruptcy courts, military courts, an alien terrorist removal court (which has never heard a case), mental health courts, juvenile courts, homeless courts, and business courts.[24] Specialized courts are usually created for specific policy reasons, and assumed to be more efficient, better able to concentrate expertise on difficult legal issues or complex facts, more consistent, and more likely to produce higher quality decisions. But specialization can also lead to narrow professional viewpoints or boredom in the judges. It can promote insularity and reduce the quality of decision making, or perhaps create an easy target for interest group pressure.[25] Specialization certainly helps the nonscientist special masters become knowledgeable repeat players, and I argue here that the robust social movement pressure they have always encountered has helped to keep pathways open to new claims.

Creating specialized health courts to handle medical injury claims has become a popular idea, though as Nora Freeman Engstrom points out, advocates of health courts often promote these virtues of expertise, efficiency, consistency, and quality without examining the many ways that the vaccine court—our current best example of a medical injury court—has failed to live up to these same expectations.[26] The vaccine court has turned out to be slow (in some cases, though not all), adversarial, and somewhat inconsistent in its rulings, particularly in what I call middle-ground cases where the evidence is ambiguous. As I show throughout this book, all these features were either built in deliberately from the start (with the choice to locate the program in a federal court with guaranteed payments for lawyers, hardly a recipe for nonadversarialism) or they are actually beneficial features of the court's adaptations of science for justice in the face of uncertainty. Delays help pace the court's rulings with the timing of scientific publication, often at the request of the petitioners themselves, and inconsistency is the result of the special masters' choices to compensate cases based on facts particular to that person's situation and to rule differently when the evidence shifts or the requirements of justice seem different for another person. Engstrom's point is to remind those who are naïvely enthusiastic about the powers of yet-to-be-tried health courts that we have a good example of how they might work in the vaccine court, and it does not live up to their vision. From my perspective, the failure of the vaccine court to "rationalize" its decisions (her term) according to the proposed virtues of health courts is not a fault, then, because its best role is not to simply transcribe scientific truths but rather to fashion justice in the immunization social order. Vaccine injuries pose highly contestable, individually variable questions based on evolving scientific understandings. It is perfectly fine that vaccine court rulings reflect those struggles.

Recognizing Vaccine Injuries

Vaccine injuries come to be recognized and known in many ways, in many places, and by many different people. The parents and adults who file claims in vaccine court and their attorneys commence these legal actions because they have recognized something as a vaccine injury and seek compensation for that harm. Movement activists understand themselves as consumer watchdogs who alert the public to vaccine injuries. Many of them are also parents or have been vaccine court petitioners themselves. Experts who testify on both sides in vaccine court—typically pediatricians, pediatric neurologists, rheumatologists, and neurologists, but also others—are hired from all over the United States to share their expertise. Researchers outside government, often grant-funded professors, perform a wide range of investigations into possible mechanisms of vaccine injury as well as epidemiological studies about whether some outcome is associated with vaccination. Another set of experts serve on periodic IOM review panels tasked with presenting conclusions from published medical research about whether adverse events after vaccination are true vaccine injuries, and the results of these reviews are supposed to guide compensation rulings.

The people I call health bureaucrats form another professional corps who are tasked with vaccine safety regulation and surveillance, including the administration of the VICP. A team of in-house doctors, called medical officers, reviews all medical records for all incoming claims and recommends a disposition of the claim. The VICP is led by a physician, typically someone who previously served as its chief medical officer. Dr. Geoffrey Evans led the VICP through the era covered in this book. The

VICP is housed within the Health Resources and Services Administration (HRSA), part of the Department of Health and Human Services (HHS), led by a secretary appointed by the president and approved by the Senate. Regulation, premarket approval, recommendations, and postmarketing surveillance of vaccines occur within the FDA and the CDC, both also under the aegis of HHS. Clinical trials tell vaccine manufacturers and FDA regulators that there may be adverse events linked to the vaccine being developed and approved, and these trials are the first step in detecting vaccine injury. Health bureaucrats formally interact with the public on mixed membership committees. Attorneys, parents, and pediatricians serve on a government advisory committee for the compensation program at HRSA, and different sets of medical and scientific experts along with consumer representatives serve on other vaccine-related advisory committees at the FDA and CDC. Whether a vaccine is causing harm is a part of what all of these advisory committees oversee as well.

Knowledge about vaccine injuries is thus produced through vaccine court hearings, but also through academic research collaborations, clinical trials, research review panels, committee meetings, and surveillance monitoring. Not all these have the same power to determine what will ultimately be considered a true causally linked vaccine adverse event, and not all are equally transparent to the public or to scholars. But at some point, the results of these meetings of people are held up and scrutinized in multiple sites within in our government through public discourse, which proceeds through polite discussion, presentation and evaluation of evidence, and argumentation. As Sheila Jasanoff has pointed out, "Some of the liveliness of contemporary democracy is to be found away from the polling booths, where one often looks for it in vain, in the less examined machinery of science and technology policy—that is, in the technical advisory committees, court proceedings, regulatory assessments, scientific controversies, and even the ephemeral web pages of environmental groups and multinational corporations."[27]

While one could dispute whether these sites and proceedings are lively, they have certainly been busy. For example, there have been at least eleven IOM panels convened to study vaccine safety questions, each of them surveying thousands of published scientific articles and publishing book-length findings.[28] The process to determine whether autism would be compensated as a vaccine injury, the OAP, included over nine hundred journal articles in the record, lasted for over eight years with nearly five thousand claimants, and resulted in multiple decisions, each hundreds of pages long. Expert testimony took weeks, and the transcripts run over five thousand pages. As I described in Chapter 2, the OAP trials replaced putative class action lawsuits in the states that would have included over 175 million people. Vaccine safety regulators monitor databases of millions of medical records from U.S. citizens. The public portal for reporting possible vaccine injuries has gathered over 200,000 reports since 1990, and the vaccine court has compensated over 4,500 claims for over $3 billion (denying over 9,000 more). Of course, the total number of vaccines given during that time would reach into the hundreds of millions. Dozens of studies are now considered pivotal in the history of vaccine safety investigation. There have been congressional hearings as well as hundreds of bills introduced in the states in response to vaccine fears, as well as conferences, marches, and endless meetings.

Some of these sites are genuinely adjudicative forums, meaning that they gather and process information about possible vaccine injuries and offer a judgment that has force and meaning for policy (as in vaccine court processing or IOM deliberations about injury causation), while others are forums for opponents and proponents of particular vaccine injury explanations to put forth their arguments and attempt to close the issue rhetorically or politically (as in congressional hearings on autism and vaccines). These different forums have different institutional characteristics that influence the type of evidence that counts as compelling and the credible forms of testimony about vaccine injury, though as I explain in Chapter 5, there is a clearly defined hierarchy of evidence for vaccine injuries. The different forums create different opportunities to shape knowledge of vaccine injury.

Becoming a Vaccine Injury Claim

Before any claim of vaccine injury begins, a parent has to recognize some health problem in her child and understand it as vaccine-related (or in an adult claimant, to recognize her own symptoms as vaccine-related). Sociolegal scholars know that to bring a lawsuit, a person first has to "name, blame, and claim," that is, to recognize a legal wrong that was not fate and not her fault and find someone or something else to blame for it. The critical point is that the entire process begins just as legal claims typically do, with individual mobilization. The person would have to find out about the compensation program and contact an attorney who knows how to file a petition, presumably through the HRSA website set up for this purpose.[29] Some parents and potential adult claimants undoubtedly fail to consider vaccine causation and never make a claim at all. A parent may experience a child's seizures, fevers, autism, or some other problem as the appearance of an inevitable genetic problem or a normal phase of childhood sickness that simply comes and goes. These claims will never appear in any record of potential vaccine injuries, except if the potential claimants belong to one of the HMOs that comprise the Vaccine Safety Datalink (VSD) described in Chapters 1 and 5.[30]

It is awkward to publicize the reality and rarity of vaccine injuries at the same time that government agencies promote widespread vaccine uptake, and the fact that a legalized process depends on individuals activating their own claims builds upon this tension.[31] Imagine, by contrast, if we had a complete national health database with records of vaccinations and subsequent diagnoses for all citizens. Someone who developed a recognized vaccine-related condition in the specified time frame could be "red flagged," notified, and led through the compensation process. Legalizing vaccine injuries turns them into moments of individual claims making in a classically American legal style, whereas an alternative society that imagined health records and national databases differently would not have to rely so much on these moments of naming, blaming, and claiming.

Parents who wonder if their child's problem could be vaccine-related will probably first raise that idea with their pediatrician in the context of treating the problem. Crucially, the three-year statute of limitations begins to toll at the emergence of the first symptom (often materialized as a pediatrician's note), not necessarily at the moment the parent or adult realizes the symptom could be vaccine-related. For a death claim, the statute of limitations requires filing within two years of the death and four years after the first symptom of the injury that would lead to the death. According to petitioners' attorneys, many of the calls they get are from people who have missed the statute of limitations for an injury claim, mainly because it can take a long time to get a diagnosis and to make the connection to a vaccine administered years before. Also, many parents and adult claimants have had a lot to deal with in the aftermath of a developing disorder.

One official starting point for a putative vaccine injury before one gets to vaccine court is the filing of a Vaccine Adverse Event Reporting System (VAERS) report. As I noted in Chapter 1, anyone can submit a VAERS report. Manufacturers submit the largest percentage of VAERS reports (about 37 percent) because they are obligated to register each adverse event discovered through their safety testing and monitoring. A similar percentage comes from health care providers (about 36 percent) as they hear about complaints from patients and parents. State immunization programs (around 10 percent) and parents or vaccine recipients themselves (about 7 percent) account for smaller shares of the reporting.[32] The final chunk, 9 to 10 percent, comes from various uncategorized sources, including attorneys representing people with vaccine injury claims. For example, VAERS reports about autism as an adverse event related to thimerosal in vaccines and to the MMR vaccine jumped dramatically in 2002, as petitioners began to organize the autism litigation and some were confirmed to be filed by attorneys related to the claims.[33]

Once recognized and registered in VAERS, a suspected vaccine injury would then proceed through medical treatment, assembling the medical record necessary for a compensation claim. Most claimants use an attorney to file their complaint at the Court of Federal Claims. The first step is a medical evaluation from HRSA medical officers, who are doctors who work for HHS and review all the claims. They can prepare their opinion of the case only after all the medical records are filed, and often there is significant delay getting all the medical records together. A petitioner's attorney may file an incomplete petition in order to make the statutory filing deadline, but it may take months or even years before the medical records are complete. Once they have all the medical records, the medical officers prepare a report outlining their view of the causation question. If they find a Table injury or recommend conceding the case, the claim proceeds straight to compensation.[34]

Table injuries can be resolved quickly because the sticky causation question has been answered, and then the case is simply about establishing that the vaccine was given, that the symptoms arose within the required time limit, and what appropriate compensation should be given the injured person's life circumstances. Doctors, HRSA medical officers, and scientific observers of the court are pleased when the Table satisfies an evidence-based standard. Lawyers for petitioners prefer the quick turnarounds for Table cases because they offer a guaranteed outcome and quick compensation and payment of attorneys' fees. DOJ attorneys are happy to process simpler and quicker Table claims, too, and having more of them helps their flow of processing look better because it lowers the program's overall time to compensation. Vaccine safety advocates and critics who believe more vaccine injuries should be acknowledged are satisfied with Table injuries because they represent agreement from the scientific and medical establishment that vaccines do in fact harm some healthy people who deserve to be compensated for those harms.

The problem is that there are very few Table injuries, and nearly all claims are off-Table disputes. As I explained in Chapter 2, the founding era of the vaccine court was defined by a more generous Table with broad definitions of encephalopathy and seizure disorders, most importantly, and many claims could be classified as Table claims that way. After IOM reviews of the evidence, however, the secretary sought to narrow definitions of encephalopathy and seizures that could be vaccine-related, closing off the path to the largest number of compensations. All the headline-grabbing health problems that advocacy groups have argued are linked to vaccines—autism, attention-deficit disorder, sudden infant death syndrome (SIDS)—are quite deliberately excluded from the Table. Since the Table largely cannot serve its intended streamlining function, the whole compensation program has become much more like a classic adversarial court proceeding. Greater specification of knowledge about vaccine injury has made processes at the vaccine court harder, not easier.

The mainstream view among doctors and researchers is that our current stable of vaccines is already very safe and there are very few firmly associated (let alone definitely causally linked) adverse events that are serious enough to meet the compensation standard. On this view the vaccine court has been regularly overcompensating people for decades and misleading the public into thinking vaccines are more dangerous than they are. Parent advocates and vaccine critics believe the range of adverse events is much wider, including conditions like asthma, autism, and attention-deficit disorder, even diabetes and obesity. On this view the compensation patterns of the vaccine court have been stingy indeed. This tension has been irresolvable among the mobilized constituents of the vaccine court, particularly between vaccine defenders in the medical profession and vaccine critics. In the actual practice of the court, however, the real challenge is deciding cases when there is very little strong evidence in existence at all about whether a vaccine caused a certain problem. Figuring out what to do then is what everyone involved with the vaccine court does at work every day.

What Counts as a Vaccine Injury? The Recognized, the Excluded, and the Middle Ground

Everyone involved in this debate agrees that vaccines can cause adverse reactions ranging from mild soreness to death and that people who have been injured by vaccines deserve justice. But this agreement does not get us very far. Much harder questions come next. How do we know when these events occur, how often and with which vaccines, and why? How much certainty about a true causal relationship is needed before we understand someone as vaccine injured and thus deserving of justice? What form of justice should a person get? Money for her own care or for her heirs, or a policy change such as removal of that vaccine from the market? Our vaccine court has been busy recognizing and addressing vaccine injuries since 1988, and there are indeed already some acknowledged vaccine injuries, some rejected ones, and a middle ground where injuries can gain legal but not scientific recognition as vaccine-related.

Vaccine-related adverse events that are recognized in the mainstream and compensated automatically at the vaccine court include anaphylaxis (a dangerous whole-body allergic reaction often involving difficulty breathing) and syncope (fainting or feeling dizzy), for example.[35] These may or may not result in injuries since what happens to a person experiencing them can vary widely. To be compensated at the vaccine court, the vaccine injury or its related aftereffects must have lasted for six months or more or resulted in hospitalization or death.[36] Death from anaphylaxis postvaccination is very rare, but if it happens within a few hours it will be compensated.[37] Injections in the shoulder can lead to deltoid bursitis, or inflammation of the fluid-filled sacs around the shoulder joints, or what the HRSA medical officers dubbed "shoulder injury related to vaccine administration." This condition is caused by the physical act of putting a needle in the body, not by vaccine components themselves, but is recognized as a vaccine injury. The vaccine court also compensates cases in which a vaccine aggravates a preexisting condition, even fairly indirectly, or for some other injury linked by a clear set of events to the vaccination, such as sustaining a head injury from fainting and falling off an exam table after vaccine administration. In one case, a young woman fainted after driving away from the doctor's office thirty minutes after her flu shot and was able to recover for her injuries from her resultant car wreck.[38]

Instances of what is called "reversion to virulence" in a live, attenuated vaccine such as the measles, varicella (chickenpox), or Sabin live polio vaccine can lead to recognized vaccine injuries when the vaccine strain virus causes infection. (We no longer use the live polio vaccine in the United States because it was capable of causing paralytic polio.) Tetanus-containing vaccines can cause brachial neuritis, characterized by shoulder pain and paralysis, and the rubella vaccine has been linked to chronic arthritis (particularly in women, although the automatic compensation is not gender-specific). Encephalopathy, which is defined as a brain disease or disorder, is a compensable condition after the MMR vaccine only when it is sufficiently severe and long-lasting. The MMR vaccine can also cause febrile seizures, which are linked with fevers and thought to be benign. Thrombocytopenic purpura, a condition characterized by low numbers of platelets in the blood, is compensable after measles-containing vaccine. There is evidence that some formulations of the flu vaccine can cause oculorespiratory syndrome, a collection of symptoms defined by red eyes, facial swelling, and tightness of breath.

Some claimed vaccine injuries are excluded because mainstream scientific and medical experts have concluded they are not plausible causes of vaccine injuries. These excluded candidates include autism and type 1 diabetes from the MMR vaccine, Bell's palsy from the flu vaccine, asthma exacerbation or reactive airway disease episodes from the flu vaccine, and type 1 diabetes from diphtheria-tetanus-acellular-pertussis-containing vaccines.[39] Excluded injuries, especially autism, remain the basis for much social movement mobilization, as I explain throughout the book, but claims based on these conditions would be routinely rejected at the vaccine court. They continue to be rejected as claims not because there is a binding precedent dictating that all such claims be denied, but because the body of scientific knowledge about these conditions is considered sufficiently conclusive that the special masters do not see any grounds for compensation. (There is no common law of vaccine injuries, and no ruling by one special master binds another to rule similarly even in cases involving the same vaccine and injury claim.)

The most intriguing category of vaccine injury cases is what I term "middle-ground" cases. These include diseases and conditions that are not on the Table but are regularly compensated by settlement. Again, because every compensation judgment stands separately and does not trigger either binding precedent for future similar cases or a Table addition, the history of compensations includes a lot of awards for injuries that do not need to be defended as wholly scientific—and cannot be on the mainstream view of what the evidence shows—but are nonetheless a critical part of the court's policy solutions. Since 2006, 80 percent of the approximately fifteen hundred non-autism-compensated claims to the vaccine court were settled through negotiation, with the other 10 percent ending in a hearing and 10 percent conceded by the government.[40] Thus, many middle-ground cases get a middle-ground solution without a scientifically dispositive answer to the question of whether the vaccine really caused the condition. Petitioners' attorneys call this class of conditions the "under the table Table," meaning that they are recognizable to court insiders as likely compensable but do not have the official recognition of a Table injury. Many of these are demyelinating disorders, or diseases of the nervous system that happen when a person's immune system attacks the myelin sheath around the nerves, leading to symptoms such as numbness or paralysis. They are autoimmune disorders in which it is difficult to pinpoint a cause, though infections and genetics are thought to play a role.[41] Claims for a demyelinating disorder called Guillain-Barré syndrome (GBS) after the flu vaccine have been compensated at a rate of 90 percent in the vaccine court for many years without the government conceding causation.[42] Other examples of middle-ground cases are acute disseminated encephalomyelitis, an inflammatory condition that damages the myelin sheath on the nerves in the brain and spinal cord, and chronic inflammatory demyelinating polyneuropathy, considered the chronic form of GBS.[43] In these settlements, the government objects to causation but agrees to pay compensation anyway, though often at less than the claimed amount of damages.

Sometimes a middle-ground case can become recognized on the Table despite its liminal status on scientific grounds. GBS after the flu vaccine will soon be added to the Table, even though a 2012 IOM review of nine "well done" epidemiological studies of the relationship gave the panel a "moderate degree of confidence" that there was no association.[44] The medical advisors to HHS who recommended the addition based their recommendation on policy rather than science. This phrase—"science versus policy"—is a term I heard regularly both at the vaccine court and within the administrative branch of the compensation program, and it refers to the balancing between the need to make decisions based on acceptable, credible scientific evidence of a true causal relationship between a vaccine and a harm and the need to compensate generously in the face of uncertainty so that the program can fulfill its mission of diverting and resolving injury claims. These middle-ground cases are the site for this balancing and negotiation. The court had already been compensating nearly every claim for GBS after the flu vaccine for years, and because the disease is quite rare as well as seasonally confounded with widespread use of the flu vaccine, it does not seem likely that considerably clearer epidemiological evidence is forthcoming anytime soon. In this case, the special masters compensated in a context of persistent uncertainty and the administrative regulation followed their lead.

Situating the U.S. Vaccine Court Globally

Recall from Chapter 2 that the U.S. vaccine court was originally envisioned as more bureaucratic, expedient, and inquisitorial than it has actually turned out to be (though I maintain that these early projections were never realistic given that policy makers chose to site it within a federal court with payment provisions for attorneys, win or lose).[45] The U.S. model is, not surprisingly, fairly unique around the world in its adoption of many features of what Robert Kagan terms "adversarial legalism," or "policymaking, policy implementation, and dispute resolution by means of lawyer-dominated litigation."[46] The key part of Kagan's definition to note in the vaccine court context is "lawyer-dominated": the vaccine act subsidized petitioners' attorneys and expert costs with a no-risk fee provision and set them against DOJ attorneys defending the secretary of HHS, guaranteeing that an essential element of American political life—lawyers—would dominate the proceedings. Nineteen other industrialized nations also have some kind of vaccine injury compensation program, but they are much more likely to be run by a national health bureaucracy (as in most Scandinavian countries) or integrated into a general no-fault process for medical injuries generally (as in New Zealand).[47] No developing countries have a vaccine injury compensation program. As reviewers of global vaccine injury systems observe, "The schemes function most efficiently when they operate alongside well established, comprehensive national social welfare systems."[48] All the programs incentivize or enforce departure from tort claims in the regular court systems, set a fairly low burden of proof of causation and require some type of medical evidence, and award monetary compensation for injuries that meet a threshold of severity or deaths (though the United Kingdom is unique in simply offering a lump-sum payment of £120,000). Some countries pay compensations directly from general revenue (Germany, the United Kingdom), while others levy a special tax on vaccines (Finland, Sweden, Norway, Taiwan, and the United States) or combine both sources (Japan). Which vaccines are eligible for compensation varies from all licensed vaccines (Taiwan) to only those recommended for administration to children (United States and United Kingdom), required or required in certain professional settings or for travel (Italy).[49]

Other countries' compensation systems are dominated by professional experts and health bureaucrats, that is, not lawyers and judges. Taiwan and Japan provide examples of expert review committees deciding cases rather than placing them within an adversarial court setting. Reports discussing these two systems at length never mention lawyers, appeals, or burdens of proof. In Japan's injury compensation system, founded in 1976, citizens file claims in different government agency review committees depending on whether the vaccine is publicly funded or in a self-paid category, and payments come from the national budget for publicly funded vaccines and from manufacturers for self-paid vaccines.[50] In Taiwan, a working group of nineteen to twenty-five experts from medical, legal, and social justice fields reviews claims.[51] Germany and the United Kingdom also use medical expert evaluation, while claims in Finland and Sweden go to an insurance claims manager.[52]

The standard of proof across countries is remarkably similar: a "balance of probabilities" must favor a connection in Finland, New Zealand, and the United Kingdom, much like our preponderance standard, while in Germany the standard is "probable cause" and in Sweden it is "preponderant probability." While it is beyond the scope of this book to examine how these standards work in practice in other systems, it is likely that reviewers around the world confront similar evidentiary challenges as I describe in Chapter 5 and even read many of the same studies. It is also difficult to compare compensation rates in the published literature because the vaccines and the populations vary, but reported rates are far less than U.S.-based vaccine critics would like to see here. The United Kingdom awarded 4 compensations in 2005 out of 106 claims (less than 4 percent), for example, and New Zealand compensated 77 claimants out of 293 from 1992 to 2000 (26 percent).[53] In Japan, publicly funded vaccine claims were compensated about 80 percent of the time as of 2007, while self-paid ones had a lower compensation rate (about 50 percent).[54] The Taiwanese compensation rate is about 39 percent as of 2013,[55] lower than our nonautism compensation rate of 49 percent.

We could have a vaccine injury compensation system run between private insurance companies, insurance exchanges, and government programs like Medicare and Medicaid. Claims could be decided by the medical officers at the HRSA, or perhaps by an expert body such as the Advisory Committee on Immunization Practices, a mixed body of laypeople and experts such as the Advisory Commission on Childhood Vaccines, or some new panel assembled for the job. We could abolish the tort system entirely, as New Zealand did, and simply pay for all injuries. But as many scholars of American law and society have noted, our policy solutions often feature citizen-driven, rights-based mobilization through courts with lawyers to represent us. We are also unique in our lack of the robust social health and welfare systems that define other countries' vaccine injury compensation programs. We have legalized vaccine injury in the most American way.

Situating the Vaccine Court among Domestic Compensation Programs

Even though I argue that our vaccine court is suffused with adversarial legalism, let us not forget that it is still an explicit departure from the tort system, the negligence standard, and several significant procedural features of litigation such as the right to discovery. Other special compensation programs have been set up as alternatives to civil litigation for several distinct purposes, and it is illuminating to situate the vaccine court among them as well as among our global neighbors.

First, Congress enacted some of these programs in response to a specific, overwhelming harm like a terrorist attack. Let us call these disaster schemes. The damages were understood to be so expensive that any private company would be overwhelmed by claims. Second, some have been devised as economic protection and incentive for a needed form of production that has such special risks and potential costs that it cannot be handled entirely privately, such as nuclear power or vaccine production. These are protective and ongoing schemes. Unlike in the first case of an accident or attack that one assumes will not be repeated, this second reason presumes that the activity must continue despite its risks, and both the producer of the risk and the people it harms need special protections. Risk in this second scenario is understood as rare but ongoing. Third, these schemes have been set up to provide economic protection and incentive for a needed form of production that is generally so important and widespread that it requires its own system beyond individual civil suits. These are broad no-fault schemes, and there are two main examples in the U.S. context: workers' compensation and no-fault auto insurance. Compensation for work-related injuries responds to a type of injury that occurs in a context—work for pay—that is both fundamental to our economy and also so commonplace that an alternate sphere is required. Car accidents are sufficiently common and driving is so fundamental to our society that these injuries have been popular candidates for removal from fault-finding tort law. In this third case, the need is ongoing, the injuries are fairly commonplace, and the activity (driving or doing a job that may result in an injury) is foundational in our society and not something we want to burden or restrict generally. And finally, there are cases in which legal claims have seemed to be getting out of hand and there was some support for an alternative scheme, but none was put into place. Injured parties are left to pursue claims through ordinary tort litigation, no matter how unwieldy, expensive, and haphazard it may become. These definitions represent ideal types, of course. It is common to see hybrid cases that combine elements of these types.

The most recent and vivid example of a disaster scheme is the September 11th Victim Compensation Fund. The VICP chief of program operations, Ward Sorensen, consulted on the implementation of the 9/11 fund since it would also involve a special master distributing funds for injuries.[56] After terrorists boarded commercial aircraft and crashed them into the World Trade Center, the Pentagon, and a field in Shanksville, Pennsylvania, on September 11, 2001, killing almost three thousand people, surviving family members could have sued the airlines for allowing security breaches. The domestic airline industry was reeling from the attacks, and it was immediately clear that there would be significant economic fallout. Congress stepped in quickly, however, and on September 22, 2001, passed a law providing for a special process for monetary awards with protections for American and United Airlines, which would have been destabilized or bankrupted by large awards from juries.[57] Survivors and their families gave up the right to bring a civil action for damages related to the terrorist attacks in exchange for filing a claim with the fund. The statute empowered the U.S. attorney general to appoint a single special master who would control the allocation of funds, paid out of general revenue. Special Master Kenneth Feinberg distributed over $7 billion to survivors of 2,880 persons killed and to 2,680 individuals injured in the attacks or the subsequent rescue efforts. Special Master Feinberg's decisions, such as how much to pay for each life lost, were controversial, but in time these debates have faded away.[58] Peter Meyers concludes that 9/11 compensation was a success because it combined "an inquisitorial posture with a friendly face," asking families to choose between filing a lawsuit or getting a nonreviewable but relatively generous amount of compensation through a process that was participatory and flexible.[59]

The first 9/11 compensation fund compensated only those physically injured on September 11, 2001, and the families of those killed. First responders, cleanup crews, and other people in the area were exposed to hazardous materials from the destroyed buildings, however, and soon began to claim that these exposures were causing lung diseases, cancers, and other health problems. A second version of the compensation program began under the Obama administration with the enactment of the James Zadroga 9/11 Health and Compensation Act of 2010, which created the World Trade Center Health Program for medical monitoring and also empowered Special Master Sheila Birnbaum to compensate people who can show they were at a 9/11 crash site and were physically harmed by it or the debris removal efforts (defined as beginning on 9/11 and ending on May 30, 2002).[60] The law published a list of presumptively caused injuries, similar to the Vaccine Injury Table, but the original law did not compensate for any nonphysical injuries such as posttraumatic stress disorder or any forms of cancer. Congress amended the law in 2012, 2013, and 2014, however, each time adding some forms of cancer to the compensation program (including prostate cancer, one of the most common cancers in men, as well as rare cancers). Claimants must show that their injuries were directly caused by the crashes or by debris removal.

The vaccine act exemplifies the second type of scheme, protective and ongoing. It protects the vaccine industry by confronting the reality that we will administer vaccines widely without being able to predict and prevent rare cases of injury, and that this situation will persist indefinitely. (Other vaccine injury compensation programs, such as the Smallpox Vaccine Injury Compensation Program, the 1976 swine flu compensation program, and California's 1986 AIDS Vaccine Victims Compensation Fund, are a hybrid with a disaster model insofar as they were created to protect manufacturers responding to a particular virus threat and were not administered widely and repeatedly.) Another example is the Price-Anderson Nuclear Industries Indemnity Act of 1957, which protects nonmilitary nuclear power facilities from damages arising from accidents by setting up a second tier of accident insurance beyond what the plants carry privately.[61] Price-Anderson embraces the idea that if we as a society want to have nuclear power plants, we must accept that accidents will be potentially very costly and thus outside the normal realm of insurability. The act paid $71 million in claims and litigation costs associated with the 1979 Three Mile Island accident, for example, and around $200 million total. The September 11th Victim

Compensation Fund came from general revenue with bipartisan political support because the airlines were already in financial trouble, there was great sympathy for the victims, and the number of payouts was reasonably limited. Protective and ongoing schemes, however, bolster an industry and thus have other options to fund the payments. For vaccines, the price of compensation is simply added to the cost of each dose, and the nuclear power plants have to insure themselves against accidents as much as possible before they obtain the extra layer of protection.

The third type of specialized compensation scheme, the broad no-fault scheme, also works as an insurance scheme with adjudications taking place within the alternative system. Workers' compensation is the primary example in the United States, and in this case employers cannot be sued in the tort system for their employees' job-related deaths or injuries. Benefits are paid from the employer's insurance, not from public funds. Workers' compensation is the oldest form of social insurance in the United States, born of what legal historian Lawrence Friedman called the need to "buy a measure of industrial peace" in the late nineteenth- and early twentieth-century United States.[62] The industrial age brought many new ways to maim and kill workers, and handling them all through the tort system proved vastly inefficient and terribly unjust. By 1920, nearly every state had enacted a statute setting up a workers' compensation system (and federal workers also have access to their own system). Co-workers are also protected from liability. There may be disputes over the validity (did the injury really happen at work?), the seriousness of the claim, or the amount and type of compensation, however, and resolution of these disputes takes place at the state-level workers' compensation board. No-fault auto insurance schemes grew out of the workers' compensation system and followed similar principles.[63] An injured driver could not sue a fellow motorist but rather would collect damages from her own insurance company, thereby removing resolution of this major risk of modern life from the fickle chaos of the tort system. No-fault auto insurance schemes have not saved money as advocates hoped, however, and they survive in only twelve states.

Other alternative compensation schemes present a hybrid structure, reflecting a combination of national security (i.e., protective and ongoing scheme) and obligation to those harmed by dangerous military-related activities (i.e., disaster scheme). For example, in the Radiation

Exposure Compensation Act of 1990, Congress apologized to those who developed cancers from above-ground nuclear weapons testing or through exposure during manufacture of those devices and offered compensation payments for certain diseases contracted in a certain time frame.[64] A 1988 act of Congress also apologized and offered $20,000 payments to people of Japanese ancestry and their heirs for their imprisonment in camps during World War II.[65] Claims based on Vietnam veterans' health problems resulting from exposure to the herbicide known as Agent Orange first went through the usual civil courts beginning in 1979, and were settled right before trial for what would turn out to be controversially small sums in the final distribution (an average of $3,400 to 52,000 claimants).[66] In 1991, Congress stepped in to establish an alternative claim structure for veterans, but it does not bar civil suits.[67]

The Veterans Administration now publishes a list of conditions such as type 2 diabetes, Hodgkin's disease, prostate cancer, lung cancer, multiple myeloma, Parkinson's disease, and various soft tissue sarcomas that are presumed to be linked to exposure to Agent Orange during Vietnam-era military service, and veterans and their children and dependents may be eligible for disability payments, medical care, and survivor benefits.[68] Like the vaccine act, the Agent Orange legislation defined a few presumptively linked diseases and directed the IOM to study the possible harms of the defoliant, but used the language of "positive association" rather than "causation" to guide compensation.[69] Veterans who had not been compensated in the settlement were able to access an alternative source of payments even as court cases continued. The litigation has not been overly burdensome to the chemical companies, however, who have been able to defend against recent claims. Agent Orange injuries were somewhat like a short-term disaster (such as a chemical spill), were not ongoing or threatening to bankrupt companies, and were limited to a certain group of people at a particular time and place. Veterans, like children and 9/11 victims, were sufficiently sympathetic that they got congressional attention when the court settlement failed so many of them.

Asbestos litigation is an example of a failed attempt at an alternative compensation structure through congressional legislation. Congress failed to pass the Fairness in Asbestos Injury Compensation Act in 2006, which would have created a federal trust fund compensation system.[70]

Instead, asbestos claims have been judicially managed through bankruptcy and tort law. Asbestos claims are the longest-running stream of tort litigation in U.S. history. One hundred U.S. companies have declared bankruptcy because of their liability for asbestos-related personal injury awards. Bankrupt companies formed trusts to pay claimants, and as of 2011 there were sixty such trust funds with assets of over $36.8 billion.[71] The first trust was formed in 1988 (also the first year of the vaccine court's operations). Since 2010 trusts have paid about $17.5 billion to settle 3.3 million claims. Claimants present their occupational and medical histories to administrators of the trust fund, who determine what diseases will be covered and how much the payouts will be.[72] People remain free to bring civil suits against still-operating companies as well. As Jeb Barnes explains, the failure to manage these numerous, costly injury claims in an alternate and more efficient way can be explained by the interactions between our different branches of government as they each responded to the litigation crisis.[73] Early asbestos claims were not covered under state workers' compensation categories, leaving workers uncompensated. Workers filed lawsuits, resulting in the expected socalled crazy quilt of outcomes in which some plaintiffs won and others lost, some sued individually and some in class actions, and some cases moved quickly while other plaintiffs died waiting for a court date.[74] The bankruptcy trusts worked well enough to deflate the urgency for Congress to act. It was a classic illustration of how members of Congress often prefer to pawn off difficult or contentious policy making to the court system instead.[75]

Another example of failed alternative possibilities is the legal problem of claims of ownership of Holocaust-era looted art. In this case, the need for an alternative structure is clear but there is no sufficiently powerful mechanism to create it at the international level. It is well known that the Nazis stole over six hundred thousand pieces of valuable art from their Jewish owners, estimated to be worth $2.5 billion in 1945 dollars, $20.5 billion today.[76] Holocaust art claims have not been part of other Holocaust asset settlements and there is no program in place to process claims in a coordinated, global way. While it is widely accepted that the art should be restored to its rightful owners or heirs (and some families have settled lawsuits or mediations and had their art returned), it is very difficult to determine where looted art is and who the rightful owners are when much evidence of ownership was destroyed in the war or scattered across many countries and after many decades have passed. Also, good-faith purchasers—who may have paid handsomely for the art many years after it was looted but were the last to hold it—are the losers in these claims, but they are not a very satisfying place to lay the blame. Attorney Owen Pell has suggested the idea of an international tribunal created by treaty to mediate Holocaust art claims using a common historical record contributed by governments and museums around the world.[77] A communal fund from museums, galleries, auction houses, and art dealers could be created to both repay rightful owners and compensate good-faith purchasers. Pell's plan has been widely discussed, but the art world has balked at creating a fund and no action has been taken to enact a treaty. Instead, the current solution consists of multiple commissions, statements of vague principles about proper provenance and return of looted items, creation of online databases, and a patchwork of U.S.-based lawsuits, none of which have the unity or enforcement power to bring together all the players, evidence, and funds that would be needed to properly reckon with the legacy of Nazi looting.

One can situate our national vaccine program in relation to these other solutions to make its political commitments more clear. We could compare vaccine injury compensation to Price-Anderson's nuclear insurance protections and conclude that domestic production of population immunity to disease ranks with nuclear power as a desirable economic activity. Or the need to maintain national immunity could be analogized to the need to keep adults in the labor force and to rehabilitate them after an injury on the job. Vaccine injury compensation was enacted for the benefit of children, a politically sympathetic group with supporters across political parties.[78] Children are similar to injured veterans in attracting sympathy (although the antipathy that Vietnam veterans faced upon return certainly puts children ahead of them as a group). Moreover, children may be similar to veterans in the sense that the state ought to take care of them if they make a health sacrifice in the interests of obtaining this national good.

Congress was willing to act for childhood vaccine injuries but not asbestos perhaps because of the relatively brief time period of parental mobilization, scientific uncertainty, vaccine supply crisis, and sense of public health peril should the vaccine supply be disrupted. The asbestos and vaccine cases are very close on an existential continuum, however; the vaccine act squeaked into becoming law while asbestos reform law barely failed. If the vaccine act had never passed, the path of vaccine lawsuits may have looked a lot like asbestos litigation, with one tremendous difference: the science proving harm from asbestos is strong, while vaccine tort claims would have had a difficult time mustering sufficient evidence in regular civil suits.

There are important differences between the vaccine compensation program and all these others, however. The Vaccine Injury Compensation Program differs from all of these systems except for workers' compensation in scale, sense and span of time, and diffusion throughout society. Vaccination is an ongoing national program that reaches nearly all citizens, often repeatedly throughout their lives. Most of these other programs are designed for one-time events or for products that are no longer legal for use in the way that caused the initial harm, such as asbestos. Workers' compensation similarly covers nearly every worker on a huge scale that is not time-delimited and is diffused throughout society. Crucially, however, workers' compensation is not run by the state, and with the exception of work requirements for welfare recipients, there are no work mandates from the state.

Vaccine injury compensation is an enduring legal innovation because it is a hybrid scheme that draws strength from several ideal types of alternative courts: it is protective and ongoing to promote the social good of herd immunity and freedom from epidemic disease; it is nearly as ubiquitous as the broad no-fault schemes because, like driving and working, immunization is part of ordinary life for nearly everyone in our society; and the threat of epidemics from new mutations of influenza or from other reemerging infectious diseases means that a disaster-like mobilization is always nearby (as in the case of the sister smallpox program and the Countermeasures Injury Compensation Program). The role of the state becomes clearer: vaccines are a form of civil defense, and immunization is a civic duty and national service. Vaccine critics are correct to frame vaccination as a national call to service by children (and now with the universal recommendation for the flu vaccine, nearly everyone) that is ongoing and far-reaching. It means that our daily lives as well as our economic and medical institutions are unburdened by many of the infectious diseases of the past. This interplay of duty, compulsion, compliance, and benefit undergirds our immunization social order. We have legalized injury claims in a uniquely American way, however. A coalition of policy makers, professionals, and mobilized parents crafted this particular solution. We invested in the role of lawyers in the process and never considered adopting a broad social safety net for injury and disability more generally instead. But most importantly, we made a court.

5

What Counts as Evidence?

There are a few widely recognized adverse events linked to vaccination that are not controversial.[1] But once we move beyond this discrete realm of agreement covering relatively few cases, we find that the claims are quite contentious and beyond easy disposition with clear and widely accepted evidence. The best way to understand the cases and decisions of the vaccine court, I contend, is to examine the types of evidence that all sides muster in vaccine injury claims and to analyze how the parties to the vaccine court tussle over them. There are explicit hierarchies of evidence for knowing vaccine injury published by the Institute of Medicine (IOM) and the Advisory Commission on Childhood Vaccines (ACCV) that value laboratory confirmation of vaccine strain virus persisting in the body and well-designed epidemiological studies at the top, with evidence such as animal studies results and case reports placed toward the bottom of the hierarchy. Everything ranked in the hierarchy of evidence is nonetheless potentially useful in a vaccine injury claim. The special masters explicitly adopt the IOM hierarchy of evidence in their decision making, and the ACCV uses its ranking to inform its recommendations for administrative changes to the Vaccine Injury Table. These listings of evidence are sufficiently similar that throughout the chapter I simply refer to the hierarchy of evidence. This chapter focuses on the questions of what counts as evidence of vaccine injury, who is entitled to produce that evidence, and through access to which knowledge pathways. I explain how the special masters decide contested cases, the place of uncertainty in the process, and how the vaccine court is itself a site of evidence making as well as evidence hearing. Not surprisingly, activists also mobilize to disrupt the hierarchy of evidence, to reorder it, and to introduce new forms of evidence, and I weave in their struggles here as well.

The Hierarchy of Evidence

There are two main moments of recognition of vaccine injuries in the compensation program: when a condition is added to the Vaccine Injury Table through administrative rule making and when either the medical officers (in their first review of the petition) or the special masters (in a hearing or settlement) decide an individual petition is compensable. What counts as evidence for these moments of recognition, who gets to produce it, and how do all the actors in and around the vaccine court play a role in these recognitions? I analyze the special masters' weighing of the evidence as well as the larger knowledge infrastructure that feeds into their judgments. As I have described in previous chapters, we have a large public-private postmarketing vaccine safety surveillance system designed to pinpoint possible vaccine injuries in near real time. Research arms of the federal health bureaucracies and grant-funded university researchers look for and publish results of vaccine safety studies, which IOM committees review and experts testify about in vaccine court. Vaccine critics muster their own evidence, often using government resources and leveraging the court itself to help them produce it. Very few pieces of evidence are considered definitive, however, and most of the time the aim is to see if enough credible evidence can be assembled to meet a contested, legalized notion of causation that is understood to be less than scientifically certain.

Congress created the first Table in the original National Childhood Vaccine Injury Act and then specifically charged the secretary of the Department of Health and Human Services (HHS) with assembling IOM panels to study the relationships between vaccines and adverse events to guide future revisions to the Table. The IOM, where my first example of a hierarchy of evidence originates, is the primary source of scientific knowledge for the vaccine program because its expert panels sort through and weigh all the published scientific literature about vaccine injury causation. The IOM produces extensive reports that present a highly systematic knowledge hierarchy about vaccine safety. In the latest review process, for example, the committee first divided the published literature into two streams, the epidemiologic (studies of populations of people) and mechanistic (biological and clinical studies of animals and individual human bodies).[2] The review committee considered "two or more [epidemiologic] studies with negligible methodological limitations that are consistent in terms of the direction of the effect" to provide "high confidence" about whether a vaccine increased risk of a medical problem. One study with negligible methodological limitations or a collection of studies that are "generally consistent" generates "moderate confidence," while only one study of a collection of studies "lacking precision or consistency" provides only limited confidence about the link to vaccines. If there are "[n]o epidemiologic studies of sufficient quality," then there is simply "insufficient" knowledge either way.[3]

For mechanistic evidence, the review committee looked for any peer-reviewed study in which "a vaccine was or may be a cause of an adverse event in one or more persons."[4] The report had to include the specific vaccine, evidence of a clinically diagnosed outcome, and a reasonable time interval. In individual medical cases, it is considered important to see if the patient suffered the same adverse event on rechallenge, which is a subsequent administration of the same vaccine. A "particularly strong piece of evidence" is laboratory confirmation that the vaccine strain of the virus remains in the patient's body.[5] Comparing symptoms after vaccination to symptoms of natural infection is another bit of evidence that the vaccine may have caused harm, though not very strong evidence. Studies in animals are helpful if the disease and the adverse event are similar in humans, and in vitro studies can be "informative," the committee said, but are "eyed with skepticism regarding their relationship to the human experience."[6] For each stream of evidence on each proposed vaccine-adverse event pairing under consideration, the IOM committee assigned a "weight-of-evidence" assessment, and then synthesized the two streams and their assessments into an overall conclusion about the causal relationship between the vaccine and the possible injury. There were four predefined conclusions possible: (1) the evidence "convincingly supports" a relationship, (2) the evidence "favors acceptance" of a relationship, (3) the evidence is "inadequate to accept or reject" a relationship, or (4) the evidence "favors rejection" of the relationship.[7]

As Stephen Hilgartner has shown, panels of scientific experts from the National Academy of Science (of which the IOM is a part) seem to speak with a unified voice of expertise from within a black box, but specific laws and rules help construct and maintain their distance, authority, privacy, credibility, and influence.[8] IOM panels enjoy a combination of privacy and the prestige of peer review. Their deliberations are exempt from the Federal Advisory Committee Act, which otherwise requires open meetings for government advisory groups. Their reports are peer reviewed, but the review comments and previous drafts are kept confidential. The vaccine act singles out the IOM as a critical knowledge resource for the compensation program. Appointees to the National Academy and the IOM vaccine review panels are accomplished university researchers at the height of their careers. Strict conflict of interest rules bolster their credibility as well. Committee members and their immediate family members cannot have financial ties to vaccine manufacturers or their parent companies, have served on federal vaccine advisory committee, have been an expert witness about vaccines, or have published on vaccine safety.[9]

As Hilgartner explains, it has been difficult but not impossible for those who disagree with IOM committees to disrupt this very solid formulation of scientific credibility and expertise. There may be a view into the "back stage" of deliberations where experts disagree or the neutrality of the panelists can be challenged. Indeed, vaccine critics have attempted to upend the disinterested scientific authority of the IOM vaccine safety panels by posting a transcript from a closed 2001 IOM meeting of the committee to investigate autism and the MMR vaccine in which the experts worry openly about all the concerned activists, the threat of immunization rates going down, and the state of uncertainty about what was happening.[10]

Vaccine critics have published journal articles based on data from passive surveillance—the Vaccine Adverse Event Reporting System (VAERS) database—that IOM panels disregard in their hierarchy of evidence. Critics charge that the IOM reviewers improperly blocked their perspectives by excluding their studies as methodologically flawed because they drew only on VAERS reports and lacked an appropriate comparison population.[11] Critics have relied heavily on publicly available databases such as VAERS because, as I describe below, they have not been able to gain access to the postlicensure safety surveillance database described in Chapter 1.[12] Vaccine critics and mainstream researchers and government safety monitors have fundamentally opposed views of VAERS as a source of evidence. For example, on the anti-vaccine blog Age of Autism, one post announces "HPV Vaccine (Gardasil and

Cervarix) VAERS Reports—Injury and Death Continue to Climb," implying that VAERS reports are a record of injury and death from HPV vaccines.[13] All official descriptions of VAERS as a reporting tool and a signal detector caution that the data cannot be used to draw causal inferences, by contrast. The official VAERS website cautions, "It is important to remember that many adverse events reported to VAERS may not be caused by vaccines. Although VAERS can rarely provide definitive evidence of causal associations between vaccines and particular risks, its unique role as a national spontaneous reporting system enables the early detection of signals that can then be more rigorously investigated."[14] When vaccine safety officials followed up about the medical details in one sample of death claims in VAERS, for example, they found deaths actually caused by choking, cancer, heart disease, and pneumonia, as well as a lower-than-expected number of SIDS cases based on the background rate of SIDS in the general population.[15] In the mainstream view, VAERS can generate only signals of possible adverse events, and then a follow-up epidemiological study would be needed to see if there is a credible causal relationship.

The manufacturers' own package inserts are another source of information that critics use as evidence of injuries in ways that mainstream experts dispute. The package inserts are required by the FDA as proper labeling, and must include a record of adverse events reported from clinical trials (for which causation is not necessarily established).[16] For vaccine critics, the package insert is the pharmaceutical company's forced confession of known and causally linked adverse events. Vaccine critics use the manufacturer's package insert as a way to raise awareness about vaccine injuries, pulling them out and reading the lists of conditions in legislators' offices, for example.[17] This knowledge gathering and deployment is designed to harness the credibility of the government's own evidence to prove that vaccine injuries are real and are being ignored. Critically, both VAERS and all package inserts are easily available online.

The advisory committee of doctors, lawyers, and parents on the ACCV are tasked with suggesting Table changes to the secretary of HHS. They compiled a set of guiding principles for deciding when to recommend adding a new vaccine injury to the Table that affirm that the Table should be "scientifically and medically credible" and should be changed "whenever possible" to the benefit of petitioners.[18] This group's deliberations mirror the elite scientific consensus about what counts as evidence of vaccine injury, and provide my second example of a hierarchy of evidence. The most convincing evidence of vaccine injury for them is also clinical laboratory data from the injured person (such as genetic confirmation of vaccine strain virus in the body),[19] followed by seeing the same adverse event in a person upon rechallenge involving generally non-relapsing symptoms or diseases. Moving down their hierarchy, the next most convincing type of evidence is controlled clinical trials, and then controlled observational studies such as cohort and case control studies, such as studies from the Vaccine Safety Datalink (VSD). The list continues with uncontrolled observational studies such as ecological studies; case series reports; data from passive surveillance systems such as VAERS; individual case reports; editorial articles on scientific presentations; and finally, non-peer-reviewed publications.[20] Critics not only dispute the hierarchy of evidence but also protest their lack of access to the resources necessary to produce it themselves.

The VSD, introduced in Chapter 1, remains the sole resource for the kind of large-scale hypothesis testing that everyone in the mainstream agrees is the gold standard for establishing population-level linkages between vaccines and adverse events. Gaining access to the records in the VSD has been challenging for vaccine critics, who want their own researchers to be able to search it for evidence of cover-ups of vaccine injuries like autism and to discover new patterns of injury. Critically, the VSD is not simply a publicly available database like VAERS but is made up of the patient health records of managed care organizations that share the de-identified information with government agencies and researchers. In other countries with national health systems and national databases, the state controls access to this information, but the mix in the United States of private health care and government regulation creates this shared control. The private health care companies whose members form the VSD database are obligated to protect patient confidentiality and so submit data to federal regulators periodically in a de-identified format.

The question then becomes how and on what terms researchers who are not affiliated with the federal vaccine safety bureaucracies will be able to use the VSD data for their own work. Prior to 2002, there was no protocol to make it possible for any researcher without an affiliation at the National Immunization Program or at one of the member managed care organizations to access the VSD.[21] The thimerosal controversy in the U.S. galvanized independent researchers who wanted to study its possible link to autism. Two vaccine-critical researchers, Dr. Mark Geier and his son David Geier, were particularly prominent in the aftermath of the revelations that the U.S. vaccine supply contained more mercury in the form of thimerosal than was considered safe under the EPA guideline for methyl mercury. In 2003 and 2004 the Geiers were granted permission to perform a study using VSD data at the CDC Research Data Center in Hyattsville, Maryland. They tried to combine and rename files in an attempt to do a broader investigation than they had received approval to do, and would have breached confidentiality of the medical records if they had not been stymied by their inabilities to use the SAS computer program. What happened during their visits became fodder for conspiratorial accounts by vaccine critics such as in David Kirby's bestseller on mercury and autism, *Evidence of Harm*.[22] To immunization supporters, this episode showed that ill-prepared anti-vaccine advocates were interested in getting data only to ineptly manipulate it. Kirby's account presents the Geiers as intrepid researchers up against the Goliath of the CDC, bent on keeping them from discovering the truth, while the CDC found that they violated research guidelines and privacy agreements while accessing the VSD data.[23] As a result of the Geiers' violations during their research visit, the private managed care companies decided they would increase protection of their patient data and would not simply hand over patient records to the CDC. For vaccine critics, this episode revealed a desperate government thwarting inquiry about vaccine safety and giving over the public resource of the VSD to private hands. For mainstream vaccine supporters, the Geiers would have been laughably incompetent had they not managed to foment considerable conspiracy theorizing as well as complicate access to patient data in a public-private health care information system.

It became clear that for vaccine safety research to be credible, however, it had to be more transparent and that access to the most definitive informational resource should be more open. In 2005, the IOM conducted a review of the transparency, fairness, and access policies for the VSD. The Geiers, Barbara Loe Fisher from NVIC, and Sallie Bernard from SafeMinds all testified to the IOM committee, along with government directors of the VSD, a manager representing one of the member managed care companies, data directors, the editor of the *Annals of Internal Medicine*, FDA and CDC officials, and others. The resulting IOM report supported "the broadest feasible use of the VSD for vaccine safety research within the constraints of law, protection of confidentiality, and VSD contract provisions," and specifically recommended minimizing bureaucratic and technical barriers to access, development and publication of guidelines for independent researchers, and implementation of a proposal system for granting them access that is transparent and timely, with costs limited to the incremental costs of access.[24] The CDC now has a VSD data-sharing program in place as well as procedures for sharing its vaccine safety datasets from published studies for reanalysis.[25] Many studies have been published using the VSD for vaccine safety analysis, but the expertise barriers remain high enough that only researchers with high-level training in epidemiology and biostatistics and the ability to secure collaborations work with it.

Using the Vaccine Court for Access and Production of Evidence

Instead of using the VSD access paths now available, vaccine critics pivoted to the vaccine court. One strategy has been to file a motion before a vaccine court special master to compel the pharmaceutical companies to turn over data or the federal government to provide access to the VSD for research and to bill the court for expert expenses in reviewing and publishing from it, in effect trying to turn the vaccine court into a granting agency for critical safety research. The major plaintiff-side firm that helped manage the autism cases (analyzed in detail in Chapter 6) had already implemented this strategy, filing extensive discovery requests and subpoenas designed to uncover putatively hidden data on injury rates. The autism petitioners attempted to get access to vaccine manufacturers' internal product studies and to documents relating to the British litigation over the MMR vaccine as a causative factor in autism (in which records were sealed), and even sought reimbursement for the costs of producing a study to be used in the autism litigation, but were not successful.[26] Petitioners have continued to try to use the vaccine court to generate epidemiological data. The Mosotovoy family asked the special master in their 2013 claim to order the federal government to provide access to the VSD to their expert, Theresa Deisher.[27] Deisher is a pro-life Catholic biotech researcher known for advocating for the use of adult stem cells over embryonic stem cells. She had attempted to get federal funding for her vaccine research but had been roundly criticized and denied funding in the National Institutes of Health peer-review process. Deisher argued that following the regular procedures to gain access to the VSD would be too burdensome, and the special master noted that her research record did not look strong enough to support an application.[28] In another recent case, a woman who had received Merck's Gardasil vaccine against HPV during pregnancy filed a vaccine injury claim alleging that it had caused her son to be born with digestive system abnormalities. She filed a subpoena in the vaccine court to obtain from Merck "[a] ny papers, reports or studies relating to a possible biological mechanism by which inadvertently [sic] exposure to Gardasil vaccination during pregnancy could cause a birth defect, abnormality, chromosomal abnormalities &/or any other adverse event."[29] Merck had already provided an annual report of its Gardasil study outcomes that showed no increased incidence of birth defects in the vaccinated population as compared to the general population (all of women giving birth). The special master interpreted the woman's request as a fishing expedition for epidemiological or mechanistic evidence that was unlikely to exist.

The special masters regarded these as requests for VSD access as requests to conduct studies and have rejected each request as beyond their powers to compel and as unnecessary for their decision making. In all of these disputes, the special masters made clear that their role and the role of discovery were very different from the analogous roles in regular civil litigation. Subpoenas and discovery in civil litigation are used for the exposure of facts that will later be presented by attorneys in an adversarial setting. By contrast, the special masters understand themselves to occupy what court scholars call an "inquisitorial" posture, by which we mean a judge-led investigation into the facts rather than a party-led presentation. Trying to use the court itself to gain access to raw data or to epidemiological studies produced elsewhere is often the only way petitioners would be able to present new epidemiological evidence. But the question was, the special masters insisted, whether *they* needed these additional documents and VSD studies to decide the cases, not whether it might be useful for the petitioners.

Critics were able to use legal and political channels as well as a vaccine court petition to scrutinize and attempt to recast evidence in a few important instances, however. The early uncertainty about the effects of thimerosal combined with high-profile publications alleging data cover-ups gave vaccine critics their best opportunity to use both the vaccine court process as well as congressional scrutiny to find hidden evidence of autism as a vaccine injury. Robert Kennedy's now-retracted 2005 *Rolling Stone* article "Deadly Immunity" focused on a 2000 meeting of scientists at the Simpsonwood retreat center outside Atlanta to discuss preliminary studies on the effects of thimerosal.[30] Activists had secured the transcript from that meeting using the Freedom of Information Act as well as a leaked transcript of an IOM committee meeting by a panel investigating the thimerosal link, and Kennedy's piece presented these transcripts as evidence of a cover-up. The article based on the researchers' VSD analysis, published in *Pediatrics* in 2003, concluded that there were no consistent significant associations between thimerosal in vaccines and neurodevelopmental outcomes.[31] But because the statistical analysis had proceeded in two phases and in different HMOs within the VSD, critics charged that the CDC had reworked the analysis to make evidence of injury disappear.[32]

The petitioners in the autism litigation were able to get some independent statistical experts at Emory University to perform a reanalysis of the contested thimerosal data and file it as an expert report in the Omnibus Autism Proceeding (OAP).[33] The reanalysis was significant because the petitioners had not otherwise been able to get new epidemiological studies as part of the discovery process, but they hoped that the reanalysis would expose hidden evidence of thimerosal's harm. Harland Austin and Cathy Lally redid the analysis in six different ways, comparing how these changes made the data look compared to how they appeared in the published paper. The published study "understated" positive associations between thimerosal and language delays and tics by separating results by the different clinical settings in which the children appeared, Austin and Lally reported, whereas these associations were clearer when they aggregated all the children together.[34] Overall, however, Austin and Lally concluded that "the methodology . . . was sound" and "their findings are valid." "Neither we, nor they," they continue, "found any positive and consistent evidence of an association between autism or attention deficit disorder and TCVs [thimerosal-containing vaccines]" although "the study design cannot rule out moderate, or small, increases in autism and attention deficit disorder potentially attributable to TCVs."[35] Moreover, the Senate Committee on Health, Education, Labor and Pensions conducted an eighteen-month inquiry beginning in 2005 into whether there had been misconduct in the early investigations of thimerosal, including the contested data and the Simpsonwood meeting.[36] After interviewing more than eighty people and examining thousands of pages of documents, the committee found that claims that thimerosal data were manipulated, among other charges, were not substantiated. Vaccine critics were not able to get validation of their interpretations of the epidemiological evidence and practices underlying it through the court or through Congress, and the safety of thimerosal is now considered solidly established in the mainstream.[37]

Compensated Cases as Evidence of Vaccine Injury

Parents who have been through the vaccine court understand their injured children as sources of evidence. One mother serving on the ACCV, Sarah Hoiberg, expressed frustration and disbelief that after her daughter had been awarded compensation for damage caused by an acute encephalopathy after the DTaP vaccine, no one from the government called to ask to study her child. Hoiberg asked Dan Salmon, then with the National Vaccine Program Office, in a March 2011 advisory committee meeting, "I personally have never received a phone call from you guys asking to look at my daughter for what happened to her, why it happened to her. I know a few of my constituents who also have vaccine injured children who have been compensated by the program and have never been contacted to say 'We'd like to find out what happened, we'd like to study your child.' So who are you guys looking at?"[38]

Salmon's response was to explain the CDC's Clinical Immunization Safety Assessment (CISA) Project, composed of a group of seven medical centers (Johns Hopkins, University of Maryland, Kaiser Permanente, Stanford, Vanderbilt, Boston University, and Columbia) and founded in 2001. CISA's charge is to "improve understandings of [adverse events following immunization] at the individual-patient level."[39] CISA experts provide clinical consultation in individual cases, store specimens, publish research on pathogenesis of the injury, and develop algorithms to guide future vaccination in people who have had a previous reaction.[40] Clinical case numbers are very small; in the first three years, the clinical case review group reviewed about one hundred cases. The CDC's Immunization Safety Office has also developed a genomics and vaccine injury research initiative using specimens gathered at CISA.[41]

But these federal programs are not really connected to the families' claims at the vaccine court because those tend to be filed many months after the event, whereas specimens need to be collected soon after the onset of the illness. These programs do not reach out to establish a personal link with parents and cannot provide the kind of emotional validation that sympathetic activists offer (such as a memorial wall for vaccine injury stories). But most importantly, confidentiality rules prevent government researchers or health bureaucrats from directly contacting compensated families. Any attempt to contact them has to come through their attorneys, and researchers cannot use their private medical information without their permission. In that same meeting in which Hoiberg expressed her frustration that no one had reached out about her daughter, Dr. Rosemary Johann-Liang, chief medical officer at the compensation program's administrative side, explained that in one instance, the doctors wanted to publish a case report about the child's vaccine reaction. They prepared a letter to the parents asking permission to use the child's medical information and routed it through the family's attorney, but never heard anything back.[42]

From the comments I heard parents and advocates make about compensated claimants as a potential treasure trove of knowledge, it seems they make the same presumption that vaccine critics make in drawing on VAERS claims: that these are records of real vaccine injuries. But medical experts would not regard people who won compensation at the vaccine court as a true sample of vaccine injuries just waiting to be studied (privacy issues aside). The compensated claims do not provide an uncontested record of recognition because of the now-dubious grounds for many of the early DTP compensations, the variation between special masters in their willingness to find causation across cases with factual differences, and the regular settlement practices in which the Department of Justice attorneys offer compensation without conceding causation in order to expedite cases. Moreover, the compensations include cases in which a vaccine aggravated a preexisting condition or set off a series of events that led to harm such as a car accident, and these cases are hard to apply more broadly.

Despite these significant barriers to building scientific knowledge from the vaccine court compensations, the program's administrators are clearly aware that they hold extensive records in their claims database. They are willing to draw on their own case reviews to recognize new vaccine injuries, but not in the way the parents imagine or with the significant findings that they seem to expect. In-house research by medical officers was responsible for discovery, publication, and inclusion of a new injury on the Table: shoulder injury related to vaccine administration (SIRVA).[43] These shoulder injuries are injection-linked rather than vaccine-linked, and are the likely result of the injection being given too deeply in the tissue or too high on the shoulder so that the vaccine reaches the subdeltoid bursa, a fluid-filled sac beneath the shoulder muscle that can become painfully inflamed. The case report the medical officers published in 2010 included only thirteen cases, but elements were sufficiently convincing to show causation.[44] Since then, the number of SIRVA cases at the vaccine court has grown quickly and SIRVA will be added to the Table. It is unlikely these cases would have been found any other way.

Vaccine critics have also used compensations for children with an autism diagnosis to show that the government is hiding something to protect the immunization social order, and that government bureaucrats have known all along that vaccines cause autism. The most famous example is the Hannah Poling case, a petition that had been slated to be part of the OAP but was pulled out and conceded to much fanfare from critics. As one critic crowed, "The government just dropped its pants."[45] The medical experts first discussed Hannah Poling's autism as a significant aggravation of an underlying mitochondrial disorder,[46] and HHS ultimately categorized her has having experienced a Table injury, namely an encephalopathy in the required time frame after the MMR vaccine, which then became "chronic encephalopathy with features of autism spectrum disorder."[47] The administrators and special masters had the difficult task of explaining how a child with an autism diagnosis (or a similar diagnosis such as developmental delay)[48] could be compensated without that compensation meaning that vaccines had caused autism, while critics took out full-page newspaper ads and declared on national television that the court had validated autism as a vaccine injury.[49] Dr. Paul Offit also responded in the *New England Journal of Medicine*, arguing that vague and unscientific standards at the vaccine court produced these confusing payouts and that they were not evidence of true causation.[50]

Critics continued to mobilize around past compensations as hidden evidence of a vaccine-autism link, publishing a law review article in 2011 in which they claimed to have found an outsized number of children with autism (or autism-like features) in the vaccine court's past compensations (usually called the Pace law review article after its school of publication).[51] Trying to contest the court's "apparent judicial clarity and finality," the authors ask, is it possible "the VICP [Vaccine Injury Compensation Program] rejected cases of 'autism' because of the hot-button label and not because of real differences in injuries or evidence?"[52] As Kevin Conway described the impetus for the article, "Their theory was that lots of autistic children have been compensated in the vaccine program because vaccines caused their autism. However, it was probably mostly before 1995, when they redefined encephalopathy. Encephalopathy means brain damage, any kind of brain damage. So it was real general. So if you could show brain damage, you know, autism is brain damage, and then you recover it. So they believe that there are lots of people, autistic people [among the compensated]."[53] The existence of these cases was never actually in dispute. "Autism cases involving Table Injuries have been compensated under the Program," Special Master Gary Golkiewicz noted when he set up the autism hearing process in 2002.[54] The question was whether they could be repackaged as evidence of an autism-vaccine linkage, of the court's duplicity and doublespeak, or both.

The critics' argument depended on autism as a broad and malleable clinical diagnosis as well as on the court's pre-1995 history of compensating for a wide range of brain injuries. The authors searched past compensations and interviewed parents to find eighty-three cases of autism or autism-like features (though only thirty-nine had a medically confirmed autism diagnosis). They argued that the *DSM-IV* definition of autism—including impaired social interaction, impaired verbal and nonverbal communication, and restricted or repetitive activities and interests[55]—looks a lot like the court's definition of altered conscious-ness after encephalopathy[56]—decreased response to the environment, decreased or absent eye contact, and failure to recognize familiar people or things. Specifically, the authors argued that "there may be no mean-ingful distinction between the cases of encephalopathy and residual seizure disorder that the VICP compensated over the last twenty years and the cases of 'autism' that the VICP has denied."[57] Attorney and anti-mercury activist Jim Moody presented the results of the study to the ACCV, arguing in his public comments that "since all of these cases come from an evidence-based compensation program, they obviously provide powerful evidence, perhaps even better than epidemiology studies, that vaccines do, in fact, cause autism."[58]

Mainstream researchers were very critical of the study, pointing out that just because a compensated child with a brain injury shares some di-agnostic features with autism (such as decreased communication) does not mean that child has autism, and that what the researchers had actu-ally done was to recast a lot of older DTP claims (and a few MMR) that had encephalopathy and seizure disorders as the compensated injuries (with a wide range of subsequent manifestations, none subject to causal scrutiny because the cases had been Table compensations) and try to redescribe them as autism or autism-like.[59] Critics took one era of com-pensations and deployed it against the credibility and settledness of the most recent court era, which has been known for its denials of compen-sation for claims like autism and its increased reliance on major studies from the IOM and other mainstream sources. Vaccine critics hoped to force congressional action against the court in the form of hearings, in-vestigations, and an amended statute that would direct compensations for previously rejected claims. They have not made much progress on these goals. Instead of using past compensations to embarrass the vac-cine compensation program and drag it before California Republican Darrell Issa's Oversight and Government Reform committee, advocates were put off in favor of a Government Accountability Office (GAO) re-port that was mildly critical of the vaccine court's delays and low profile but did not identify any pressing injustices (and endorsed none of the conspiratorial vision critics offered).[60] The story of the Pace law review article shows how critics used the court for evidence and for political mobilization, effectively utilizing interest group pressure and prompting a GAO review, which had not been done since 1999. They did not get what they wanted, but they had access and resources and their efforts redounded to the public good in the form of increased democratic oversight of the vaccine compensation program.

Interpreting Uncertainty and Lack of Evidence

The previous sections described evidence hierarchies and disagreements about the results of studies, observations, or compensations. But what about the studies that have not been done, the populations that have not been included, or the signals in vaccine safety monitoring systems that have not appeared? The federal vaccine safety system establishes a "regime of perceptibility," as Michelle Murphy would call it, which is the cumulative vision that all its systems of injury detection use to see vaccine injury. Our surveillance systems see vaccine injuries through monitoring signals, as I describe in Chapter 1. "Imperceptibility," Murphy warns, can be both "inevitably produced . . . [but] also at times purposefully generated and maintained."[61] Vaccine critics consistently argue against closure in vaccine safety debates, promoting uncertainty and arguing we need more studies.[62] If the vaccine injuries have not been confirmed, perhaps we just do not know enough yet. So if the FDA and CDC monitor health outcomes and reports in real time to watch for vaccine injuries (as they do, explained in Chapter 1), then what does it mean if these systems detect nothing? What is the absence these systems detect? Can not seeing be reassurance and even certainty of safety?

In 2009, there was a comprehensive IOM review of all the vaccines that had been added to the Table over the years since the last major revisions in 1995, after considerable efforts by then–VICP director Dr. Geoffrey Evans to secure the necessary funding. The panel reviewed the scientific evidence from over twelve thousand studies to see if there was evidence for or against a causal link with eight vaccines (for varicella or chickenpox, influenza, hepatitis B, HPV, tetanus, measles-mumps-rubella, hepatitis A, and meningococcal disease) and 158 possible vaccine-adverse event pairs.[63] Most of the adverse events were drawn from the history of claims at the vaccine court, and the IOM team added a few of their own. The IOM found fourteen adverse event-vaccine pairs in which evidence "convincingly supports" a causal relationship[64] and four in which they "favored acceptance" of a causal relationship.[65] None of the announced causal relationships were at all controversial or surprising to anyone, such as the live attenuated chickenpox vaccine causing infections (which live vaccines are well known to be able to do, albeit rarely) or anaphylaxis and fainting, acknowledged possibilities after injections generally. There are proposed changes to the Table to take account of these new IOM findings currently making their way through the lengthy rule-making process and expected to be finalized within a year or so. Five relationships were rated "favors rejection," including an old favorite, the MMR vaccine and autism.[66]

The absence of evidence in the review, not its fairly unsurprising affirmative findings, was its notable feature. The IOM was unable to infer any causal relationship one way or another based on the evidence in 135 vaccine-adverse event pairs (85 percent). There simply was not sufficient, reliable research on these relationships in existence at all. In one sense this is not surprising. Scientific and medical research is expensive and time-consuming, and it is unlikely to be directed at rare occurrences or possible routes of injury that are biologically less plausible, particularly when the main sources of those claims are vaccine court petitions and research grant funding is scarce. When there have been a large number of alleged cases (such as autism) or a credible signal detected through VAERS (such as intussusception), there are researchers and funders eager to research the question (or the CDC does the study). Vaccine supporters interpreted the IOM review as further evidence that vaccine adverse events are hard to find because they are extremely rare. A headline in *Contemporary Pediatrics* announcing the review read "Reassure Worried Parents: Vaccines Rarely Have Serious Adverse Effects."[67] Critics of the vaccine court and the compensation program, however, were quick to pounce on the 135 "insufficient evidence" vaccine-adverse event pairs and to characterize the vaccine establishment as uninterested in scientific knowledge about vaccine safety. A headline on the popular website of Dr. Joe Mercola, a well-heeled funder of vaccine skepticism, read "Vaccines Have Serious Side Effects—The Institute of Medicine Says So!," and NVIC noted in a press release that "the current state of science holds no answers for parents and doctors, who for many years have reported multiple vaccine injuries to the government's Vaccine Adverse Event Reporting System (VAERS)."[68]

Vaccine safety studies are prompted by curiosity about an adverse event that surfaces as a signal in the surveillance databases. But researchers and government monitors have also studied their own detection processes to try to understand better what makes a real signal. From 2006 to 2009, vaccine safety researchers from the CDC and the managed care organizations monitored five vaccines for five to seven possible outcomes each on a weekly basis using Rapid Cycle Analysis in the VSD.[69] Of the thirty possible vaccine-outcome pairs, twenty-one showed no signal, that is, no uptick in those watched conditions around vaccination. One signal turned out to be a twofold increased risk of febrile (with fever) seizures in children receiving the combination MMR and varicella vaccine (MMRV) as opposed to separating those shots (in the same visit), or one additional febrile seizure per 2,300 to 2,600 children. After getting a report of the preliminary data from this monitoring, the Advisory Committee on Immunization Practices revised its recommendation that preferred the MMRV over separate shots to a neutral recommendation that either would be fine and formed a working group to consider more changes.[70] A 2010 update continued to endorse both the combination vaccine and the two separate shots, but stated that unless the parents prefer the combination vaccine, the MMR and varicella vaccines should be given separately for the first dose in children ages twelve to forty-seven months (97 percent of febrile seizures happen in children younger than forty-seven months).[71] The researchers did not find the remaining signals to constitute evidence of vaccine injury, rather concluding they were explained by changes in coding, confounding, use of an inappropriate comparison group, miscoding in the medical records, bias from uncertainty in background rates, and chance.[72] "When concerns about the safety of a specific vaccine have arisen from another source," they write, "the absence of signals in our system has provided rapid reassurance about vaccine safety."[73] So while vaccine critics decry the failure of government to initiate studies of proposed vaccine injuries, government researchers and safety monitors listen and watch elsewhere. Their monitoring systems detect acute or at least clearly diagnosable conditions that generate a medical record. These events can become intelligible signals.[74] Lack of a signal thus becomes evidence of safety, of vaccine injuries not happening.

Deciding Cases from the Bottom of the Evidence Hierarchy

The special masters decide cases in an overall evidentiary context in which the IOM did not find evidence sufficient to draw scientific conclusions about 135 out of 185 vaccine-adverse event pairs drawn directly from the vaccine court docket. An easy case would feature convincing direct evidence of a link between a condition and a vaccine from atop the evidence hierarchy, such as a biomarker or "footprint" from the vaccine or, as former Chief Special Master Golkiewicz has explained, an epidemiological study "indicating a relative risk greater than two" for a risk group in which the petitioner belongs.[75] But often, none of the highly rated forms of evidence are available (and if they are, the government typically concedes the case and the injury is a candidate for being added to the Table). More often the special masters hear evidence drawn from further down the hierarchy of evidence such as, as Golkiewicz explained, "epidemiology (evidencing a relative risk less than two), animal studies, case reports/case series studies, anecdotal reports, manufacturing disclosures, Physician Desk Reference citations, journal articles, institutional findings (such as those reported by the Institute of Medicine), novel medical theories, treating physician testimony, and non-dispositive but inferential clinical and laboratory findings."[76]

For example, a treating physician who performed a differential diagnosis (meaning she eliminated most other possible causes) and was left with vaccine injury as a reasonable clinical conclusion might be pitted as a testifying expert against a researcher arguing that there is no epidemiological evidence to suggest the vaccine raises the risk of such a condition. Both witnesses are likely to be credible, but they have very different perspectives. Petitioners' attorneys prefer to raise up the treating physician, who is more likely to be an obtainable witness and whose perspective does not rest on epidemiology.[77] On the one hand, the treating physician's notes offer contemporaneous evidence of what was happening that special masters value (particularly to establish timing), but clinical observations leave out the possibility that something else is causing what is being observed. The researcher relying on epidemiology can say there are no convincing population-level data to suggest a problem, but her evidence cannot serve as a direct rebuttal to this particular person or to a series of compelling case reports of similar problems.

And what if there is epidemiology, but it is limited methodologically or multiple studies point different ways? What about a single published case report and a petitioner who seems to match well to the person described in the report according to her doctor, who has no other idea of what could have caused her condition? Is that enough evidence, or simply one mysterious case being used to bolster another? The IOM limits its conclusions to the strongest evidence, but at the vaccine court, the special masters must decide each case. The persistent reality of case filings based on often-meager evidence has led to contradictory decisions (because there is no clear decision path through this evidence that enjoys consensus) and delays (as petitioners wait for new evidence to be published or search for experts willing to testify).

In 2001, Golkiewicz tried to clarify the muddled and contradictory ways special masters had been deciding off-Table cases. His *Stevens* test would have required (1) proof of medical plausibility, that is, that the vaccine could cause such an injury; (2) confirmation of medical plausibility from the medical community and peer-reviewed literature; (3) an injury recognized by the medical plausibility evidence and literature; (4) a medically acceptable temporal relationship between the vaccination and the onset of the alleged injury; and (5) the elimination of other causes.[78] The major innovation would have been the second prong, requiring something affirmative from the medical community in the form of research that would support the injury claim. Otherwise, in cases with two equally credible experts on both sides, one asserting a causal connection and the other doubting it but neither with much published research to back it up, special masters would continue to lean one way or another for reasons that would be difficult to formalize between them.

The 2005 case of *Althen v. Secretary of HHS*, however, overturned the *Stevens* test. Specifically, the *Althen* court found that the second prong of the *Stevens* test, requiring support from the medical literature, went beyond the original statutory language and could not be required. The vaccine act requires medical records or medical opinion to find causation, but it does not mention published studies. A causal mechanism story is not necessary to prevail, either. "The purpose of the Vaccine Act's preponderance standard," the *Althen* court noted, "is to allow the finding of causation in a field bereft of complete and direct proof of how vaccines affect the human body." The *Althen* factors, as they are now called, describe the petitioner's burden to provide (1) "a medical theory causally connecting the vaccination and the injury," (2) "a logical sequence of cause and effect showing that the vaccination was the reason for the injury," and (3) "a showing of a proximate temporal relationship between vaccination and injury."[79]

As petitioners' attorneys frequently repeat, petitioners do not have to produce medical or epidemiological studies in support of causation.[80] Nonetheless, they argue that the special masters have illegitimately raised the bar for proving a vaccine injury by requiring more and more scientific evidence and by casting doubt on the truthfulness and credibility of their experts.[81] As longtime petitioners' attorney Kevin Conway explained, citing the difficulty in obtaining good epidemiology on their side in the autism cases, "Yeah, that really wasn't part of our case, the epidemiology. That's what the other side uses, epidemiology. And, you know, we don't have any. Vaccine injuries are just so rare, to detect this rare result, you're just, you're not going to find it. And also people have no interest in doing it, or the money to do it. You know, we're not required to show epidemiology. Petitioners aren't required. Because it doesn't exist."[82] They must put forth a "reputable medical or scientific explanation that pertains specifically to [their client's] case," but case law dictates that explanation need only be "legally probable, not medically or scientifically certain."[83] A simple notation in the medical record by the treating physician that there was a link to the vaccine would certainly count as causation evidence, for example. The problem is assembling enough of this kind of evidence—the kind that occupies the lower ranks of the hierarchies of evidence certified by mainstream bodies—to get over the preponderance standard of "more likely than not" that the vaccine caused the injury. It is even more difficult if the government has evidence from the top of the evidence hierarchy that points the other way.

If the petitioner manages to satisfy the *Althen* factors by the preponderance of the evidence, she is entitled to compensation unless the Department of Justice attorneys prove, also by the preponderance standard, that the injury was caused by a "factor unrelated" to the vaccine. The "factor unrelated" must be a specific cause and not a broad and mysterious alternative category such as sudden infant death syndrome. A "factor unrelated" to the vaccine can be rooted in genetic evidence, which easily displaces more conjectural theories about vaccine causation. The special masters regularly deny claims based on seizures and subsequent developmental problems after vaccination, even if the first seizure occurred within a day or so of a vaccination, if the child tests positive for what is known as the SCN1A gene mutation.[84] This gene mutation is highly associated with a type of epilepsy called Dravet syndrome, and vaccines cause neither the mutation nor the epilepsy. If a family refuses to have a child tested for the mutation when it appears from the medical record that she may have Dravet syndrome, special masters refuse to move the case forward until they have that information and will dismiss the case if the parents refuse to test.[85]

Absent something such as genetic test results that are considered a definitive alternate explanation, the special masters are often left weighing experts against experts, each testifying from within a wide range of evidence from clinical observations to published journal articles to biological mechanisms. Petitioners do not have to submit an expert report or put on an expert to testify in a vaccine court case, but if they do, the special masters are entitled to evaluate the expert's credibility using the *Daubert* standard. The Supreme Court's 1993 ruling in *Daubert v. Merrell Dow Pharmaceuticals* was an attempt to equip judges with better tools to evaluate the credibility of expert testimony so as to prevent embarrassing "junk science" endorsements.[86] In civil trials, *Daubert* motions function to keep juries from even hearing noncredible experts, including experts who have testified in vaccine court.[87] By contrast, *Daubert* does not block any expert from testifying in vaccine court. Judges weigh (1) the proffered testimony's general acceptance in the scientific community, (2) whether the theory has been subjected to peer review and publication, (3) whether it can and has been tested, and (4) the known potential rate of error.[88] As Sheila Jasanoff explains, the *Daubert* ruling endorsed the "myth" that "law can simply transpose the project of science, without further ado, into its own projects of fact-finding and reality representation."[89] But Jasanoff argues that judges have been able to use *Daubert* to actively construct what real science should be under the pretense of simply pointing to it, when scientific knowledge is actually created in many different ways with different methods, within and across different communities, with objects and instruments that are themselves variable human creations, and negotiated to points of consensus or kept open for many reasons, such as time and money.[90]

Expert witnesses are the primary route for the introduction of all of the forms of evidence discussed here. In practice, the special masters hear expert testimony from a small pool of individuals well known to them: the medical officers (appearing only through their reports, not as witnesses) and the few physicians and researchers in the country who regularly serve as petitioners' expert witnesses. Each of these experts may have testified before the same special masters in dozens of cases. The name of one petitioners' expert in the autism litigation appeared in the case database 185 times, for example. The petitioners' experts are often poorly matched in status and expertise to the respondents' experts. Petitioners' attorneys complain that it is so hard for them to get credible experts to testify about vaccine injury because the professional norm against blaming vaccines for any harm is so strong that would-be experts suffer career harms if they agree to appear. In one public example, Dr. Derek Smith, a Harvard neurologist who had testified that the tetanus vaccine could trigger transverse myelitis in vulnerable individuals, withdrew as a vaccine court expert in 2002 after his supervisors heard that he "was ruining his reputation by his testimony in the vaccine program."[91] From the petitioners' attorneys' perspectives, this shows that real coercion undergirds our immunization social order, not merely disinterested scientific perspectives. From the perspectives of medical experts on the government's side, however, there is nothing wrong with criticizing a colleague whose opinion goes further than the evidence supports. If there is very little evidence available from the top of the hierarchy of evidence, it will be difficult for many professional scientists and researchers to feel comfortable helping petitioners cobble together bits and pieces of less compelling evidence into a case. What I have called the middle-ground cases are an example of just that, however.

Middle-ground cases involving damaged nerves and autoimmune reactions after vaccinations are an excellent illustration of the interplay between epidemiological studies (at the top of the hierarchy of evidence) and expert theories about possible biological mechanisms without such grounding (pulled from lower on the hierarchy). For example, in 2006 and 2007 Special Master Laura Millman compensated petitioners in a set of hepatitis B claims for GBS,[92] multiple sclerosis,[93] chronic inflammatory demyelinating polyneuropathy,[94] and transverse myelitis.[95] In its causality review of injuries and the hepatitis B vaccine, the IOM noted that there was not much evidence that the vaccine caused demyelinating conditions and some evidence showing no association in epidemiological studies, but there were some plausible mechanistic theories in the wider medical literature describing how infections might lead to damaging autoimmune responses.[96] This support was enough in the vaccine court, but not for the court's critics from the medical side. In a 2008 *New York Times* op-ed titled "Inoculated Against Facts," Dr. Paul Offit singled out the hepatitis B decisions granting compensation for multiple sclerosis for lacking scientific merit. "Now," he wrote, "petitioners need merely propose a biologically plausible mechanism by which a vaccine might cause harm—even if their explanation contradicts published studies." Dr. Offit noted that "[t]wo large studies had clearly shown that hepatitis B vaccine could neither cause nor exacerbate multiple sclerosis." The vaccine court had wrongly "elevat[ed] a hypothesis above epidemiological evidence."[97] In the broad class of cases involving autoimmune diseases and nerve damage disorders, the vaccine court did exactly that: compensate based on an otherwise plausible but imprecisely connected theory of injury (if the timing otherwise makes sense) in the face of population-level evidence showing no positive association with that injury. As I argue in Chapter 6 on the autism cases, the petitioners' attorneys were banking on the special masters once again putting aside epidemiological evidence in favor of a biologically plausible mechanism that could connect vaccines to autism.

Reputable experts who testify regularly at the vaccine court about the connection between vaccines and multiple sclerosis and other demyelinating and autoimmune conditions, such as Dr. Carlo Tornatore, a neurologist and head of Georgetown University Medical Center's multiple sclerosis center, argue from the basic plausibility of a few mechanistic theories applicable to a vulnerable subpopulation. Dr. Tornatore emphasizes the limits of epidemiological explanations that can never prove a negative: "Epidemiologic studies are never going to be able to say something does not happen."[98] These experts are mainstream professionals with no ties to anti-vaccine researchers. They testify only in these middle-ground cases, not for excluded causes with no plausible mechanism account in the mainstream (as autism turned out to be). Opposing experts treat them with respect but agree with Dr. Offit about the superiority of epidemiologic evidence. An opposing government expert, a neurologist at Johns Hopkins, agreed that "[Tornatore's theory of] molecular mimicry is an excellent theory" but "does not believe it is relevant in hepatitis B and MS [multiple sclerosis]" because epidemiological studies fail to support a connection.[99] More recent claims of multiple sclerosis after the hepatitis B vaccine have been settled informally, with the government agreeing to pay a lump sum but entering a denial that the hepatitis B vaccine actually caused the claimed injury.[100]

A compensation does not automatically mean that the injury is added to the Table or that other special masters have to follow a common law of vaccine injuries, and thus this curious state of compensated cases that do not themselves supply evidence of injury persists. The fact that another special master had a similar fact pattern and ruled in a certain way does not create any obligation for her colleague to cite that decision and rule in a similar way. The special masters explain that what they do is render factual conclusions, not interpret legal doctrine, and thus it does not make sense to create a common set of rules about vaccine injuries at the vaccine court. Pointing out how two special masters came to the opposite result in two very similar cases is a favored way of critiquing the court and attempting to damage its credibility, however. The insistence that every award is individual combined with the widely known but not formally enforced set of common law–type rules (the informal settlement of these middle-ground cases) leaves the special masters vulnerable to criticism on both jurisprudential and scientific grounds. Yet it is unsurprising that a court processing relatively large numbers of claims with so-called repeat players would develop mutually understood shorthand practices such as settlement of off-Table cases to manage most claims.

A longtime petitioners' attorney, Curtis Webb, argues that the vaccine compensation system ought to embrace uncertainty and lack of knowledge and, in the context of uncertainty, simply rule more generously. "I think [the court] should afford a simplified end remedy," he says, "a remedy that is more generous than traditional court and a system that operates on less information, that is willing to make rough guesses."[101] In a knowledge-driven legal context, however, no one at the court or on the government side seems comfortable with rough guesses. I heard the term "close call" frequently, but it was often invoked in a hortatory and conclusory fashion, most often by petitioners' attorneys who argued that their cases should have been interpreted as close when the special masters saw them as falling well short of the preponderance standard. Close calls are indeed supposed to go in favor of the petitioners at the vaccine court, but the evidentiary challenges of vaccine injury claims do not often fit the metaphors of closeness or distance very well. The term "close call" suggests multiple reasons for either accepting or rejecting a proposition, where both sides have a chance of prevailing. More commonly, the two sides draw from opposite ends of the hierarchy of evidence without the overlap necessary for a close call or a rough guess. In the end, it is sometimes possible for credible expert witnesses to pull together enough bits of evidence from further down the hierarchy to create a plausible account of individualized injury. These accounts, unsatisfying to medical experts, are well suited to emerge in a court that is trying to construct an account of what is likely to have happened and to do justice to a person.

6

The Autism Showdown

The most important thing the vaccine court has ever accomplished is the Omnibus Autism Proceeding (2002–2010), denying claims that autism is a vaccine injury. Our vaccine court was the sole institution in the world to conduct full and public hearings of one of the most important and divisive questions of our time. The fact that the vaccine court existed and could handle the autism claims as it did was monumentally important for containing the further harm the erroneous hypothesis could have done if it had been put before juries all over the United States before dispositive studies were completed and published. It may seem with hindsight that the outcome was inevitable, but as the autism claims began to roll into the court in the early 2000s, things were not so clear at all. As I described in Chapters 4 and 5, the special masters at the vaccine court have devised a way of handling off-Table claims that turns on whether a credible expert can articulate a plausible theory for how the vaccine injury could have happened in the petitioner's body. If there is epidemiology to support the injury claim, so much the better, but if there is a plausible theory of causation gathered up from the bottom of the evidence hierarchy and articulated by a credible expert, it can support a claim even if epidemiology points away from a link. The formal rules of the vaccine court do not require petitioners to put forth epidemiological studies or to prove a causal mechanism, but as a practical matter as soon as experts start to talk about how a vaccine could be responsible for an injury, this must be the way they talk.

In the years leading up to the autism decisions in 2009 and 2010, the special masters had been wrestling with how to decide these middle-ground cases with some plausible theory but lacking epidemiological support. Recall that in 2006 and 2007 Special Master Laura Millman compensated petitioners for Guillain-Barré syndrome (GBS), multiple sclerosis (MS), chronic inflammatory demyelinating polyneuropathy, and transverse myelitis, for which the court received a scolding in the

New York Times by Dr. Paul Offit. Within a few years, the handling of these types of claims shifted somewhat, from traditionally ordered compensations after a causal finding to stipulations permitting payments but without concessions of true causation from the government. The autism cases, tried in 2007–2008 and decided in 2009–2010, were a showdown over the application of this new approach at the vaccine court. Would autism be seen as similar to MS, a mysterious condition with a plausible-enough underlying story of how vaccines could cause it in the body? Would the causal theories about what took place in the body be compelling enough to set aside the epidemiology, which by 2003 was stacking up fast against a relationship between vaccines and autism?

Most discussions about the evidence in the vaccine-autism controversy treat epidemiological studies as the site of the debate and as the definitive evidence that settled it, and this attention is well deserved. But my analysis of the autism cases at the vaccine court shows that the critical focus was really on the theories of causation at the bodily, molecular, cellular, and subcellular levels. The vaccine court created a unique site for what Steven Epstein calls a credibility struggle, or a dispute over knowledge in an attempt to shape policy and create certainty.[1] The pages of scientific and medical journals no longer presented the autism-vaccine link as an open question after about 2004, but the pace, relative openness, and financial support from the vaccine court kept the issue officially open there for several more years. The petitioners kept asking for delays so they could produce research aimed at showing a plausible chain of events in the body, and always maintained that the epidemiology could not disprove that a small number of children had come down with vaccine-induced autism. Understanding what evidence could win a middle-ground case in that era shows why the autism petitioners focused so much on the story within the body: if they could demonstrate a plausible-enough mechanistic theory of causation, they might be able to win, and close court observers knew it. But as I explain here, neither of the causal stories put forward in the autism litigation was able to get any traction at all, and the petitioners' experts were beset with credibility problems.

The autism controversy settled in the vaccine court as parents claimed autism as a vaccine injury beginning in the late 1990s and early 2000s and were forced to seek redress in the vaccine court instead of state courts. The vaccine court was still using a paper-based filing system when claims first started to flood in, and there was not even enough space to house the paper files that would result from so many claims.[2] In July 2002, the then-chief special master Gary Golkiewicz created the OAP. Three hundred claims had come in the previous six months, and the total would rise to more than fifty-six hundred after it became clear that suits against vaccine manufacturers would have to go through the vaccine court. Special Master Golkiewicz's order set up a two-phase program in which three special masters would hear six test cases on the general causation issues and then use the results to decide on compensation for the remaining thousands of claims. The first three test cases were to decide whether thimerosal and the measles-mumps-rubella (MMR) vaccine together triggered autism. The second set of three cases considered whether thimerosal-containing vaccines alone triggered autism.[3] The litigation would drag on for eight years, involving dozens of expert witnesses, hundreds of scientific articles, thousands of pages of transcripts, and teams of lawyers on both sides.

The stakes were very high. Linking vaccines and autism could cause widespread vaccine refusals and imperil public health's greatest achievement: the banishment of many infectious diseases from childhood in the developed world. Verdicts for the thousands of families would bankrupt the compensation fund. Verdicts against the families would leave them uncompensated for a lifetime of expensive care for their children in a society with a meager safety net. Used to processing cases in almost total obscurity, the special masters of the vaccine court judges found themselves adjudicating the most volatile public health question of our day. Its business is normally closed to the public because of the private medical issues involved, but the Petitioners' Steering Committee and the Justice Department agreed to open the test case hearings to the public and to place nearly all filed documents online.

The proceedings against both thimerosal and the MMR vaccine began with the case of *Cedillo v. Secretary of HHS* at nine o'clock in the morning of June 11, 2007. Eight hundred people were listening in on a public phone line on that first day of testimony. The next trial, *Hazlehurst v. Secretary of HHS*, took place over four days in mid-October 2007, followed by *Snyder v. Secretary of HHS* for five days in early November 2007. The second cluster of three cases, *Mead v. Secretary of HHS*, *King v.*

Secretary of HHS, and *Dwyer v. Secretary of HHS*, focused on thimerosal and went to trial in the spring and summer of 2008. The petitioners in the first set of test cases argued that thimerosal-containing vaccinations had disrupted the children's immune systems via mercury toxicity such that when they received the MMR vaccine (which never contained thimerosal), the virus was able to persist in their guts and cause inflammation (called theory 1). The virus then traveled to and affected their brains, causing autism.[4] The second theory in the next three test cases was that thimerosal-containing vaccines alone caused autism by provoking neuroinflammation in the brain. This brain environment then led to the behavioral expressions labeled autism, petitioners argued.[5]

As I described in Chapter 4, middle-ground, off-Table claims are regularly compensated with only indeterminate scientific evidence. Typically such cases settle before reaching a hearing or following a hearing of only a day or two and involving perhaps one or two expert witnesses. Autism was different. The first MMR-thimerosal test case to go to hearing, *Cedillo v. Secretary of HHS*, featured twelve days of testimony from seventeen experts (six for the family of Michelle Cedillo, eleven from the government). The lead case for the second thimerosal-only theory, the combined hearing for *Mead v. Secretary of HHS* and *King v. Secretary of HHS*, lasted fourteen days with testimony from sixteen experts (five for the families and eleven for the government, with only a couple of experts testifying for both theories). Originally slated to go to hearing in 2004, the autism cases were not heard until 2007 and 2008 because the petitioners asked for delays to wait for new studies to be published and attempted a full-scale discovery process not normally seen in vaccine cases.

What Is Autism? Brain Injury, Genetic Problem, or Neurodiversity?

The petitioners and the mainstream scientists in the OAP disagreed about many things, of course, but the most foundational disagreement was over what autism is. The reigning conception of autism is a condition defined by impaired social abilities, communication, and restricted, repetitive habits and interests. It is usually diagnosed in toddlers as they fail to reach developmental milestones. The diagnosis is clinical, meaning it is made using observational criteria rather than, say, a blood test.

It varies widely in its severity and prognosis, though in the mainstream it is considered an incurable lifelong condition. But what would autism be if it were the outcome of a toxic tort injury? The injury frame is critical for any winning legal claim. Parents who think vaccines triggered their child's autism typically think of it as a reversible, treatable brain injury. Mainstream researchers emphasize genetic and perhaps prenatal environmental factors without much treatment hope. A small group of autistic people and their disability rights supporters prefer to frame it as neurodiversity, or a variation on human wiring that should not be portrayed as a curse on families and ought not be stamped out. These neurodiversity advocates see treatments as miserable and eugenic. These three groups are quite separate and mistrustful of each other. The neurodiversity perspective is not represented in the legalization of vaccine injury because it does not presuppose that an injury has taken place; I focus for the rest of this chapter on the competing views of injury as the parties to the autism cases described them.

As Generation Rescue founder J. B. Handley describes it, "autism is brain injury."[6] The OAP was the big chance for these parent advocates to prove the scientific basis for their account. In the OAP litigation, the theory of autism was a dual genetic-brain injury theory based on the notion that some children are genetically hypersusceptible to the mercury in vaccines or are unable to clear the measles virus from the MMR from their bodies. The first point in most vaccine-blaming arguments is to highlight the "autism epidemic" and note that such an increase cannot be explained by genetics and must be environmental. But the OAP petitioners had to narrow down the class of autistic children who were injured by vaccines to a subset they termed the "clearly regressive" cases, estimated by their expert statistician to be about 6 percent of all cases. Creating that group was necessary because the petitioners needed to define a condition that could be linked to a vaccine and to distinguish it from the dominant account of autism as a developmental disorder likely present before birth and manifesting over time, but not caused by an environmental provocation. A key part of advocacy arguments, as I noted in Chapter 4, is that children are suffering from epidemic levels of a variety of diseases, including ADHD, asthma, allergies, immune problems, and autism, and that over-vaccination is the cause. There the emphasis is on very large numbers of children, not on vulnerable genetic subgroups. Advocates use this disabled children frame and the vulnerable minority frame to tap into support from the widest possible net of fearful parents while also drawing on the highly resonant moral principle of minority rights.

The medical and scientific experts on the government's side in the OAP litigation voiced the mainstream consensus view of autism causation—it seems to be traceable to developmental moments occurring before birth. I call this the "wiring" explanation, in contrast to the "injury" explanation. It is understood as heavily though not entirely genetic, with both sides agreeing that autism cannot be wholly explained by genetics.[7] Twin and family studies show that sharing genes with someone with autism greatly increases the risk of having autism, but even for identical twins the outcomes are not always the same (there is, for example, a 60 percent chance one has autism if one's identical twin also has it, a 300 percent increase from the general population risk).[8]

The special masters were impressed by evidence that autopsies of the brains of autistic children show abnormalities linked to specific points in prenatal development.[9] The government's experts described these as systemic or structural abnormalities in the number, location, and interconnections of neurons in the brain.[10] One autopsied brain showed, for example, that the part that controls facial expressions had failed to develop in the autistic child at the fourth or fifth week of gestation.[11] Neurons had failed to migrate from the part of the brain where they were made to take up their proper places,[12] and there were found to be too many local neuronal connections and not enough long arcs of neurons connecting different parts of the brain.[13] One government expert explained that the reason some children could seem to develop normally and then regress is that as they age and need a new part of the nervous system to "come on line" and "switch to the new system," "they can't because it's missing."[14] Experts frequently noted that there are other examples of conditions that are genetic but do not manifest themselves until later in life, such as schizophrenia (thought to be heavily genetic, but not entirely) and Huntington's disease (a clear case of genetic causation).

There are some known causes of autism from prenatal exposure: thalidomide and valprioc acid, if exposed between twenty and twenty-four days after conception, and misoprostol and rubella virus if exposed during the first twelve weeks of gestation. (The MMR vaccine, by keeping rubella from circulating in the population, *prevents* autism.) So it is not

that mainstream researchers testified that autism was definitely genetically determined but they just had not decoded it yet; rather, they felt
confident ruling out ethyl mercury as a postnatal cause based on conclusions about its properties and dose, but did not know if there could
be other environmental causes (occurring at any point) or what those
might be besides the few (and rare) exposures already known. In his
Cedillo ruling, Special Master Hastings noted that "medical science does
not at this time completely understand the causation of autism, and is
open to the *possibility* of postnatal factors playing a causal role,"[15] though
he concluded the evidence for that was "weak."[16] In the popular media,
autism is often explained as a thoroughgoing mystery that has scientists
and doctors baffled. In the OAP, by contrast, the government experts
testified at length about what is currently known about autism (which
has been a relatively well-funded research area for some years now) and
succeeded in portraying it as a condition with some fairly definite features that are well understood: some aspects of causation, prevalence
and incidence, variations, progression, and clinical presentations. There
is no known cure and no particularly effective treatments.[17]

Defenders of the mainstream position subsequently argue that the
supposed epidemic of autism can mostly be explained by the broadening
of diagnostic factors for autism, increased awareness and support, and
diagnostic substitution (as those who would have otherwise been labeled intellectually disabled move over into the autism spectrum disorders category), and that there are simply not enough good data to be able
to measure a true increase accurately.[18] Dr. Michael Rutter testified that
he was quite confident that contemporary measures of autism captured
cases pretty well, but he emphasized that it was very difficult to look
back and apply current criteria in the past to see if more cases should
have been diagnosed but were not. He did not "rule out the possibility
that . . . there has been a true rise due to some as yet to be identified
factor."[19] Since the OAP concluded, sociological and epidemiological
research by Peter Bearman has found provocative geographic patterns
of autism cases, with some areas having dramatically higher rates than
others. His data are inconsistent with the vaccine theory since vaccines
are not geographically specific, but suggest other social avenues for pro-
liferating diagnoses of autism through mechanisms such as networking
and clustering among parents.[20]

The Case against Thimerosal

The petitioners argued that thimerosal exposure caused damage through its ability to impair sulfur metabolism at a subcellular level, disrupting metabolic pathways that regulate brain chemistry. (In the first theory, the role of mercury was said to be weakening the immune system, thus allowing the measles virus to persist; in the second theory, it was the gradual buildup that caused brain damage.) The petitioners' expert on this theory, Dr. Richard Deth, a pharmacologist from Northeastern University in Boston, testified that this disruption would lead to impaired methylation and chronic oxidative stress in the brain.[21] The idea was that mercury toxicity, a result of very low doses, would keep critical processes of cell regulation and amino acid production chronically off-kilter, producing autistic symptoms. Dr. Deth described this stressed state as neuroinflammation.[22]

A second and closely related version of the thimerosal theory came from Dr. Marcel Kinsbourne, a pediatric neurologist who had also testified in the first theory cases and made a report in the U.K. litigation over the MMR. Dr. Kinsbourne testified that inorganic mercury in the brain from vaccines could cause neurons to release too much glutamate, an excitatory brain chemical. Astrocytes are immune cells in the brain that regulate and absorb excess glutamate, but Dr. Kinsbourne argued that they would be damaged or killed by the inflammatory processes set off by the inorganic mercury. Methyl mercury at doses much higher than the ethyl mercury doses in vaccines had been shown to inhibit astrocytes' uptake of glutamate.[23] The excess glutamate would then cause excitotoxicity, Dr. Kinsbourne proposed, a state in the brain characterized by too many neurons firing, which can bring on seizures and cell death. Dr. Kinsbourne's "overactivated brain" theory of autism was that the repetitive behaviors and agitation often seen in people with autism are expressions of this abnormal brain function. Both versions of the thimerosal injury theory depended on the processes occurring at a chronic level rather than worsening to cause degeneration and cell death (because people with autism do not die from it and may improve over time, unlike people with neurodegenerative conditions such as Alzheimer's disease).

To account for why such small doses might have such significant effects for only for some children, the petitioners needed to provide a new interpretation of toxicology. Dr. Vasken Aposhian, a toxicologist from the University of Arizona, testified for the families that autism is possible from vaccines because of a mercury efflux disorder in a subpopulation.[24] Some people are genetically unable to excrete mercury properly, on this account, and it builds up and causes autism. He compared the children to people with Wilson's disease, a genetic condition in which the body cannot excrete copper. Wilson's disease is caused by a single gene mutation and can be cured by chelation therapy.[25] Wilson's disease is an easy analogy to understand, but the special masters never accepted that it was more likely than not that a similarly vulnerable group exists for mercury excretion. Dr. Aposhian built his theory from a set of studies purporting to show that autistic children had very low mercury levels in their hair and teeth, inferring that they were unable to excrete it normally from within their internal organs.[26] The special masters came to regard these studies as unreliable advocacy science of low quality. The hair from the autistic children in one study that petitioners continue to rely on as evidence, what I term the Holmes baby haircut study, was actually within the normal range for children, while the control children's hair had fifteen times the expected amount of mercury, for example. Five studies have failed to replicate the Holmes results, but a petitioner's expert continued to give testimony relying on it as late as 2015.[27]

"Well-Established Factual Predicates"

Special Master Denise Vowell explained that the thimerosal theory took hold because "some of the factual predicates for the hypothesis are well established."[28] "Initially," she observed, "to someone unacquainted with mercury's toxicology, autism spectrum disorders, or biochemistry, Dr. Deth's opinions on mercury, oxidative stress, and sulfur metabolism might appear to be solidly based and plausible."[29] How did the case go from some compelling "factual predicates" to a resounding rejection by the special masters? What were these factual predicates, and how did they fail to build a credible case?

First, everyone agreed that mercury generally is a dangerous neurotoxin. Its vapors made hatters mad. It is second only to lead as an element for public concern, and from the lead scares of previous decades we learned that even tiny amounts of a toxic substance can have ongoing subclinical effects.[30] Despite general agreement that mercury is a known neurotoxin, what exactly that meant was highly contested throughout the autism case process. The petitioners' cases relied on an approach to mercury that resisted line drawing and differentiation. It was better for them to emphasize mercury's well-known toxicity and to extrapolate from studies that used much higher doses than the vaccine schedule or that obtained results indicating damage at the cellular or in vitro level. The special masters, however, would adopt the perspective on mercury toxicity that the Department of Justice (DOJ) attorneys urged. That meant paying close attention to the type of mercury (methyl mercury, the much-studied kind found in fish, or ethyl mercury, the kind in thimerosal), the dose (similar to the vaccine schedule or much higher), the exposed subject (a child, an adult, a mouse, a cell, an adult monkey, or an infant monkey), and the clinical outcome (autism, nothing at all, or something else). The special masters carefully differentiated the properties and effects of mercury by type and granted less credibility to studies that did not closely fit the question of ethyl mercury in humans.

The special masters refused to make inferences between the small doses of ethyl mercury in vaccines and large-dose methyl mercury poisonings, instead constructing mercury as an element with a wide variety of properties that can be benignly present in healthy bodies.[31] Everyday adult mercury exposure comes almost entirely from dental amalgams and fish consumption (of which canned tuna is the largest single source in the United States) and is almost entirely methyl mercury. The special masters understood human contact with mercury as a gradual, lifelong absorption process, beginning from gestation to normal adulthood, with adult brain mercury levels averaging fifteen parts per billion.[32] They regarded mercury as functionally benign in the usual ranges found in human bodies, and noted that observable effects do not begin until brain concentrations reach 150 to 200 parts per billion and perhaps higher.[33]

All the parents in the OAP cases testified that their children had mercury toxicity confirmed by alternative lab tests. The special masters came to see these alternative mercury testing labs as unreliable sites that produced artificially alarming results that Defeat Autism Now! (DAN!) practitioners could use to bolster the notion that autism is caused by mercury toxicity. Special Master Hastings noted that Dr. Elizabeth Mumper, a DAN! pediatrician who testified about the lab results on behalf of the families, seemed able to get to a diagnosis of vaccine-induced autism no matter what the lab results looked like.[34] Under cross-examination, she admitted that some of the labs she relied on had significant reliability problems.[35] But this alternative lab testing was the source of the parents' notions of the legal wrong done to their child. The test results were part of what tied them into the alternative autism community and gave them hope their children could be cured. One mother testified that she first believed vaccines had caused her son's autism when she saw the lab report for mercury toxicity: "And when we got those results back, we saw that he was in the 96th percentile for mercury, and that just—you know, even just visually on the page seeing that line go all the way over to the far right of the page is very upsetting to me, and I thought, oh, no, we're being exposed to something toxic, and that's what happened to Jordan."[36] Those urine test results had been obtained following chelation therapy, a popular alternative treatment for autism based on this paradigm of mercury toxicity. A chelating agent is administered to draw out heavy metals from the body, so from the mainstream toxicology perspective, one would expect higher levels of mercury. The lab results that upset his mother were keyed to the normal range for an unprovoked sample, however, a diagnostic practice that the American College of Medical Toxicology calls invalid and harmful.[37] Jordan had a blood test a month before that showed mercury levels in the reference range.[38] Another child in the first theory cases had five mercury level blood tests, all within the normal range despite being post-chelation.[39] Another's mercury came back in the "nondetectable" range.[40] Despite these results, the children had continued to be treated as if their autism was the result of mercury toxicity. The mainstream toxicology and medical communities and the alternative autism community drew on incommensurable understandings of what counted as evidence of injury, therefore, with different labs, test standards, practices, and foundational assumptions.

The second factual predicate was evidence showing that mercury from vaccines could cross the blood-brain barrier and persist in the brain. Studies from the 1990s in adult monkeys showed that when given very large doses of methyl mercury, the monkeys' brains showed neuroinflammation (though the animals remained behaviorally normal).[41] The autism controversy then made it critical to extend that body of knowledge to baby monkeys and thimerosal. The Burbacher infant monkey study (which the petitioners' lawyer identified as the most important study for them and which the special masters also accepted as credible) investigated how the different types of mercury behave in the developing brain.[42] Infant monkeys received dosages of both types of mercury and were sacrificed to see what had happened in their brain tissue. The infant monkeys got thimerosal via vaccines administered at birth and at one, two, and three weeks of age (about two and a half times the human infant amount and at a faster schedule to account for the monkeys' faster maturation rate). This study was unusual evidence in the OAP because it was important to both sides, credible, and highly ranked in the hierarchy of evidence.

The Burbacher infant monkey study showed that the two types of mercury were indeed different. Mercury from thimerosal injections (ethyl mercury) cleared the body faster than the mercury from the oral doses (methyl mercury), but a larger proportion of the inorganic mercury that was left in the monkeys' brains was from thimerosal. The petitioners relied on Burbacher's work to show that ethyl mercury crossed the blood-brain barrier and settled in infants' brains. The persisting inorganic mercury could trigger damaging subcellular processes, they argued. While everyone conceded the Burbacher study showed some persisting inorganic mercury from vaccines, the special masters were convinced by the government expert Dr. Brent's interpretation of the study that actually more *methyl* mercury would persist as inorganic mercury (because we are exposed to so much more methyl mercury), making it hard to pin the blame for any damage (if there was any) on the vaccines.[43] The Burbacher study was thus a strong circumstantial piece of evidence for the petitioners, but once the special masters endorsed the dominant framework for understanding mercury (as different varieties, with methyl deposits vastly outnumbering ethyl deposits), it lost most of its implications for the vaccine injury theory.

It was also accepted that damage to the immunological cells in the brain can cause neurological dysfunction.[44] And so on to the third factual predicate: it was not in dispute that brains of autistic people from autopsy studies showed neuroinflammation. Inflammation meant something was damaged, the attorneys argued. That brain damage could cause susceptible children to regress into autism. Research from a well-regarded group at Johns Hopkins University established the existence of inflammation though two critical papers, called the Vargas autopsy study and the Pardo neuroinflammation study. In his opening statement in the second theory hearings of May 12, 2008, the petitioners' attorney noted that this work from Dr. Carlos Pardo's neuropathology research group, which showed activated immune responses in the brains of autistic people, would be critical to proving their case. The resulting neuroinflammation, the petitioners would claim, was provoked by the ethyl mercury in thimerosal.

Mainstream researchers would not permit the petitioners' attorneys to use their work to hop over an expertise barrier, however.[45] Ten days later, the DOJ called Dr. Thomas Kemper, a neuropathologist from Boston University. Dr. Kemper told the special masters how he had talked with his friend Dr. Pardo about their research and its implications for autism. Dr. Kemper flatly contradicted the petitioners' construal of the Pardo research group's work on the stand[46] and introduced a letter he had received from Dr. Pardo dated May 13, 2008, just one day after the petitioners had announced their reliance on his work. Recall that the vaccine court does not use the Federal Rules of Evidence (under which this testimony would be hearsay), and anything that would help the special master decide is heard. The Pardo letter does not mention the court cases at all. Its tone is professionally closed in its technicality and direct address to a fellow scientist, but it clearly makes the case for another interpretation of the neuroinflammation.

In the letter, Dr. Pardo explained his aim was to "clarify some of the misconceptions" about his group's work on neuroinflammation and autism. He noted that the inflammatory response the petitioners were relying on was "associated with the neuro-innate immune response rather than an adaptive immune response" and that the particular cells, astrocytes, that the petitioners claimed were affected did not actually decrease in number.[47] "These findings are inconsistent with the hypothesis of a potential toxic effect on astrocytes by neurotoxins or toxic material," he wrote. "At present, we are not able to conclude that these neuroglial reactions are deleterious for the central nervous system." The immune reaction might even be helpful or protective, his group speculated. Moreover, the activation of immune processes in autistic brains, he concluded, "resulted likely from prenatal and early exposure rather than late exposure."[48] The special masters noted that neither the government experts on neuroinflammation nor the Pardo researchers were willing to infer a causal link and that experts thought maybe the inflammation was protective or an effect of the body's response to autism.[49] Special Master Hastings made a special note of the Pardo letter on this point.[50] To accept the petitioners' theory, the special masters would have had to embrace an interpretation of key evidence over the explicit written dissent of the scientist whose lab (in one of the world's most prestigious sites for medical research) generated that evidence.

The petitioners still needed the final piece of the story: evidence showing that genetic vulnerability could produce injuries from thimerosal in some subjects while leaving others unaffected. Studies by Jill James of the Arkansas Children's Hospital Research Institute and Mady Hornig of Columbia's School of Public Health purportedly filled the lacuna. Hornig and James had been part of the inner circle of anti-mercury activists,[51] and both received funding from the anti-mercury parents' group SafeMinds as well as from mainstream governmental sources. The petitioners had delayed the autism hearings numerous times, awaiting the results of these and other studies. James aimed to find out if autistic children had different metabolic and genetic profiles than nonautistic children that might show that they suffered from impaired methylation and oxidative stress. The James glutathione study, as it was called in the cases, found that autistics had lower levels of glutathione, a crucial antioxidant, in their blood plasma than nonautistic controls.[52] For Dr. Deth (who testified about the James studies), that indicated that autistic children are under chronic oxidative stress because they do not have enough glutathione. A James study on genetic polymorphism revealed differences between autistic and nonautistic children's genes that Dr. Deth also argued showed their vulnerability to autism.[53] Dr. Deth also relied on what was termed the Hornig mouse study, which compared the effects of thimerosal on two strains of lab mice, one with a preset vulnerability to autoimmune disorders.[54] Mark Blaxill, a prominent anti-vaccine, anti-mercury activist with SafeMinds, trumpeted the Hornig study as showing "clear evidence of developmental delay and altered brain development" in the genetically vulnerable mice.[55] Unfortunately for the petitioners, these last pieces of the story were understood not as established factual predicates, but as discrete pieces of circumstantial evidence that were not scientifically compelling for reasons of study design and execution.

Credibility Failures in the Thimerosal Theories

As Special Master Vowell put it, after producing the factual predicates—that mercury could be toxic, that organic mercury would persist in the brain, and that autistic brains showed neuroinflammation—the petitioners' case nonetheless "f[e]ll apart."[56] The first credibility failure was a failure of implication: the special masters concluded that the studies the petitioners had waited for so hopefully did not imply enough to link thimerosal and autism in susceptible children. This failure was not a negative judgment on an expert's credibility, just a limit on the findings. As Special Master Campbell-Smith observed, James "carefully avoided overstating the significance of [her] findings."[57] Even though she had been intimately involved in the development of the scientific case against thimerosal, James was clearly unwilling to cede her legitimacy in her papers (and neither she nor Hornig testified at the hearings). Her conclusions, though reputable, simply could not stretch far enough. The special masters adopted the opposing experts' view of her work that blood plasma levels of glutathione were so local as to hold no implications for brain levels (a point Dr. Deth conceded) and that genetic differences were not surprising in a study comparing a group of children with a heavily genetic condition to children without that condition.[58] Moreover, the metabolic problems the autistic subjects have are commonly found in people with many diseases and thus seem more like effects of disease than a cause of autism. Even if someone did have a genuine problem with these cellular processes, the result would be continual deterioration and death, not a chronic damaged state like the petitioners described, and certainly not autism. The special masters were convinced that nothing that any kind of mercury poisoning does to humans seems to resemble autism at all.

The second credibility failure was descriptive. The petitioners' description of the body was one of great vulnerability to a tiny dose, at least in cases of preexisting susceptibility. The alternative account was of robust bodies that could commonly and easily excrete and manage small amounts of dangerous substances on their own, and where there was no credible evidence of a special subgroup that could not do so. I noted above that the special masters considered the amount of mercury added to the body burden by thimerosal-containing vaccines to be very tiny compared to the usual amounts any person, even a newborn, would be expected to carry without harm. They were also impressed by the government's experts' alternative accounts of our bodies as resilient in response to all kinds of biochemical stresses, particularly the very tiny insult of a thimerosal-containing vaccine. Our bodies handle oxidative stress constantly and easily on this account (exercise, for example, causes it and could be one of the reasons why it is beneficial), and we have so much glutathione in our cells that it would take less than one minute for an infant's body to replace the glutathione needed to process the first six months' worth of vaccines even if they were given all at once.[59] The descriptive scale just did not make sense, in other words.

The third type of credibility failure was reputational, in both absolute and relative terms. These reputational failings are the classic ones well identified in previous studies on credibility in the courtroom.[60] The opinions portray the elderly Dr. Aposhian as a bumbling and confused witness who took up the anti-vaccine cause after his scientific career was over. The opinions note his numerous calculation errors, how he could not remember many details in his testimony and simply read from his slides, and how he discounted the foundational dose theory of toxicology.[61] The opposing attorneys had cross-examined Dr. Deth on how many rejections a key article had received (four)[62] and how his work had not been cited by other scientists even though he had emailed them about it,[63] and intimated that he was much more circumspect when writing about autism causation for a peer audience than he was as an expert in the OAP.[64] The research he presented at the OAP had been almost entirely supported by parent advocacy organizations such as SafeMinds in the years leading up to the trials because he could not get mainstream grant funding. Although Dr. Deth's primary theory was that oxidative stress in the brain triggers autism, he had published only one review paper on oxidative stress.[65] (By contrast, government expert Dr. Jackson Roberts of Vanderbilt had researched oxidative stress for over twenty years, with 180 original research publications and four patents related to it.) Dr. Deth claimed he had detected cellular effects of mercury at levels one hundred to one thousand times below what other researchers had found, but the work had not been published. The special masters entirely disregarded this evidence as simply not believable.[66] Dr. Kinsbourne's credibility suffered because though he is a pediatric neurologist, he had not seen patients in eighteen years and was perceived as a "frequent flyer," or professional expert witness who appeared at the vaccine court many times. He had also been the expositor of the measles causation theory in the first set of trials, and the government attorneys suggested in cross-examination that he had done nothing more than replace the words "measles virus" with "thimerosal-containing vaccines" in his second expert report.[67] Finally, all the special masters emphasized that epidemiological studies across multiple countries had failed to find any association between thimerosal in vaccines and autism.

The government's experts, on the other hand, successfully presented paradigmatic scientific credibility: publication in prestigious places of results that could be replicated, long careers with many achievements, and highly professionalized ways of describing the strengths and limits of their evidence without seeming to stretch or embellish. The mainstream researchers' credibility did not entirely speak for itself, however, and there were skirmishes over whether the experts were advocating "crossing the line from scientific testimony to public health advocacy."[68] The petitioners presented one witness with prestigious credentials and mainstream credibility, UCLA epidemiologist and statistician Sander Greenland. Dr. Greenland was not eager at first to testify for the petitioners, but when he read Dr. Steven Goodman's expert report for the government, he realized he "had to go through with it."[69] He read the Goodman report as a case of an "expert witnesses interpret[ing] their role as a lawyer, like they're just sort of a lawyer with scientific credentials and they're there to create rhetoric to support the case, to persuade a jury and a judge." He testified that "[a]n association between TCVs [thimerosal-containing vaccines] and regressive autism, especially clearly regressive autism, would have been seriously diluted in all the available epidemiologic studies, if there were such an association."[70] In other words, studies showing no association left open the possibility that the number of children affected by vaccines was so small they did not show up. Dr. Greenland did not think vaccines were causing an epidemic of autism, however.[71] Science requires a special adherence to uncertainty about statistical estimates, in Greenland's view, and it is wrong to portray the evidence as positively establishing that there is no link between a small subset of autism cases and thimerosal when the mathematics just cannot rule it out.[72] So while the petitioners were able to bring along at least one prestigious outsider to push back against what he saw as a violation of scientific disinterestedness, this fact was unable to change the outcome by positively meeting the petitioners' burden.

The Case against MMR

A British medical researcher and gastroenterologist, Dr. Andrew Wakefield, is credited with first proposing the connection between the MMR vaccine and autism in a now-famous *Lancet* paper and in a related press conference.[73] Dr. Wakefield's rise and fall has been widely discussed,[74] and my emphasis here is the OAP process and its interaction with U.K. litigation that Dr. Wakefield had been supporting against MMR manufacturers (who can be sued directly there, unlike in the United States). Plaintiffs can get public funds to start litigation in the United Kingdom, and a team had used such funds to found a lab to test autistic children's gut samples for evidence of persisting vaccine-strain measles virus. The causal account was that the virus persisted in their guts, causing inflammation that traveled to the brain and caused autism. (Recall that persisting virus in the body is usually considered top-quality evidence.) After the U.K. public funding authority for litigation reviewed sixty expert reports on the MMR-autism link, the case was defunded in 2003 on the grounds that it was not meritorious.[75] The PCR (polymerase chain reaction) lab, called Unigenetics, set up to find vaccine-strain measles virus in the guts of autistic children, closed in 2005. There was never a trial, and the records of the case remain sealed. The American OAP became the trial venue for the MMR theory instead. The OAP children introduced as evidence their gut sample analyses from the Unigenetics lab. Michelle Cedillo's samples showed a positive PCR result for vaccine-strain measles RNA.

Some of the most dramatic testimony of the whole OAP came from British researchers who had been expert witnesses for the pharmaceutical companies in the first round of lawsuits over MMR in the United Kingdom. A molecular biologist from the University of London, Dr. Stephen Bustin, most damaged the credibility of the Unigenetics lab's PCR work. Allowing him to testify about his conclusions from the sealed British litigation reports was controversial because the underlying materials were unavailable to the petitioners. The vaccine court's more permissive evidentiary rules permit any evidence that is helpful, and generally nothing is barred. From the petitioners' perspective, Dr. Bustin had been paid by pharmaceutical companies to dig (for fifteen hundred hours of work time) until he found some evidence of lab misconduct, which was then unfairly used to besmirch everything the lab touched, even though Michelle's own sample did not show all those same problems.[76] After examining the Unigenetics lab, Dr. Bustin concluded that the finding of measles RNA was likely a false positive due to contamination. In one practice he called simply "unacceptable," Dr. Bustin found that when two samples from the same source tested differently (one negative and one positive, when the result should have been the same), it would be recorded as a positive result.[77] He also found that the lab's notebooks had been tampered with to change results, perhaps fraudulently. The special masters were able to examine pages of the notebooks themselves and see the alterations.

Testimony indicted both the Unigenetics lab work and Dr. Wakefield's own lab work, which he used to develop the idea that autistic children with bowel symptoms suffered from a condition he called autistic enterocolitis, caused by the MMR vaccine. Nicholas Chadwick, who had been a Ph.D. student in Dr. Wakefield's lab when he was testing for the measles virus, testified that he had personally done PCR testing on gut samples. In each case either the samples were negative or sequencing showed that an initial positive result was a false positive.[78] (Sequencing is follow-up genetic testing done on a purportedly positive sample to confirm the result.) Dr. Chadwick also testified that he told Dr. Wakefield about the negative results and the false positives and asked to have his name removed from any publications in which any of the PCR data appeared. Petitioners' expert Dr. Krigsman testified that one of these published papers using these results sparked his initial interest in treating autistic children (though he referred to the article by a co-author's name rather than invoke Dr. Wakefield).[79] Dr. Wakefield has continued to insist that he did find measles virus in the guts of autistic children, though his recent book neither mentions nor responds to Dr. Chadwick's testimony.[80] The Chadwick testimony was devastating, and Wakefield's failure to respond to it is a classic case of what Elizabeth Anderson calls a failure of epistemic responsibility through dialogic irrationality, that is, reasserting that he had indeed found vaccine-strain measles virus in the children he tested without addressing Chadwick's quite credible story that he had not.[81]

Credibility Failures of the MMR Case

All three special masters doubted that the PCR results really showed vaccine-strain measles virus persisting in the children. The experts and special masters came close to pronouncing the lab's work downright deceptive, and certainly understood its obscurantism to be a failure of professional scientific responsibility. "[T]he *most important* points in my rejection of the Unigenetics testing," Special Master Hastings explained in *Cedillo*, "were (1) the fact that the laboratory failed to publish any sequencing data to confirm the validity of its testing, (2) the failure of other laboratories to replicate the Unigenetics testing, and (3) the demonstration by the D'Souza group that the Uhlmann primers were 'nonspecific.'"[82] A nonspecific primer would amplify other materials in addition to the target material, thus giving a false positive result. Replication attempts found that at first the samples would appear to be positive, but follow-up tests of the RNA that had been amplified revealed it to be human genetic material and "in no case did [researchers] find measles virus genomic material."[83]

The government also pointed to epidemiological evidence from researchers in the United States, Europe, and Japan showing no association between autism and the MMR vaccine. According to Special Master Hastings, "the best form of evidence consists of epidemiologic studies."[84] Writing in the *Cedillo* decision, Hastings concluded that "*all of those studies failed to find such an association.*"[85] The families argued that the epidemiological evidence against them was irrelevant because it was about the link between vaccines and autism generally, while their claim was tailored to the small subset of regressive cases. The special masters responded that some of the studies had indeed looked at regressive cases and MMR in particular and found no association and that the lack of broader associations did indeed render their subset association less likely.[86]

Special Master Hastings concluded that the petitioners had "failed to demonstrate that [Michelle Cedillo's] vaccinations played any role at all" in her medical problems.[87] The evidence was "overwhelmingly contrary" to the claims, Hastings wrote, and the expert witnesses for the government were "far better qualified, far more experienced, and far more persuasive than the petitioners' experts concerning most of the key points."[88] The expert who represented Dr. Wakefield's line of research for the families, Dr. Krigsman, received a particularly critical appraisal. Not only had he listed items under the heading "Publications" on his C.V. that turned out not to be real publications, he had also been disciplined in his role at a previous hospital for performing unwarranted tests on autistic children and was "grossly mistaken" about the timeline of Michelle Cedillo's symptoms. It was as if he had not really even read her records, Special Master Hastings concluded, or at best badly misread them.[89]

The petitioners' attorney tried to show that the government experts violated their own norms of scientific inquiry to show that vaccines are safe. One of the most emotional points in all the test cases was when psychiatrists testified about having watched the Cedillo family's home videos of their daughter Michelle, noting early signs of autism that predated the MMR vaccine and that her parents had missed. They claimed an expertise in observing Michelle objectively that her parents lacked, that is. But the family's attorney pressed Dr. Max Wiznitzer, one diagnostic expert who viewed the videos: "You know [that she became autistic] and you're looking back and you're identifying things that support the outcome, correct?"[90] Dr. Eric Fombonne, a leading figure in research about both autism rates and clinical diagnostics, parried in cross-examination about the home videos when asked what he believed: "Actually, I have no beliefs in general." Invoking classic Mertonian scientific norms, he continued, "I'm a scientist. What I look at is the evidence, which I generate myself in studies, or when I review studies of others. So I have no particular set of beliefs which drive my opinion."[91] Both experts argued that the purpose of the videotapes was only to pinpoint the time when early signs of autism appeared and that for that purpose not being blind to the eventual diagnosis was not problematic.

There was high drama around the most famous name of the whole vaccine scare—Dr. Andrew Wakefield—and around the insinuation that real corruption, real manipulation of results, had occurred. The Unigenetics lab became a locus for a credibility struggle—both a real space and a trace of connected researchers—that loyal parents stood by but the special masters found to be rotten through. Even leaving Wakefield aside (which the petitioners' lawyers were quite eager to do), the evidence upon which they relied came to be seen as scientifically suspect because it did not hold itself out for the kind of scrutiny that characterizes the most prestigious science: testing and retesting, transparency, and replication. When other groups not affiliated with the litigation tried to replicate the PCR results, they failed. Contentment with false positives was the most damning implication for scientific credibility in the first theory cases. The fact that Dr. Bustin's investigation was litigation-funded research and the fact that the diagnostic experts viewed Michelle Cedillo's tapes already knowing her diagnosis were not understood as real credibility problems. Credibility in an adversarial contest is relational: who is more credible than the other? The significant imbalance in the OAP meant that deviations from the model of scientific rationality ("I have no beliefs in general") did not weaken scientific credibility.

The Aftermath of the Autism Showdown: From Scientific Credibility to Procedural Justice

The vaccine court was supposed to be an attractive tort reform alternative for families to pursue vaccine injury cases, but paradoxically, the flexibility of its procedures and the thoroughness of the government's defense in the OAP also helped produce confirmation for many families that the vaccine program was hopelessly corrupt. How could the same legal process look so different to different people? How can powerful institutions wage credibility battles with advocates for highly publicized causes that may not be well supported by mainstream authorities without incurring backlash from overreaching? The autism challenge to vaccines was particularly tricky: here was a growing childhood diagnosis with no cure and an incomplete account of its origins, affecting mobilized families with resources. The paradox is that even when the credibility struggles are otherwise wholly lopsided, when the Goliath of government pushes back strongly against a highly publicized and emotionally salient cause (vaccine-injured children), the pushback itself may reinforce the challenger's credibility in some ways and for some audiences. The autism-vaccine theory has been on the decline in the past few years, and groups and individuals who still insist on the connection have been relatively marginalized.[92] The overall effect of the OAP outcome was to further diminish the respectability of the vaccine-autism link, but it nonetheless handed critics a new way to talk about their loss in vaccine court.

Instead of continuing to fight on the scientific merits of the theory, critics—the losing families and the vaccine critics who support them—pivoted to a procedural justice argument against the vaccine compensation program instead. Their continued belief in their own version of scientific truth continues to be bolstered by alternative researchers, journals, labs, and activist community networks. But instead of continuing the causation argument primarily (although many still do), losing petitioners and their advocates transformed their overwhelming loss on the credibility of the science into a case that the institutional power of government immunization was hopelessly stacked against them. It seems likely that court critics will not be able to separate their failed scientific arguments from their institutional criticisms because the relatively small number of advocates are very closely tied to discredited figures such as Wakefield. Yet, just as creationists argue for teaching "both sides" and climate change skeptics indict clannishness among scientists striving to close that question, these vaccine critics have nonetheless managed to shift some of the debate from the merits of their scientific evidence to broader questions of procedural justice and governmental power.

From the petitioners' and advocates' perspectives, the large scale of the process and the harsh appraisals of experts were simply the federal government doing everything in its power to defeat the threat to national immunization coverage that a link between vaccines and autism would have brought. The losing attorneys for the families protested that the special masters had unfairly raised the burden of proof in the OAP. From their perspective, they had children injured soon after receiving shots, they articulated theories to explain why, they provided a story of cause and effect, and thus they felt entitled to win at a fairly forgiving level of proof where close calls are supposed to go to the injured party. They had won lots of middle-ground cases that way before.

The test case families were not convinced by the evidence to change their minds about causation. Furious at the treatment of Dr. Krigsman, Rebecca Estepp, an activist mother with a case in the OAP, told the special masters that in her house, he was a "saint."[93] She characterized the special masters' treatment of petitioners' witnesses as "a public flogging" and complained that because of the outcome of the OAP, families could not find any experts willing to testify for them anymore. The root of her anger is the belief that vaccines really do cause autism and the OAP reached the wrong conclusion. But instead of continuing to insist on that, she reframed her complaint to the media in procedural terms: the vaccine court is a stacked deck in which "[g]overnment attorneys defend a government program, using government-funded science before government judges. Where's the justice in that?"[94]

What the petitioners really wanted was a chance to sue pharmaceutical companies with the right to discovery in front of a jury for punitive damages as well as the families' costs. What they got instead was a hearing in a forum with sufficient institutional flexibility to expand into a full-scale, in-depth proceeding populated by a small group of actors who had been working together on vaccine cases for many years. Their claims were against the trust fund, not vaccine manufacturers, and since there is a presumption against outside discovery in vaccine court, the petitioners were not able to compel pharmaceutical companies to open their files to scrutiny. Especially after the Supreme Court's ruling in *Bruesewitz v. Wyeth* that design defect claims (that a vaccine could have been made in a safer formulation, say without thimerosal) are preempted by the vaccine act and must go to the vaccine court exclusively, families and vaccine critics feel forced into a hostile forum for their claims. As Mary Holland charged in a press conference post-*Bruesewitz*, "[The vaccine court] is not remotely a court. There are no rules of evidence or procedure or discovery or juries of one's peers. It's a program that is stacked against families because let's face it, vaccine injuries make vaccines look bad."[95] Rolf Hazlehurst, the father of one of the OAP children and an attorney himself, holds the compensation court responsible for the rise in autism rates: "In vaccine court, the rule of law in the American system has been replaced by what is known as a special master. A special master is nothing more than a politically appointed government attorney. The vaccine court is nothing more than a procedural hurdle that has kept the vaccine-autism issue out of court for twenty-five years. I truly believe that if it were not for the vaccine act of 1986, the autism epidemic would not be possible."[96]

For mainstream researchers and vaccine supporters throughout the federal government, however, the OAP had been an exhaustive effort to hear every bit of evidence, to give the families every delay they requested to build the best possible case, and to open their hearings to public scrutiny in an unprecedented way. From their perspective, the OAP allowed the vaccine-autism theory a much better hearing than it ever could have gotten in any other forum because evidentiary rules would have excluded some of the less reputable experts (as Dr. Mark Geier had been excluded in cases filed outside the program) and where the financial risk to the attorneys would have been greater. Unlike in regular civil litigation where the contingency fee means a losing plaintiff's attorney may collect nothing, recall that the vaccine court pays attorneys' fees and expenses regardless of the outcome. The unanimity of the rulings and the release of each set of decisions on the same day helped consolidate their bid for closure. Each opinion describes how vast the record was, details each special master's evaluation process for all the important pieces of evidence, and describes exactly how much weight was assigned to each piece. Though much of this explanation is for appellate review, the rhetorical effect of these accounts is to present the OAP as thorough, fair, open, and precise. The special masters consider themselves independent from the rest of the vaccine program because they are appointed by the judges on the U.S. Court of Federal Claims and serve within the judicial branch, not at the whim of Congress (the source of the original statutory setup) or the health bureaucracy of HHS (where the rest of the vaccine compensation program is housed). Special masters' four year terms are nearly always renewed. The more flexible rules of the vaccine court (those that permitted Dr. Bustin's testimony from the U.K. litigation, for example) had previously garnered bipartisan praise for showcasing a workable alternative to unwieldy traditional products liability suits.

We cannot learn this lesson too many times: scientific evidence, no matter how clear it seems to be to the people who produce it and vouch for it, does not have magical power to change minds. It exists within interested communities and, in the law, enters into a charged adversarial context within which social norms and institutional values play an important role in what the evidence is ultimately said to mean. The OAP was a tremendous effort to bring closure to one of the most controversial causation questions of our day, and legitimacy of the outcome was a crucial goal of its design and execution. Features of its overwhelming exactitude and procedural accommodations did not have fixed benevolent meanings, however, and could be transformed into critiques of the power imbalance between the parties. Just because a design meant to produce legitimacy ends up being used to upend legitimacy among dissatisfied citizens does not mean government and courts should not strive for the most thorough, transparent, and validated procedures possible. But we should not be surprised when the controversies they are meant to settle nonetheless stumble on.

Conclusion

The Epistemic Politics of the Vaccine Court

In the contemporary United States we have opted to manage the techno-scientific, legal, political, and ethical challenges of vaccine injury claims in the classic American way: by creating a court with judges, lawyers, and experts, waiting for individuals to bring claims, and then letting them hash it out. We could have done this many other ways. It need not have been a court. An administrative panel, an insurance company, a panel of doctors, or some other blend of these nonlegal professionals could have been put in charge of vaccine injury claims. It need not depend on individual rights claims. A more generous system of social welfare or medical and disability insurance for all would provide for needs after vaccine injury without all the fuss over causation. A more robust administrative state would be able to seek out possible conditions and provide care rather than having individuals and families make the first move. The other industrialized nations with vaccine injury compensation programs have drawn on all of these alternatives, which presume alternate political realities that do not exist in the contemporary American state. Congress designed the vaccine court that we have as a particular policy solution at a certain moment. Like many institutions, it has proven to be both adaptive and influential in its field, shaping and being shaped by vaccine safety science, activist mobilization, and political and bureaucratic oversight. If it were not a court, the story of what it has done might look very different.

I argued at the start of the book that the vaccine court *as a court* exemplified many of the features that are worth wanting in solving contentious social and scientific problems. It has helped to democratize inquiries into vaccine safety and vaccine injury; that is, it has created mechanisms, practices, interactions, resources, and routes for different kinds of knowledge about vaccine injury to be placed into dialogue and cogently debated. It falls short in some ways, to be sure. Some problems are long-standing struggles between science and law, such as how judges can interpret scientific testimony in the courtroom when experts are hired by the parties, which historian Tal Golan reminds us have been with us since the nineteenth century.[1] Other shortcomings are specific to its particular history, such as the inability to get even simple amendments to the program with broad support through Congress. Nonetheless, both its procedures and its outcomes have been very helpful in managing vaccine controversies and vaccine injuries over the past thirty years.

We should evaluate the vaccine court not by its ability to transcribe science into law, as Jasanoff argues, but rather by its sociological and political profile as a site of contestation that can do justice. Has the vaccine court been just? Does the vaccine court reflect, create, and distribute power relations in a way we should support given a certain view of the appropriate balance between citizens, experts, and the state in these contentious scientific matters? The citizen-activists in this story are not shut out or downtrodden. I have scrutinized their contributions very closely, arguing that they assist in democratization while relying on and reinforcing their own privilege. If we want citizen participation in scientific debates, we must have institutions that can fairly amplify, guide, and evaluate their arguments along with those of the professional experts who already enjoy access to elite conversations. Scholars have been understandably sympathetic to activists seeking health-based rights and raising critical knowledge-based arguments, but we should remember that their activism may itself retrench inequalities or fail to live up to standards of reasonable claims making. We need accountability that extends in many directions: to politicians, to judges, to attorneys, to regulators, but also to movement leaders and the quality of their claims over time. The case of the vaccine court shows how a legal institution can both nurture dissent in technoscientific debates and tame it at the same time.

The vaccine court's timing and pacing of decisions is more adapted to scientific inquiry than is generally the case with courts, and its ability to delay has been crucial to supporting mainstream research conclusions. The mismatch of timing and pace in science and in court has been much criticized in cases such as the silicone gel breast implant litigation, in which court rulings against Dow Corning came before the studies showing no association between the claimed disorders and breast implants.[2] The fact that there is no common-law precedent from one case to another in vaccine court or protection for the secretary from being repeatedly subject to the same claim means that attorneys can bring similar claims over and over as the evidence evolves. Cases do not get thrown out on motions from the other side, and petitioners can wait for studies to be completed and evidence gathered. The autism hearings, for example, were delayed for about four years because the petitioners were awaiting development of research they thought would help them. The vaccine court thus takes on more of the scientific pose of repeated consideration rather then the law's impulse to deliver a final judgment that settles a question. Sometimes, still, the special masters make decisions about medical questions in middle-ground cases even before any scientific consensus has formed. Legal answers to scientific questions before the science is conclusive may seem flawed to scientists and doctors (many of whom have criticized the court over the years), but if we understand them as serving a unique social and political need for justice and order, or perhaps providing a pressure valve against anti-vaccine mobilization, the court's rulings look much more successful. Moreover, most of these more uncertain decisions are settlements rather than judicial decisions. The settlements bring an end to controversies through negotiation rather than through the accumulation of sufficient evidence to convince everyone about what really happened.

There has been a vigorous social movement claiming vaccine injuries that has also had its own research wing. Those activist researchers have been regular witnesses in the vaccine court, and some such as the Geiers have also worked extensively with government sources such as the Vaccine Adverse Event Reporting System (VAERS) to try to make their case about widespread vaccine injuries. These same experts were blocked by *Daubert* or *Frye* motions from testifying in civil court, but they were able to act as go-betweens in social movement activism and at the vaccine court for many years. The special masters hear every witness, by contrast, and then reimburse their fees. The vaccine court elevates expertise by not having juries of laypeople decide vaccine cases, however. The special masters are not scientifically trained, but their status as repeat players in a topically specialized court helps them to learn a lot on the job about vaccines and claimed conditions. The small, contained culture of the court also allows for familiarity with experts over time. As I argue in this conclusion, these features promote the kind of knowledge production and multifaceted accountability that we ought to want.

Upholding the Immunization Social Order

Admittedly, the vaccine court is an obscure specialized court. Most people are unaware that it exists, and only attorneys, health profession-als, researchers, activists, and government officials know much about the substance of its rulings, which do not carry any precedential weight in other courts. As law professor Joëlle Anne Moreno notes, because the autism decisions were made in a specialized court that does not use the Federal Rules of Evidence, federal judges and legal scholars may not regard the special masters' extensive reasoning about the expert testi-mony as part of the vast post-*Daubert* literature on how courts handle scientific problems.[3] The vaccine court sits within a massive research and governmental enterprise of immunization law and policy that gets a lot more attention. Yet I have claimed here that it has helped to stabilize and maintain our immunization social order. How?

First, it has fulfilled its original *gatekeeping* mission of keeping law-suits out of the tort system, thereby shielding vaccine manufacturers and our vaccine supply from the unpredictability and volatility of large jury verdicts. Its existence and rulings have been vital to affirming vac-cine safety even without public attention. The courts' rulings have been relatively obscure in part because they have not ventured far from the mainstream scientific consensus. Consider a counterfactual, however. If the vaccine court had not existed in the early 2000s and the well-organized plaintiffs' efforts to get a case about thimerosal and autism before a jury in a regular civil suit had succeeded prior to 2003, a jury likely would have returned an alarming and erroneous verdict that vac-cines were responsible for at least some cases of autism. A clear endorse-ment at the end of the Omnibus Autism Proceeding of a vaccine injury theory for autism would have been spectacular news around the world. If the court were to issue rulings based on evidence from outside the mainstream and for widely known conditions, social movement activ-ists would be able to use them to advance their agendas in many ways, including getting congressional attention for vaccine policy changes and advancing the cause of exemption expansions in the states. Recall that even without the tide of evidence turning their way, advocates were able to get multiple congressional hearings and a few new state exemptions. The eight special masters serve four-year terms, and even a determined political intervention to oust troublemakers would take several years to accomplish. Widespread fear of real or perceived vaccine injuries would severely undercut the immunization social order through legal changes, noncompliance, or likely both. The vaccine court has helped quell these fears. We avoided these damaging outcomes.

Second, the court is both an *audience and an engine for evidence.* Anticipation of its review helps promote the creation of evidence in the form of published studies, and it is also an engine of evidence production through its payment rules and the special masters' requests for evidence. Many vaccine safety studies would be done anyway because of requirements in the vaccine approval and postmarketing surveillance process, but the vaccine court creates an audience for these and additional studies that must be satisfied. Because researchers and health bureaucrats know that without good evidence of safety, the special masters will compensate petitioners and the social movement activists will amplify fears, they are under pressure to produce evidence from the top of the hierarchy. Let us not forget that the vaccine act requires the production of vaccine safety reviews, too. The Institute of Medicine (IOM) review panel reports are driven directly by the need to produce guidance for revising the Table, and these reviews show researchers that vaccine research is something that gets noticed. Advocates funded some of their own studies, but in relatively small amounts, and having a stable of experts who are sure to be paid assists them in making their cases.

Third, the vaccine injury compensation system with the court at the center *expresses our ethical obligations* to injured vaccinees. As Michelle Mello convincingly argues, we should compensate people injured by vaccines because legal requirements limit people's choices and because any reasonable person receiving a vaccine would choose the cheap form of insurance against harm that the seventy-five-cents-per-dose excise tax offers.[4] As she notes, we as a society have these ethical obligations even if the availability of compensation does not really influence individual vaccine choices (because people do not know about it).[5] But for those who do use it, the court provides a forum for individuals and families to have their injuries discussed and examined on an individual level. The other venues for exploring vaccine injury questions are nonindividual-ized and population-focused, by contrast. Even sites like the Clinical Immunization Safety Assessment network address people as potential donors to a biobank, not as families with a story to tell. The compensa-tion decisions in favor of the petitioners provide for the injured and acknowledge that in the nation's public health quest for population im-munity, some individuals will be harmed through no fault of their own. If a mainstream consensus develops that there is a specific vulnerable subpopulation of people who are predisposed to react more strongly to vaccines, but we are not able to identify them and screen them out, then the moral case for the vaccine court becomes even stronger.

Legitimation of the immunization social order requires squarely ad-mitting its costs, then, and I argued that a comparative look at the vac-cine court within other compensation schemes shows that we consider vaccination to be a critical civic duty and a form of national service. These compensations have a moral cast as well as pragmatically remove the burden of costly care from the private realm of familial (often moth-erly) labor and from public sources such as Medicaid and Social Secu-rity. Compensations are paid from a trust fund filled by an excise tax on every dose of covered vaccine given, not from general tax revenue, and this direct linkage makes it clear that vaccine injuries come directly from vaccine administrations. (Arguably, however, the benefit of vacci-nation accrues to everyone, not just those who get vaccinated, and so it would be fairer to pay compensations from a general fund. The people who get the greatest benefit, after all, are those who avoid vaccination themselves but enjoy the absence of disease secured by others' vaccine uptake.) Mothers and fathers often want to tell their story to someone who is officially responsible for hearing it. The vaccine court provides this official attention. Being able to testify in their child's vaccine court hearing and to explain why they believe vaccines were responsible can be uniquely powerful even if compensation is not awarded.

The vaccine court should be a legitimating court process, then, but only if citizens share a normative commitment to the basic account of justice it upholds and internalize a sense of obligation to obey the law.[6] Has the vaccine court operated as a safety valve for vaccine fears, drawing off people who would have otherwise mobilized and engaging them in the court process instead? It is impossible to know for sure. We should carefully distinguish the actual petitioners from the movement activists because they often do not overlap. The people who bring claims are those who went themselves or brought their children to be vaccinated. They are very different from the organized activists, many of whom resist vaccines for deeply held ideological or philosophical reasons and not because of a personal bad experience. In fact, compensated parents can react with anger at activists' suggestions that the vaccine court is wholly illegitimate and should be disbanded. As one mother put it, "For me, the vaccine injury compensation program has, in a way, given life back to my daughter. I have been able to get her therapy that I never would have been able to afford on my own." She continued, responding to an activist claiming that past autism compensations show the court trying to hide the truth: "That is why I am angry [at his arguments], because I feel like the program did something good in compensating these people."[7] It is likely that there are at least some would-be activists who are instead caring for themselves or their children with compensation funds rather than organizing against vaccines.

But of course the fact that people who received money were satisfied is not surprising; Tyler's research asks why people who do not get a benefit still comply. The third accomplishment—a place for individuals to be heard that is ethically required—leads to only a partial fulfillment of a fourth: *diffusing dissent*. Because of privacy protections, it is not possible to trace how many *un*compensated people became anti-vaccine court activists, although some certainly have mobilized. A 2009 survey of petitioner satisfaction by administrators at the vaccine program—including people who had both won and lost—had a very low response rate (107 out of 716 petitioners contacted) and included a lot of complaints about the amount of payments they received and the time their claims took, among other things.[8] But on some questions, at least half of the petitioners were at least somewhat satisfied, and the vast majority of people simply did not respond, which suggests they did not have much to say. Vaccine court petitioners are also people managing injury or disability and are thus less likely to have the time and energy for activism that healthy people have. It is likely that if the 1986 vaccine act had not passed, some of the several thousand people who have gone on to be compensated would have remained unsatisfied and joined the vaccine-critical movement, which would have then included a wider range of people with more scientifically legitimated claims. As it happened, the quick success of the 1986 act left activists adrift. When the thimerosal, MMR, and autism controversies arose in the late 1990s, there were so many routes for activism to develop, particularly through popular culture, informal networks, and parental experiences with diagnosis, that the vaccine court had little chance of diverting and absorbing it.

Despite its general obscurity, the vaccine court has been a focus of the social movements and their legal mobilization since its inception. Movement leaders have never tried a bolder, broader litigation strategy to overturn *Jacobson v. Massachusetts*, the 1905 Supreme Court case that affirmed the state's police power to require vaccination to preserve the public health.[9] The vaccine court attracts dissent as well as diffuses it, then, but with several important features. It attracts claims and the attention of vaccine critics and worried parents, but channels them into engaging a relatively obscure, private, slow adversarial process within a small community of attorneys, experts, and special masters. Most importantly, it requires some basis in evidence for claims and a responsiveness to counterevidence. Sociolegal scholars have documented many ways in which making a harm into a legal claim narrows it and transforms it, and indeed the pressure to produce evidence forces vaccine injury claims onto entirely different ground than activists prefer. In the case of vaccine injury claims, the transformation occurs as petitioners' attorneys try to enlist experts and assemble medical records to move a claim into the middle ground of the autoimmunity or nerve damages cases, or perhaps an aggravation claim. Social movement activists trying to use the vaccine court as a basis for dissent—by pointing to "gotcha" moments of past compensations and trying to present them as duplicity, for example—run up against the overwhelming scientific and medical consensus that vaccines do not cause autism, making it hard for their procedural justice critiques to stick.

The autism showdown at the vaccine court, as I argued, helps us to see how important that particular debate has been to shaping the relationship between the organized vaccine-critical groups and the vaccine compensation program. It also shows us a fifth way the vaccine court has upheld the immunization social order: by *holding critics account-*

able for their claims. There is no other institutional way to ask critics to back up their claims. All those organizations still endorse a vaccine-autism link. All their policy suggestions stand against that now quite unflattering background. (There is a clear epistemic shortcut for anyone sorting the debate: does this advocate still believe vaccines cause autism or organize with those who do without clarification?) The situation has developed so that now vaccine critics have lost all their credibility in the institutions in which they have to present reasons and evidence but maintain an audience among the like-minded and in forums they choose for themselves online or in public advertising.

Interactions between the court and the social movement have stabilized the immunization social order a bit too much in some ways, however, because these tensions have kept widely supported reforms at bay. Concerns about liability exposure based on autism claims diverted otherwise widely supported political changes to the vaccine court that probably would have passed years ago, such as extending the three-year statute of limitations to six years. Congress most certainly should pass legislation to reform the vaccine compensation program in ways that have been widely endorsed for years among insiders: extending the statute of limitations, paying for family expenses such as counseling or setting up a guardianship, adding an adult injured by a vaccine to the advisory committee overseeing the program, raising the caps on death benefits and pain and suffering payments (and indexing them so they maintain apace), making information about cases more transparent and easily accessible to the public, and funding more advertising of the court's existence. It is hard to get anything through the current Congress, let alone a relatively small set of reforms to a specialized court. Program administrators and the HHS secretary share some of the blame for failing to push harder, but activists can hardly expect cooperation when they are accusing those same leaders of covering up the mass poisoning of children. There is unfortunately no real movement of vaccine supporters pushing such legislation again, and its other supporters lost credibility over the autism issue. When one continues to make arguments that have been discredited, it is not a problem that one's reputation in politics diminishes. It is really regrettable, however, that these reforms, which would help families and their attorneys, have always been framed within the battle lines over autism and have lost out as a result.

Extending the Vaccine Court Model?

Given the useful deployment of this specialized court design in resolving questions of vaccine injury, it is natural to ask to what other kinds of scientific and political problems this kind of court structure could extend. Should we copy the vaccine court structure for other medical and scientific questions in the law that we now handle through the tort system? Specialized courts have been a popular answer to the perceived need to obtain better, smarter, and more efficient judgments from courts, as Lawrence Baum and Nora Freeman Engstrom have described in detail.[10] Specialized health courts for medical malpractice claims are especially popular now: legislation has been introduced in the states and both houses of Congress, President Obama's 2012 budget included funding for state medical justice reforms such as health courts, and prestigious institutions such as the IOM, the U.S. deficit commission, the American Medical Association, and policy think tanks from the right and left have come out in support of this "reform du jour."[11]

Health courts would be a solution for medical malpractice claims; the other problem area is mass toxic tort lawsuits, which often turn on the presence or absence of a scientific consensus about injury causation. Edward Cheng describes other tort reform solutions that have been proposed to fix the problem of courts misunderstanding scientific evidence or having to make decisions without sufficiently developed science, such as moving such cases to administrative agencies and out of the courts entirely.[12] Government agencies could require corporate defendants to have insurance against insolvency, administrators could fund their own studies, and they could draw on their own sources of expertise. But Cheng points out they may be captured agencies that fail to initiate enforcement, and if the individual right to sue were removed there would be no way to commence an action.[13] These administrative alternatives are also unlikely to succeed as radical reform.

Cheng points out other more moderate reforms that may be more possible to achieve, such as dismissing cases if the evidence seems too immature, allowing stays for scientific maturity that keep the lawsuit alive but delay it until further studies are complete, or allowing postjudgment relief if the science underlying the original judgment shifts enough.[14] As I have argued, the special masters and petitioners use delays at the vaccine court in exactly this way, holding onto cases that would not be compensable at the moment until an expert can be located or an anticipated study is published. These delays allow petitioners to meet the tight statute of limitations and then track down the evidence. But delays impose painful waiting costs on both vaccine court petitioners and plaintiffs in toxic tort suits. The original vaccine act was supposed to be "quick and certain" and resolve cases within one year to prevent "injustice upon the petitioner."[15] When petitioners cannot muster evidence of causation in the end, however, the delay does not displace anything that would have been better for them.

I would not support extending the vaccine court solution to other types of tort litigation for several reasons. The vaccine court serves a very unique function in maintaining our immunization social order. Recall the CDC's estimates that our vaccine program will prevent 322 million illnesses, 21 million hospitalizations, and 732,000 deaths during the lifetimes of the children born in the United States between 1994 and 2013.[16] Vaccines are a unique product because they are the material keystones to this immunization social order. Vaccines come with legal requirements that impose burdens if one does not use them, they touch nearly everyone, levels of uptake across and within communities can have very broad societal effects, and they are a technoscientific, government intervention on healthy people. Other pharmaceutical and medical products do not share these features or serve the same function. We also have a robust and well-functioning vaccine safety surveillance system that protects against harm. Jury verdicts against doctors or corporations, even big ones or poorly grounded ones, are not the same kind of problem for the social order. Concerns for the costs of medical malpractice and defensive medicine are a commonsense reason for wanting an alternative system that protects against liability, but these fears are not well supported by the evidence. One study found that the cost of defending medical malpractice claims in the United States is only 0.46 percent of our total health expenditures, for example, while our high costs can be traced to the fact that we charge and pay much higher prices for pharmaceuticals, hospital stays, and physician visits than is the case in other comparable countries.[17] Plaintiffs get nothing in two-thirds of U.S. claims and payments to winners are lower on average than in Canada and the United Kingdom.[18] How much defensive medicine adds to health care costs is difficult to measure, and HHS and the Congressional Budget Office (CBO) have reached different conclusions (from 5 to 9 percent of spending in an HHS estimate to a CBO failure to replicate those results, with their projection that savings from tort reform would be "small").[19]

Moreover, removing access to judges and juries in our regular state and federal courts and channeling disputes to a special tribunal is a very serious restriction on one form of justice and should be used rarely. In another example, we see that federal preemption of state tort lawsuits against managed care organizations' coverage decisions under the Employee Retirement Income Security Act (ERISA) can leave patients with limited options for relief after a coverage denial.[20] Interpretation of ERISA currently takes away the same kinds of rights that vaccine critics wanted in *Bruesewitz* (access to possibly more sympathetic state courts), leans far in favor of protecting employee benefit plans over patients, and impedes state health reform experiments.[21] As I described in Chapter 4, we have created special tribunals only occasionally in the United States and for certain kinds of social problems: disaster schemes, like the 9/11 Commission, schemes for ongoing protection of certain vital but dangerous industries, such as nuclear power production, and broad no-fault schemes for activities of daily life so commonplace and essential to our economy that we cannot afford to burden them with the vagaries of the tort system as an injury solution, namely working and driving. Any additional alternative solution must offer something significant to claimants to make up for removing a legal path and not simply stack the deck. Even though critics of the vaccine court argue that it should not be as difficult to win a compensation claim there, it is extremely unlikely that vaccine injury claims would fare better in the tort system with its tighter rules and higher bars to expert testimony. So while I am satisfied that the vaccine court is better for both petitioners and the general public than not having an alternative at all, I doubt the same conditions would justify other medical or health courts.

The Epistemic Politics of the Vaccine Safety System

The court is part of a larger governing structure for vaccines that includes congressional oversight and funding, administrative agency regulation, and state laws requiring vaccines for school children. These institutions overwhelmingly endorse pro-vaccine policies, but activists accuse them of violating human rights and being captured by powerful pharmaceutical interests. How then shall we evaluate the broader epistemic politics of vaccine injuries? Epistemic politics means the power relationships and institutions that help us know things as citizens. How well does the vaccine court help us know vaccine injury? Elizabeth Anderson proposes the following questions for evaluating whether our governing institutions make good decisions to solve problems, or what she terms the "epistemic powers of particular democratic institutions": "Are there diverse, open, accessible channels for people from all walks of life, in all social positions, to publicly express dissent? Do social norms welcome the expression of dissent by all discontented parties? Do they require decision makers to take dissent seriously, and hold them accountable if they don't?"[22] Anderson also argues that ordinary people—meaning nonscientists, in our case nearly everyone involved in vaccine cases except for some of the witnesses—are capable of second-order judgments of scientific expertise by evaluating whether someone making a claim is in a position to do so ("whether they have access to the evidence and the skills to evaluate it"), whether the person is being honest, and whether the person is "responsive to evidence, reasoning, and arguments others raise against their beliefs."[23] "The mark of epistemic responsibility," Anderson argues, "is responsive accountability to the community of inquirers."[24] We rightfully mistrust those who keep arguing the same thing in the face of counterevidence or simply insist that we should trust them with no accountability.

Anderson analyzes the climate change debate based on online resources an ordinary person would find accessible, arguing that the evidence for a correct second-order evaluation of that debate is readily available to laypeople. For example, the so-called hockey stick controversy over a particular modeling showing rapid recent temperature increases in the past one thousand years shows how denialists challenged the article. A National Academy of Sciences investigation into the controversy found some errors but confirmed the basic results. Yet denialists still talk about the original paper as a fraud "as if nothing has happened since." "The claims live on forever," Anderson explains, "as if no one had answered them."[25] Similarly, vaccine critics repeat their claims about autism and vaccines as if Nicholas Chadwick had never testified that he confirmed Andrew Wakefield's lab tests were wrong, as if the Emory University re-review of the thimerosal data had never happened, as if a Senate committee had not spent eighteen months investigating and interviewing eighty people over that same data, and as if the petitioners' own epidemiologist had not rejected the analysis behind the Geiers' publications in the autism cases. It is simply not epistemically responsible to continue to cite VAERS reports as causal confirmation of vaccine injury. Petitioners' doctors repeatedly ordered dubious lab tests for children and described them as disordered as a result even though results were in the reference range. Petitioners continued to present one study (the Holmes baby haircut study) years after the special masters had pointed out that five studies had attempted to replicate it and had failed, without acknowledging this follow-up. The special masters, by contrast, must write opinions for each decision that confront and weigh the evidence presented to them and justify their reasoning. Legalization of vaccine injury requires this repeated confrontation and explication of reasons and thus builds in epistemic responsibility. The case of the quickly withdrawn RotaShield vaccine in 1999 showed that our current system is capable of self-correction when vaccines turn out to have newly detected risks. We should continue to strengthen requirements for epistemic responsibility throughout our vaccine safety and injury compensation system, but it would be silly to pretend that the epistemic responsibility displayed by both sides is anything but wildly lopsided.

Debates over vaccine injuries are a fairly strong case in support of the epistemic powers of our democratic institutions, I conclude, with the outlying problem that members of racial and ethnic minority groups, poor people, and others from the margins of society such as the undocumented do not seem to use available channels to either express dissent or make vaccine injury claims (or we do not know enough about their attempts to do so to know how they fare). There is a second order problem that we do not know how much of a problem this lack of representation is. Injuries may be very rare, but there may be forms of dissent that cannot be recognized within the current social movement organizations or within political structures, and given the importance of vaccination, that is a problem in itself. It is worth recounting the contributions vaccine critics have made before dwelling on these limitations, however.

Vaccine injury claims have been the basis of a vigorous social movement that achieved national legislation within just a few years of its initial mobilization, a remarkable achievement for any group. The National Childhood Vaccine Injury Act of 1986 then created even more channels for political and legal dissent: the parent-activist positions on the National Vaccine Advisory Committee and on the Advisory Commission on Childhood Vaccines (ACCV); the provision that any citizen may petition the secretary to have an injury added to the Table with a mandate that the ACCV discuss it and issue a recommendation; the guaranteed payment of fees for attorneys and experts for people bringing injury claims; the requirement that parents receive information about possible adverse effects and about the Vaccine Injury Compensation Program with each vaccine administration; a right of action against the secretary of HHS for failing to perform any act or duty of the vaccine act; a mandate to conduct specific vaccine safety reviews; and the creation of VAERS. We should be grateful to vaccine critics for these remarkable achievements that have strengthened the relationships between law, science, and democratic governance.

Some of the better-organized vaccine critics have generated considerable publicity in the past fifteen years as well as used official avenues to express their views. The IOM review panels of vaccine safety issues have held public hearings and taken comments, and critics have regularly participated in these as well as open meetings and rule-making comment periods (such as the open comment periods at each Table change). Some, like the National Vaccine Information Center, the group formed in the 1980s that helped pass the vaccine act, are sufficiently well funded by holistic health entrepreneurs that the organization in 2011 bought advertising space on the CBS Jumbotron in Times Square to share its vaccine choice message.[26] Celebrities Jenny McCarthy and Jim Carrey famously led a "Green Our Vaccines" rally in Washington, D.C., in 2008 that received nationwide mainstream news coverage. And as I argued with my co-authors in a recent study of vaccine politics at the state level, vaccine critics have introduced dozens and dozens of bills to advance their legislative agendas in the past fifteen years, filled legislative hearing rooms, hired lobbyists, and achieved some limited successes.[27] Lack of resources or blocked channels of dissent cannot explain the fact that critics have failed to win over many legislators, scientists, health bureaucrats, or even parents.

The organized vaccine critics are drawn from the relatively privileged classes, however. They lack any discernible representation of poor people, undocumented immigrants, non–English speakers, and racial or ethnic minority groups. They have a history of articulating claims in terms that appropriate minority identity-based oppression but reframe it in individualistic, libertarian, private family-focused, and responsibilizing terms. I argued that this version of health libertarianism whitens vaccine criticism while also making it relatively useless for anyone interested in structural solutions from the left of the political spectrum, such as truly universal, single-payer government health care with robust medical monitoring and automated detection of possible vaccine injuries, for example. Despite my generally positive evaluation of the vaccine court, it is regrettably the kind of solution typical of a society steeped in individual rights and adversarial legalism and opposed to simply attending to the health needs of all its citizens who are ill or disabled for any reason.

So while it is clear and perhaps not surprising that the social movement does not represent all views, unfortunately government channels for either dissent or injury recognition are also not as open to minority groups and socially marginal people as they should be. The reporting features created under the vaccine act as well as the vaccine court's records do not tell us whether there are racial disparities in vaccine injury claiming. The active surveillance databases that experts use to monitor the population for vaccine injuries do not include people without insurance coverage and so their vaccine injuries are not tracked. Even as the reach of vaccine coverage looks more racially equal than is often the case in the distribution of health resources, there are still some gaps based on race. Do pediatricians listen more to worried white middle- and upper-class mothers describing vaccine anxieties than to parents of color describing what may be vaccine adverse reactions? Are parents or individuals with fewer resources and lower status less likely to describe adverse reactions in the first place, perhaps out of greater deference to doctors or for fear of discriminatory treatment? These forms of inequality may provoke us less because vaccine injuries are reassuringly rare generally and other health inequalities are more urgent. Yet once again we see a health debate taking place over several decades in which less powerful minority groups are functionally unrepresented. Legal arguments once crafted to serve their interests have been co-opted by the organized groups dominating the dissenting conversations.

As is fitting in a democracy, we have gotten the immunization social order we deserve. We have social movements and a vaccine court that reflect the deep organizing values of American society, including our racial hierarchies, mothering and health ideologies, and meager social safety systems as well as our embrace of attorneys and judges as social problem solvers. Fortunately, the vaccine court has shown us that a court is capable of of legalizing the question of vaccine injuries in an epistemically responsible way. The vaccine court has adapted the law to science in practices such as delays for the development of evidence. Vaccine safety science has adapted to the court, too, and been judicially molded into legal conclusions in what I called the middle-ground cases. The vaccine court could be more visible and more easily reformed through democratic legislative channels. I hope that this book can help raise its public profile and help achieve some of those long-endorsed reforms.

NOTES

INTRODUCTION

1 Mariam Siddiqui, Daniel A. Salmon, and Saad B. Omer, "Epidemiology of Vaccine Hesitancy in the United States," *Human Vaccines and Immunotherapies* 9 (2013): 2643–48.

2 I focus on the United States here, but as Melissa Leach and James Fairhead have noted, "vaccination is . . . at one and the same time micro-technological and macro-political experience" that varies around the world depending on "particular notions of the body and the body politic that reinforce each other." Leach and Fairhead, *Vaccine Anxieties: Global Science, Child Health and Society* (London: Earthscan Press, 2007), 166.

3 Michelle Mello, "Rationalizing Vaccine Injury Compensation," *Bioethics* 22 (2008): 32–42; Tom R. Tyler, *Why People Obey the Law* (New Haven, CT: Yale University Press, 1990).

4 Cynthia G. Whitney et al., "Benefits from Immunization during the Vaccines for Children Program Era—United States, 1994–2013," *Morbidity and Mortality Weekly Report* 63, no. 16 (2014): 352–55.

5 Ibid.

6 Monica J. Casper and Laura M. Carpenter, "Sex, Drugs, and Politics: The HPV Vaccine for Cervical Cancer," *Sociology of Health and Illness* 30 (2008): 887.

7 Ibid., 887.

8 Booster shots and the annual flu vaccine are recommended through the teen years, as is vaccination against human papillomavirus (HPV) and meningococcal disease at around age twelve, so vaccinating a child is a persistent parental responsibility that is highly salient over many years.

9 Siddiqui et al., "Epidemiology of Vaccine Hesitancy," 2643–44.

10 Saad B. Omer et al., "Vaccination Policies and Rates of Exemption from Immunization, 2005–2011," *New England Journal of Medicine* 367 (2012): 1170–71. The highly publicized measles outbreak originating at Disneyland in the winter of 2014–2015 brought a lot of media attention to the issue of vaccine exemptions and galvanized the California state legislature to remove religious and personal belief exemptions.

11 Saad B. Omer et al., "Nonmedical Exemptions to School Immunization Requirements: Secular Trends and Association of State Policies with Pertussis Incidence," *Journal of the American Medical Association* 296 (2006): 1757–63.

12 James Keith Colgrove, *State of Immunity: The Politics of Vaccination in Twentieth-Century America* (Berkeley: University of California Press, 2006); Nadja Durbach, *Bodily Matters: The Anti-Vaccination Movement in England, 1853–1907* (Durham, NC: Duke University Press, 2005).

13 I explain the workings of the vaccine court in much more detail throughout the book. The web pages for the administration of the program and the court's website are helpful sources. The vaccines currently covered by the Vaccine Injury Compensation Program (VICP) are diphtheria, tetanus, pertussis (DTaP, DTP, DTP-Hib, DT, Td, and TT), measles, mumps, and rubella (MMR, MR, M, R), polio (IPV and OPV), Haemophilus influenzae type b (Hib), hepatitis B (HBV), varicella/chickenpox (VZV), rotavirus (RV), pneumococcal conjugate, hepatitis A, influenza, meningococcal, and HPV. A vaccine must be FDA approved, ACIP recommended, and recommended for universal use in children and have an excise tax attached to it to qualify for the VICP.

14 Peter H. Meyers, "Fixing the Flaws in the Federal Vaccine Injury Compensation Program," *Administrative Law Review* 63 (2011): 785–851; Mary Holland and Robert Krakow, "The Right to Legal Redress," in *Vaccine Epidemic: How Corporate Greed, Biased Science, and Coercive Government Threaten Our Human Rights, Our Health, and Our Children*, ed. Louise Kuo Habakus and Mary Holland (New York: Skyhorse, 2011), 39–44; Wayne Rohde, *The Vaccine Court: The Dark Truth of America's Vaccine Injury Compensation Program* (New York: Skyhorse, 2014).

15 Tyler, *Why People Obey the Law.*

16 Center for Personal Rights, "Vaccine Justice Press Conference," last modified March 3, 2011, www.ustream.tv, accessed July 27, 2011.

17 Sheila Jasanoff, "Law's Knowledge: Science for Justice in Legal Settings," *American Journal of Public Health* 95 (2005): S50–51.

18 Annelise Riles, *Collateral Knowledge: Legal Reasoning in the Global Financial Markets* (Chicago: University of Chicago Press, 2011), 25.

19 Sarah S. Lochlann Jain, *Injury: The Politics of Product Design and Safety Law in the United States* (Princeton, NJ: Princeton University Press, 2006).

20 Rachel E. Dubrofsky and Shoshana Amielle Magnet, eds., *Feminist Surveillance Studies* (Durham, NC: Duke University Press, 2015).

21 Ibid., 2.

22 Wendy Brown, *States of Injury: Power and Freedom in Late Modernity* (Princeton, NJ: Princeton University Press, 1995).

23 Claire Laurier Decoteau and Kelly Underman, "Adjudicating Non-knowledge in the Omnibus Autism Proceedings," *Social Studies of Science* 45 (2015): 471–500.

24 Martyn Day and John Kelleher, "Lessons from MMR and the Future of Group Litigation Funding," *Journal of Personal Injury Law* 1 (2005): 98–105.

25 Andrew J. Wakefield et al., "Ileal-Lymphoid-Nodular Hyperplasia, Non-specific Colitis, and Pervasive Developmental Disorder in Children," *The Lancet* 351 (1998): 637–41.

26 Day and Kelleher, "Lessons from MMR," 100.

27 Simon H. Murch et al., "Retraction of an Interpretation," *The Lancet* 363, no. 9411 (2004): 750.

28 Editors of *The Lancet*, "Retraction—Ileal-Lymphoid-Nodular Hyperplasia, Non-specific Colitis, and Pervasive Developmental Disorder in Children," *The Lancet* 375, no. 9713 (2010): 445.

29 Fiona Godlee, Jane Smith, and Harvey Marcovitch, "Wakefield's Article Linking MMR Vaccine and Autism Was Fraudulent," *British Medical Journal* 342 (2011): c7452.

30 Wakefield has continued to insist that his research is valid and that the GMC charges were unjust; Andrew J. Wakefield, *Callous Disregard: Autism and Vaccines—The Truth Behind a Tragedy* (New York: Skyhorse, 2010).

31 Jeffrey P. Baker, "Mercury, Vaccines, and Autism: One Controversy, Three Histories," *American Journal of Public Health* 98, no. 2 (2008): 244–53. The MMR vaccine has never contained thimerosal, so these two hypotheses were initially in competition with each other (a detail easy to forget now). David Kirby, *Evidence of Harm: Mercury in Vaccines and the Autism Epidemic* (New York: St. Martin's Griffin, 2005), 92.

32 Baker, "Mercury, Vaccines, and Autism." Thimerosal remains in some multidose vials of flu vaccine (25 µg and 12.5 µg for a version administered to children under three), and federal regulations require a preservative in multidose vials. U.S. Food and Drug Administration, "Thimerosal in Vaccines," www.fda.gov.

33 American Academy of Pediatrics (AAP) and the United States Public Health Service (USPHS), "Joint Statement of the American Academy of Pediatrics (AAP) and the United States Public Health Service (USPHS)," *Pediatrics* 104, no. 3.1 (1999): 568–69.

34 Arthur Allen, *Vaccine: The Controversial Story of Medicine's Greatest Lifesaver* (New York: Norton, 2007), 380–83; Paul Offit, *Autism's False Prophets: Bad Science, Risky Medicine, and the Search for a Cure* (New York: Columbia University Press, 2008).

35 Sallie Bernard et al., "Autism: A Novel Form of Mercury Poisoning," *Medical Hypotheses* 56, no. 4 (2001): 462–71.

36 Elsevier, "*Medical Hypotheses*—Guide for Authors," www.elsevier.com.

37 Transcript from the combined Omnibus Autism Proceeding hearings for *King v. Secretary of HHS*, No. 03–584V (2008), 17; *Mead v. Secretary of HHS*, No. 03–215V (2008), 24–25, 3009.

38 SafeMinds, "Accomplishments," www.safeminds.org.

39 Institute of Medicine, *Thimerosal-Containing Vaccines and Neurodevelopmental Disorders* (Washington, DC: National Academies Press, 2001).

40 Karin B. Nelson and Margaret L. Bauman, "Thimerosal and Autism?," *Pediatrics* 111, no. 3 (2003): 674–79.

41 Institute of Medicine, *Immunization Safety Review: Vaccines and Autism* (Washington, DC: National Academies Press, 2004).

42 World Health Organization, "Thiomersal," last modified June 26, 2013, www.who.int, accessed April 8, 2016.

43 Denise Lillvis, Anna Kirkland, and Anna Frick, "Power and Persuasion in the Vaccine Debates: An Analysis of Political Efforts and Outcomes in the States, 1998–2012," *Milbank Quarterly* 92, no. 3 (2014): 475–508.

44 Rebecca Estepp, "Second Round of Autism Omnibus Cases Decided," *Age of Autism*, last modified March 12, 2010, www.ageofautism.com, accessed February 3, 2014.

45 Francesca Polletta, *Freedom Is an Endless Meeting* (Chicago: University of Chicago Press, 2004).

46 Betsy J. Grey, "The Plague of Causation in the National Childhood Vaccine Injury Act," *Harvard Journal on Legislation* 48 (2011): 343–414.

47 The office of special masters posted copies of every publicly available document filed in those cases from 2002 to the present as well as the dozens of expert reports, the six rulings, the appeals court rulings upholding the decisions that were appealed, and related court cases on vaccine injury.

48 Barbara Loe Fisher of the National Vaccine Information Center (NVIC) declined to be interviewed for this project, as did the next two leaders I approached. I chose not to continue seeking interviews where there was already a published record of the person's views on the vaccine court. Many of the important actors have been making their arguments publicly for many years. The audio recordings of the 2009 NVIC conference provided me with over thirty hours of primary source material of public arguments, some of which I had professionally transcribed and rely on here. I also attended much of the event in person.

49 Jennifer Reich, *Calling the Shots: Why Parents Reject Vaccines* (New York: New York University Press, 2016); Chloe Silverman, *Understanding Autism: Parents, Doctors, and the History of a Disorder* (Princeton, NJ: Princeton University Press, 2012).

50 Janet Shim, *Heart-Sick: The Politics of Risk, Inequality, and Heart Disease* (New York: New York University Press, 2014); Ruha Benjamin, *People's Science: Bodies and Rights on the Stem Cell Frontier* (Palo Alto, CA: Stanford University Press, 2013).

51 Laura Beth Nielsen, *License to Harass: Law, Hierarchy, and Offensive Public Speech* (Princeton, NJ: Princeton University Press, 2006); David M. Engel and Frank W. Munger, *Rights of Inclusion: Law and Identity in the Life Stories of Americans with Disabilities* (Chicago: University of Chicago Press, 2003).

52 Anna Kirkland, "Revisiting Rights across Contexts: Fat, Health, and Antidiscrimination Law," *Studies in Law, Politics and Society* 48 (Fall 2009): 121–45 and "Think of the Hippopotamus: Rights Consciousness in the Fat Acceptance Movement," *Law & Society Review* 42, no. 2 (June 2008): 397–431.

53 This approach is similar to Gordon Silverstein's wide-ranging evaluation of the place of the Supreme Court in American politics in *Law's Allure: How Law Shapes, Constrains, Saves, and Kills Politics* (New York: Cambridge University Press, 2009).

54 Kirby, *Evidence of Harm*; David Kirby, "Capitol Hill Briefing on Autism," September 24, 2008, www.ageofautism.com.

55 Paul A. Offit, *Deadly Choices: How the Anti-vaccine Movement Threatens Us All* (New York: Basic Books, 2010).

56 Saad B. Omer, Daniel A. Salmon, Walter A. Orenstein, Patricia DeHart, and Neal Halsey, "Vaccine Refusal, Mandatory Immunization, and the Risks of Vaccine-Preventable Diseases," *New England Journal of Medicine* 360 (2009): 1981–88.

57 Anna Kata, "A Postmodern Pandora's Box: Anti-Vaccination Misinformation on the Internet," *Vaccine* 28 (2010): 1709–16.

58 Cornelia Betsch, Frank Renkewitz, Tilmann Betsch, and Corinna Ulschöfer, "The Influence of Vaccine-Critical Websites on Perceiving Vaccination Risks," *Journal of Health Psychology* 15 (2010): 446–55.

59 Patricia Ewick and Susan S. Silbey, *The Common Place of Law: Stories from Everyday Life* (Chicago: University of Chicago Press, 1998); Robert A. Kagan, *Adversarial Legalism: The American Way of Law* (Cambridge, MA: Harvard University Press, 2001); Stuart A. Scheingold, *The Politics of Rights: Lawyers, Public Policy, and Political Change* (Ann Arbor: University of Michigan Press, 2004).

60 Sheila Jasanoff, *States of Knowledge: The Co-Production of Science and Social Order* (New York: Routledge, 2004).

61 A great deal of work from both social scientists and scientists, generated mostly in the context over debates about climate change, has bemoaned the tendency of science to get messed up by politicians (or judges, or bureaucrats). For example, Wendy Wagner and Rena Steinzor, *Rescuing Science from Politics: Regulation and the Distortion of Scientific Research* (Cambridge: Cambridge University Press, 2006).

62 Gilbert Ross, "Science Is Not a Democracy," *Washington Times*, June 14, 2007.

63 Sheila Jasanoff, *Science at the Bar: Law, Science, and Technology in America* (Cambridge, MA: Harvard University Press, 1997), xv.

64 Thomas F. Gieryn, *Cultural Boundaries of Science: Credibility on the Line* (Chicago: University of Chicago Press, 1999); Dorothy Nelkin, *Controversy: Politics of Technical Decisions* (Beverly Hills, CA: Sage, 1979).

65 Harry M. Collins, *Are We All Scientific Experts Now?* (Cambridge: Polity, 2014).

66 Jasanoff, "Law's Knowledge," S51.

67 Ibid., S52.

68 Elizabeth Anderson, "The Epistemology of Democracy," *Episteme: A Journal of Social Epistemology* 3 (2006): 8–22 and "Democracy, Public Policy, and Lay Assessments of Scientific Testimony," *Episteme: A Journal of Social Epistemology* 8 (2011): 144–64.

69 Michael McCann, "Law and Social Movements: Contemporary Perspectives," *Annual Review of Law and Social Science* 2 (2006): 25.

70 Catharine MacKinnon, "Privacy v. Equality: Beyond Roe v. Wade," in *Application of Feminist Legal Theory to Women's Lives: Sex, Violence, Work, and Reproduction*, ed. D. Kelly Weisberg (Philadelphia: Temple University Press, 1996).

71 Beth Richie, *Arrested Justice: Black Women, Violence, and America's Prison Nation* (New York: New York University Press, 2012).

72 Lynn Mather and Barbara Yngvesson, "Language, Audience, and the Transformation of Disputes," *Law & Society Review* 15, nos. 3–4 (1980): 775–821.

73 Tyler, *Why People Obey the Law*.

74 It is worth noting that their social movement is moderate and law focused as opposed to extralegal or violent. The contemporary movement does not advocate civil disobedience, violence toward vaccine manufacturing facilities or pediatricians' offices, or open rebellion against government vaccine mandates. (Imagine an anti-abortion movement that speaks only in terms of abortion safety and would never even mention bombing a clinic or banning all abortions. The contrast is stark.) Rather, advocates work for legislative, regulatory, and litigation-driven changes within the current social order of the contemporary U.S. state, even as they regularly accuse it of being thoroughly malevolent and untrustworthy.

75 Michael McCann, *Rights at Work: Pay Equity Reform and the Politics of Legal Mobilization* (Chicago: University of Chicago Press, 1994).

76 Shobita Parthasarathy, "Breaking the Expertise Barrier: Understanding Activist Strategies in Science and Technology Policy Domains," *Science and Public Policy* 37 (2010): 355–67.

77 Ann Southworth, *Lawyers of the Right: Professionalizing the Conservative Coalition* (Chicago: University of Chicago Press, 2008); Steven Teles, *The Rise of the Conservative Legal Movement* (Princeton, NJ: Princeton University Press, 2008).

78 Charles R. Epp, *Making Rights Real: Activists, Bureaucrats, and the Creation of the Legalistic State* (Chicago: University of Chicago Press, 2009).

79 Lillvis et al., "Power and Persuasion in the Vaccine Debates."

80 Nelkin, *Controversy*.

81 Mark A. Largent, *Vaccine: The Debate in Modern America* (Baltimore: Johns Hopkins University Press, 2012). Jacob Heller's work also describes the firm, generalized mainstream narrative about vaccines, which explicitly resists talking about vaccines and the diseases they prevent as variable or contingent. The vaccine narrative frames each vaccine as equally necessary and resists parsing them by how serious, transmissible, costly, or rare each disease prevented actually is, for example, though vaccines and the diseases they prevent vary considerably. Tetanus, for example, is not contagious from person to person, rubella is not a dangerous disease for children or adults but can be devastating for a fetus, and polio is now confined to a few of the poorest and most war-torn parts of the globe, but measles is highly contagious, is endemic in many countries, and can be very serious and even deadly. Jacob Heller, *The Vaccine Narrative* (Nashville: Vanderbilt University Press, 2008).

82 Phil Brown, *Toxic Exposures: Contested Illnesses and the Environmental Health Movement* (New York: Columbia University Press, 2007).

83 Colgrove, *State of Immunity*; Elena Conis, *Vaccine Nation: America's Changing Relationship with Immunization* (Chicago: University of Chicago Press, 2015); Durbach, *Bodily Matters*; Robert D. Johnston, "Anti-Vaccine Movements in His-

torical Perspective," in *The Politics of Healing: Histories of Alternative Medicine in Twentieth Century America*, ed. Robert D. Johnston (New York: Routledge, 2004), 259–86.

84 Sharon Hays, *The Cultural Contradictions of Motherhood* (New Haven, CT: Yale University Press, 1996); Annette Lareau, *Unequal Childhoods: Class, Race, and Family Life* (Berkeley: University of California Press, 2003).

85 Sharon R. Kaufman, "Regarding the Rise in Autism: Vaccine Safety Doubt, Conditions of Inquiry, and the Shape of Freedom," *Ethos* 38, no. 1 (2010): 8–32.

86 Reich, *Calling the Shots*.

87 Omer et al., "Vaccination Policies and Rates of Exemption."

88 Sarah Moore, "Is the Healthy Body Gendered? Toward a Feminist Critique of the New Paradigm of Health," *Body & Society* 16, no. 2 (June 2010): 95–118; Anna Kirkland, "The Legitimacy of Vaccine Critics: What Is Left after the Autism Hypothesis?," *Journal of Health Politics, Policy, and Law* 37, no. 1 (February 2012): 69–97.

89 I develop these arguments more fully as applied to workplace wellness programs in "Introduction: What Is Wellness Now?," *Journal of Health Politics, Policy, and Law* 39, no. 5 (October 2014): 957–70 and "Critical Approaches to Wellness," *Journal of Health Politics, Policy, and Law* 39, no. 5 (October 2014): 971–88.

90 Amanda Grigg and Anna Kirkland, "Health," in *Oxford Handbook of Feminist Theory*, ed. Mary Hawkesworth and Lisa Disch (Oxford: Oxford University Press, 2015).

91 Elena Conis describes the roots of the mothers' movement against vaccines in the 1970s and 1980s against the backdrop of the Carter administration's call for volunteerism among mothers to promote immunizations as well as the feminist women's health movement. Conis, *Vaccine Nation*, 105–29.

92 Grigg and Kirkland, "Health"; Sandra Morgen, *Into Our Own Hands: The Women's Health Movement in the United States, 1969–1990* (New Brunswick, NJ: Rutgers University Press, 2002). Jordynn Jack has recently analyzed autism, revealing all the ways that this condition is gendered as well. Jack, *Autism and Gender: From Refrigerator Mothers to Computer Geeks* (Champaign: University of Illinois Press, 2014).

93 Morgen, *Into Our Own Hands*.

94 Susan M. Reverby, "Feminism and Health," *Health and History* 4, no. 1 (2002): 5–19.

95 Trudy K. Landwirth, "The Women's Health Movement," *Serials Librarian* 12, nos. 3–4 (1987): 89–105.

96 Philip J. Smith, Susan Y. Chu, and Lawrence E. Barker, "Children Who Have Received No Vaccines: Who Are They and Where Do They Live?," *Pediatrics* 114, no. 1 (July 1, 2004): 187–95; Reich, *Calling the Shots*.

97 Feifei Wei et al., "Identification and Characteristics of Vaccine Refusers," *BMC Pediatrics* 9 (2009): 1–9.

98 Elizabeth T. Luman et al., "Maternal Characteristics Associated with Vaccination of Young Children," 111 *Pediatrics* (2003): 1215–18.

99 Reich, "Neoliberal Mothering and Vaccine Refusal: Imagined Gated Communities and the Privilege of Choice," *Gender & Society* 28 (2014): 695.

100 A. T. Walker et al., "Reduction of Racial/Ethnic Disparities in Vaccination Coverage, 1995–2011," *Morbidity and Mortality Weekly Report* 63 (2014): 7–12.

101 Without all these additional policies, vaccine coverage for adults slips back into the racial, ethnic, and class disparities that are so familiar. Peng-jun Lu et al., "Racial and Ethnic Disparities in Vaccination Coverage among Adult Populations in the U.S.," *American Journal of Preventive Medicine* 49, no. 6 (2015): S412–25.

102 World Health Organization, "Global Vaccine Safety," www.who.int, accessed October 24, 2013.

103 Leach and Fairhead, *Vaccine Anxieties.*

CHAPTER 1. HOW ARE VACCINES POLITICAL?

1 Colgrove, *State of Immunity.*

2 Conis, *Vaccine Nation*, 5.

3 Jasanoff, "Law's Knowledge," S51.

4 Engel and Munger, *Rights of Inclusion*, 242. Emphasis mine.

5 Sheila Jasanoff, "Ordering Knowledge, Ordering Society," in Jasanoff, *States of Knowledge*, 17, emphasis original.

6 Peter W. Huber, *Galileo's Revenge: Junk Science in the Courtroom* (New York: Basic Books, 1993). Huber's tone of impending crisis and colorful anecdotes have also been roundly criticized for being an inaccurate portrayal of law's treatment of science. Jeff L. Lewin, "Calabresi's Revenge? Junk Science in the Work of Peter Huber," *Hofstra Law Review* 21, no. 1 (1992): 4.

7 Scott Frickel, *Chemical Consequences: Environmental Mutagens, Activism, and the Rise of Genetic Toxicology* (New Brunswick, NJ: Rutgers University Press, 2004), 13.

8 Stanley A. Plotkin, Walter A. Orenstein, and Paul A. Offit, "The Vaccine Industry," in *Vaccines*, 6th ed. (Philadelphia: Saunders/Elsevier, 2013).

9 Dan M. Kahan, "Vaccine Risk Perceptions and Ad Hoc Risk Communication: An Empirical Assessment," last modified January 27, 2014, http://ssrn.com, accessed September 25, 2014.

10 Kirkland, "Legitimacy of Vaccine Critics."

11 Lauren Silverman, "Texas Church at Center of Measles Outbreak," National Public Radio, last modified September 1, 2013, www.npr.org, accessed September 29, 2014.

12 Centers for Disease Control, "Notes from the Field: Measles Outbreak among Members of a Religious Community—Brooklyn, New York, March–June 2013," *Morbidity and Mortality Weekly Report* 62 (September 13, 2013): 752–53.

13 Pamala Gahr et al., "An Outbreak of Measles in an Undervaccinated Community," *Pediatrics* 134, no. 1 (July 1, 2014): e220–28.

14 National Cancer Institute, "Cancer Vaccines," www.cancer.gov, accessed June 26, 2014.

15 Tetanus is not infectious between people, and so the tetanus vaccine protects the recipient but not surrounding people who have not been vaccinated.

16 Centers for Disease Control and Prevention, "Hepatitis B FAQs for the Public," last modified June 9, 2009, www.cdc.gov, accessed October 24, 2014.

17 Largent, *Vaccine*.

18 Smith et al., "Children Who Have Received No Vaccines."

19 Norman W. Baylor and Valerie B. Marshall, "Regulation and Testing of Vaccines," in Plokin et al., *Vaccines*, 1431.

20 U.S. Food and Drug Administration, "Vaccines, Blood & Biologics: Vaccine Product Approval Process," last modified June 18, 2009, www.fda.gov, accessed October 29, 2013.

21 Paul A. Offit and Frank DeStefano, "Vaccine Safety," in Plotkin et al., *Vaccines*, 1465.

22 U.S. Food and Drug Administration, "Vaccines, Blood & Biologics."

23 Centers for Disease Control and Prevention, "The Advisory Committee on Immunization Practices," last modified February 2013, www.cdc.gov, accessed June 26, 2014. Exceptions can be made if someone's expertise is needed and the conflict of interest is declared publicly. Jean Clare Smith, "The Structure, Role, and Procedures of the U.S. Advisory Committee on Immunization Practices (ACIP)," *Vaccine* 28, no. 0, suppl. 1 (April 19, 2010): A68–75.

24 Stanley A. Plotkin, Walter A. Orenstein, and Paul A. Offit, "Immunization in the United States," in Plotkin et al., *Vaccines*.

25 Centers for Disease Control and Prevention, "Vaccines for Children Program," last modified February 14, 2014, www.cdc.gov, accessed October 24, 2014.

26 Patricia M. Danzon, Nuno Sousa Pereira, and Sapna S. Tejwani, "Vaccine Supply: A Cross-National Perspective," *Health Affairs* 24, no. 3 (2005): 707.

27 Plotkin et al., "Vaccine Industry."

28 Angela K. Shen, Paul S. Mead, and Charles B. Beard, "The Lyme Disease Vaccine—A Public Health Perspective," *Clinical Infectious Diseases* 52 (2011): S247–52. The recommendation was not extended to younger children because of a lack of data about safety and immunogenicity. Other problems with a Lyme disease vaccine include the limited geographic distribution of cases (the Northeast and Upper Midwest) in a relatively limited population (people who spend time in the outdoors around ticks, which transmit the disease). The disease itself is also treatable and not particularly severe, and vaccinated people would likely need booster shots and to maintain preventive measures against ticks because of the other diseases they transmit. Here market forces, features of the disease and the vaccine, and concerns about the social reception spelled failure for a vaccine.

29 Amanda C. Cohn et al., "Prevention and Control of Meningococcal Disease: Recommendations of the Advisory Committee on Immunization Practices (ACIP)," *Morbidity and Mortality Weekly Report* 62 (March 22, 2013): 1–22.

30 Lorry Rubin, "Infant Meningococcal Vaccination: Advisory Committee on Immunization Practices (ACIP) Recommendations and Rationale," *Morbidity and Mortality Weekly Report* 62 (January 25, 2013): 52–54.

31 The well-known Princeton University outbreak of 2013 was serotype B meningitis, which is rare in the United States and for which we then lacked a licensed vaccine. The CDC authorized emergency importation of Novartis's Bexsero vaccine against serotype B, which was approved in Europe. After an accelerated approval process, we now have two licensed and approved serogroup B meningococcal vaccines in the United States (Bexsero and Wyeth's Trumenba) meant for children and adults at increased risk. Temitope Folaranmi et al., "Use of Serogroup B Meningococcal Vaccines in Persons Aged ≥10 Years at Increased Risk for Serogroup B Meningococcal Disease: Recommendations of the Advisory Committee on Immunization Practices, 2015," *Morbidity and Mortality Weekly Report* 64 (June 12, 2015): 608–12.

32 Frankie Milley, "Parents Weep as CDC Only Recommends Vaccine for High Risk Infants Instead of All Infants," *Meningitis Angels*, November 1, 2013, www.meningitis-angels.org, accessed October 7, 2014, emphasis original.

33 National Vaccine Information Center, "49 Doses of 14 Vaccines Before Age 6? 69 Doses of 16 Vaccines by Age 18?," last modified 2013, www.nvic.org, accessed October 24, 2014. I count combination vaccines as one shot that covers multiple diseases, but it would be reasonable to say it is multiple vaccines in one syringe. The NVIC count for younger children would have to include double doses of the influenza vaccine each year, though this sequence is unlikely. Children who may need a second dose include those who have not received the vaccine before, so it is more likely that getting two doses one year would mean there had been none in prior years. Christine Vara, "Why Some Kids Need a Second Dose of Flu Vaccine," *Shot of Prevention*, last modified December 5, 2012, http://shotofprevention.com, accessed October 24, 2014.

34 Centers for Disease Control and Prevention, "Recommended Immunization Schedule for Persons Aged 0 through 18 Years—United States, 2014," www.cdc.gov, accessed October 24, 2014.

35 Children's Hospital of Philadelphia, "History of the Vaccine Schedule," last modified April 2013, http://vec.chop.edu, accessed October 24, 2014.

36 Not all immunization advocates see complete eradication of polio as worth the expense and dangers involved. Global polio rates have dropped by 99 percent, but that last 1 percent will be nearly impossible to stamp out given the political instability and war in its holdout locations such as remote Pakistan. At least thirty health workers, nearly all of them women, have been murdered by the Taliban since 2012 while trying to immunize children against polio. Immunization efforts became associated with U.S.-sponsored anti-terrorist operations after the CIA used it as a ruse to attempt to gather DNA from occupants of Osama bin Laden's compound. The U.S. government has since changed its policy and will not use vaccination in espionage campaigns, and the Taliban has also recently backed away from targeting polio aid workers. Lawrence O. Gostin, "Global Polio Eradication: Espionage, Disinformation, and the Politics of Vaccination," *Milbank Quarterly* 92, no. 3 (2014): 413–17.

37 Children's Hospital of Philadelphia, "History of the Vaccine Schedule."

38 Lillvis et al., "Power and Persuasion in the Vaccine Debates."

39 National Conference of State Legislatures, "States with Religious and Philosophical Exemptions from School Immunization Requirements," July 6, 2015, www.ncsl.org.

40 Law professor Dorit Reiss argues that we should abolish religious exemptions because people invoke them dishonestly and because it is too difficult to investigate the sincerity of a person's religious claims. Reiss, "Thou Shalt Not Take the Name of the Lord Thy God in Vain: Use and Abuse of Religious Exemptions from School Immunization Requirements," *Hastings Law Journal* 65 (2014): 1551–1601.

41 Daniel A. Salmon et al., "Compulsory Vaccination and Conscientious or Philosophical Exemptions: Past, Present, and Future," *The Lancet* 367, no. 9508 (February 4, 2006): 436–42.

42 *In re Christine M.*, 157 Misc 2d 4 (NY Fam Ct 1992).

43 *Mason v. General Brown Central School District*, 851 F 2d 47 (2d Cir NY 1988).

44 *Caviezel v. Great Neck Public Schools*, 701 F Supp 2d 414 (EDNY 2010).

45 *Sherr v. Northport–East Northport Union Free School District*, 672 F Supp 81 (EDNY 1987).

46 *McCarthy v. Boozman*, 212 F Supp 2d 945 (AR Dist Ct 2002).

47 Drew Harris, New Jersey Public Health Institute, interview with the author, July 2013.

48 *Department of Health v. Curry*, 722 So 2d 874 (FL Dist Ct App 1st Dist 1998). Florida remains somewhat ambiguous even after the court decision rendering their religious exemption a de facto philosophical exemption, because it was heard in the First District in Tallahassee but did not get reviewed and affirmed in Florida's Supreme Court. The Wyoming case, by contrast, was a state Supreme Court ruling that would apply statewide, but we count it as unclear because citizens may not know that religious claims have no restriction on their meaning if they do not know about the ruling.

49 *In re Exemption from Immunization Requested by Susan Lepage v. State*, 2001 WY 26 (Wyo 2001).

50 Dawn Richardson, "How We Achieved the Conscientious Belief Exemption in Texas" (speech, NVIC Fourth International Public Conference on Vaccination, Reston, VA, October 2, 2009).

51 Lillvis et al., "Power and Persuasion in the Vaccine Debates."

52 Mike Adams, "What's Really in Vaccines? Proof of MSG, Formaldehyde, Aluminum and Mercury," October 24, 2012, www.naturalnews.com, accessed August 1, 2013. The varicella (chickenpox), rubella, hepatitis A, and shingles vaccines and a version of the rabies vaccine use fetal cells lines in the manufacturing process that were obtained from two elective abortions in the 1960s. Vaccine Education Center, Children's Hospital of Philadelphia, "Do Vaccines Contain Fetal Tissues?," last updated April 2013, http://vec.chop.edu, accessed September 26, 2014. Vatican policy still supports immunization, but would strongly prefer alternatives to the

particular vaccines developed with those cell lines. Donald J. Henz, "Infant Immunization: A Catholic Parent's Guide," Children of God for Life, www.cogforlife.org, accessed October 24, 2014.

53 Michael Pollan, *Food Rules: An Eater's Manual* (New York: Penguin, 2009), 17.

54 UNEP News Centre, "Minamata Convention Agreed by Nations: Global Mercury Agreement to Lift Health Threats from Lives of Millions World-Wide," January 19, 2013, www.unep.org, accessed July 23, 2013.

55 Mercury Free Vaccines Act of 2009, H.R. 2617, 111th Cong. (2009).

56 Michael Nguyen et al., "The Food and Drug Administration's Post-licensure Rapid Immunization Safety Monitoring Program: Strengthening the Federal Vaccine Safety Enterprise," *Pharmacoepidemiology and Drug Safety* 21, suppl. 1 (2012): 291–97.

57 Centers for Disease Control and Prevention, "Rotavirus Vaccine (RotaShield®) and Intussusception," last updated April 8, 2014, www.cdc.gov, accessed October 29, 2014.

58 Paul A. Offit and H. Fred Clark, "Rotavirus Vaccines, Part II: Raising the Bar for Vaccine Safety Studies," in *History of Vaccine Development*, ed. Stanley Plotkin (New York: Springer, 2011), 323.

59 Centers for Disease Control and Prevention, "Rotavirus Vaccine (RotaShield®) and Intussusception."

60 Centers for Disease Control and Prevention, "Withdrawal of Rotavirus Vaccine Recommendation," *Morbidity and Mortality Weekly Report* 48, no. 43 (November 5, 1999): 1007.

61 Jason L. Schwartz, "The First Rotavirus Vaccine and the Politics of Acceptable Risk," *Milbank Quarterly* 90, no. 2 (2012): 278–310.

62 Centers for Disease Control and Prevention, "Rotavirus Vaccine (RotaShield®) and Intussusception."

63 Centers for Disease Control and Prevention, "Withdrawal of Rotavirus Vaccine Recommendation."

64 Schwartz, "First Rotavirus Vaccine," 278–310.

65 Ibid., 298.

66 Ibid., 295.

67 Ibid., 292.

68 Lizell B. Madsen et al., "Reduced Price on Rotavirus Vaccines: Enough to Facilitate Access Where Most Needed?," *Bulletin of the World Health Organization* 90, no. 7 (2012): 554–56.

69 W. Katherine Yih et al., "Active Surveillance for Adverse Events: The Experience of the Vaccine Safety Datalink Project," *Pediatrics* 127, suppl. 1 (2011): S54–64.

70 Centers for Disease Control and Prevention, "Vaccine Safety Datalink," last updated October 10, 2014, www.cdc.gov, accessed October 29, 2014.

71 Michael McNeil et al., "The Vaccine Safety Datalink: Successes and Challenges Monitoring Vaccine Safety," *Vaccine* 32, no. 42 (2014): 5390–98.

72 Nguyen et al., "Food and Drug Administration's Post-licensure Rapid Immunization Safety Monitoring Program," 291–97.

73 W. Katherine Yih et al., "Surveillance for Adverse Events Following Receipt of Pandemic 2009 H1N1 Vaccine in the Post-Licensure Rapid Immunization Safety Monitoring (PRISM) System, 2009–2010," *American Journal of Epidemiology* 175, no. 11 (2012): 1120–28.

74 Ibid., 1125.

75 The relative informality of flu vaccination and its appearance in malls, workplaces, and pharmacies is controversial between vaccine critics and vaccine promoters because while these practices boost immunization rates, critics argue that informality may mean that the conditions are not as safe. Flu shots are much more accessible in these locations, and there is no evidence they are unsafe places to get immunizations. Lucinda L. Maine, Katherine K. Knapp, and Douglas J. Scheckelhoff, "Pharmacists and Technicians Can Enhance Patient Care Even More Once National Policies, Practices, and Priorities Are Aligned," *Health Affairs* 32, no. 11 (November 2013): 1956–62.

76 Yih et al., "Surveillance for Adverse Events Following Receipt."

77 FDA Amendments Act of 2007, H.R. 3580, 110th Cong. (2007).

78 FDA, "The Sentinel Initiative," July 2010, www.fda.gov, accessed June 27, 2014.

79 Mini-Sentinel Data Core, "Mini-Sentinel Distributed Database Summary Report Year Four, Version 1.1," August 2014, www.mini-sentinel.org, accessed June 27, 2014.

80 Susan Forrow et al., "The Organizational Structure and Governing Principles of the Food and Drug Administration's Mini-Sentinel Pilot Program," *Pharmacoepidemiology and Drug Safety* 21, suppl. 1 (2012): 12–17.

81 Institute of Medicine, *The Childhood Immunization Schedule and Safety: Stakeholder Concerns, Scientific Evidence, and Future Studies* (Washington, DC: National Academies Press, 2013).

82 Kreesten Madsen et al., "A Population-Based Study of Measles, Mumps, and Rubella Vaccination and Autism," *New England Journal of Medicine* 347, no. 19 (2002): 1477–82. This study using the Danish databases examined 537,303 children, 440,655 of whom had received the MMR vaccine, while the rest had not. There was no association between the MMR vaccine and any autism diagnosis.

83 John Gilliom and Torin Monahan, *SuperVision: An Introduction to the Surveillance Society* (Chicago: University of Chicago Press, 2013), 45.

CHAPTER 2. THE SOLUTION OF THE VACCINE COURT

1 Advisory Commission on Childhood Vaccines (ACCV), December 1993 meeting minutes (on file with the author).

2 Edward A. Mortimer, Jr., "Pertussis Vaccine," in *Vaccines*, 2nd ed., ed. Stanley A. Plotkin and Edward A. Mortimer (Philadelphia: Saunders, 1994), 91–135.

3 Harris L. Coulter and Barbara Loe Fisher, *DPT: A Shot in the Dark* (San Diego: Harcourt Brace Jovanovich, 1985), 26–77.

4 Diana Brahams, "Medicine and the Law: Pertussis Vaccine Litigation," *The Lancet* 335 (1990): 905–6.

5 Thomas F. Burke, *Lawyers, Lawsuits, and Legal Rights: The Battle over Litigation in American Society* (Berkeley: University of California Press, 2002), 145. Burke is the primary scholar of the founding of the vaccine court, and I draw significantly from his research on the congressional debates and internal Reagan administration memos in this section. My analysis of the ACCV committee meeting minutes—not previously obtained by any researcher prior to my FOIA request— adds an original perspective on the early days of the court and on the thimerosal litigation because it is the site where every vaccine compensation program issue is regularly discussed. Jeb Barnes and Thomas F. Burke continue their analysis of the law and politics of vaccine injury compensation in *How Policy Shapes Politics: Rights, Courts, Litigation, and the Struggle over Injury Compensation* (Oxford: Oxford University Press, 2015).

6 Burke, *Lawyers, Lawsuits, and Legal Rights*, 145.

7 Ibid., 151–52.

8 Marie Bismark and Ron Paterson, "No-Fault Compensation in New Zealand: Harmonizing Injury Compensation, Provider Accountability, and Patient Safety," *Health* 25, no. 1 (2006): 1278–83.

9 *Toner v. Lederle*, 779 F.2d 1429 (1986) and *Johnson v. American Cyanamid Co.*, 718 P.2d 1318 (1986). The Toner family received $1,131,200 in damages, but the Johnson judgment was overturned.

10 Kagan, *Adversarial Legalism*.

11 Barnes and Burke, *How Policy Shapes Politics*, 159; Burke, *Lawyers, Lawsuits, and Legal Rights*, 143.

12 American Law Institute, Restatement of Torts (Second), Section 402a, comment k (1965).

13 Wendy K. Mariner and Mary E. Clark, "Confronting the Immunization Problem: Proposals for Compensation Reform," *American Journal of Public Health* 76, no. 6 (1986): 704. Observers have also noted that the federal government's previous experience with vaccine injury compensation during the 1976 swine flu epidemic (which did not really turn into an epidemic) also helped shape today's vaccine court. Lainie Rutkow, Brad Maggy, Joanna Zablotsky, and Thomas R. Oliver, "Balancing Consumer and Industry Interests in Public Health: The National Vaccine Injury Compensation Program and Its Influence during the Last Two Decades," *Penn State Law Review* 111 (2007): 681; Barnes and Burke, *How Policy Shapes Politics*, 162.

14 Burke, *Lawyers, Lawsuits, and Legal Rights*, 155.

15 Ibid., 156.

16 Ibid., 157.

17 Ibid., 157.

18 Amicus brief of the National Vaccine Information Center, Its Co-Founders, and 11 Other Organizations in Support of Petitioners in *Bruesewitz v. Wyeth*, No. 09–152.

19 Barbara Loe Fisher, statement to the ACCV, ACCV, November 18, 2008, meeting minutes.

20 Barnes and Burke, *How Policy Shapes Politics*, 152.

21 Wendy K. Mariner, "The National Vaccine Injury Compensation Program," *Health Affairs* 11, no. 1 (1992): 262.

22 Feminist scholars are used to asking these questions about the family, for example. Stephanie Coontz, *The Way We Never Were: American Families and the Nostalgia Trap* (New York: Basic Books, 1992).

23 Peter Meyers argues for a more lenient interpretation of the causation standard in close cases, but there are not large numbers of close cases. Meyers, "Fixing the Flaws," 845–47. The autism cases, for example, which are a large proportion of rejected claims, were not close cases that any adjustment to the causation standard could have salvaged. As I describe in Chapter 5, the metaphor of closeness does not accurately describe the situation that the special masters often face, which is a battle of the experts that is heavily lopsided, or the situation in which there are very little data on the question either way. Meyers's many reasonable suggested reforms would not change the outcome for the autism cases, for example, and he sidesteps the fact that most critics still think vaccines cause autism and that the loss of that large bolus of cases is a major source of their dissatisfaction.

24 Most critics of the vaccine court fall in this second category, including Barbara Loe Fisher and NVIC, advocates at the Birt Center, and contributors to *Vaccine Epidemic: How Corporate Greed, Biased Science, and Coercive Government Threaten Our Human Rights, Our Health, and Our Children*, ed. Louise Kuo Habakus and Mary Holland (New York: Skyhorse, 2011).

25 The original Table was written into the statute and included the DTP, MMR, and polio vaccines (live and inactivated). 42 U.S.C. 300aa-14 Sec. 2114(a). It presumed a causal link between the DTP vaccine and anaphylaxis or anaphylactic shock within twenty-four hours, encephalopathy or encephalitis within three days, and residual seizure disorder within three days plus any acute complication or related problems (termed sequelae, including death). It presumed a causal link between the MMR vaccine and anaphylaxis or anaphylactic shock within twenty-four hours, encephalopathy or encephalitis within fifteen days, and residual seizure disorder within fifteen days plus any acute complication or related complication. For the live oral polio vaccine, the original Table presumed causation between paralytic polio in a child with a normally functioning immune system within thirty days, in an immunodeficient one in six months, and in a child who acquired polio from someone in the community who had gotten the vaccine at any time plus any acute complication or related complication.

26 Malcolm Feeley, *The Process Is the Punishment: Handling Cases in a Lower Criminal Court* (New York: Russell Sage Foundation, 1992).

27 The special masters were not the only ones who were swamped. By 1991, vaccine claims accounted for 20 percent of all Justice Department Civil Division caseloads, and the appropriations for pre-1988 claims were running low. ACCV, March 1991 meeting minutes (on file with the author).

28 ACCV, March 2011 meeting minutes (available at www.hrsa.gov/vaccinecompensation/commissionchildvaccines.html).

29 Ibid. In 1991, amendments to the court process ensured that the court could retain jurisdiction of claims past the deadline for a decision with the consent of the petitioner, and this mechanism kept claims within the court for the several years it took to process them. Health Information, Health Promotion, and Vaccine Injury Compensation Amendments of 1991, H.R. 3402, 102nd Congress (1991–1992).

30 ACCV, May 1989 meeting minutes (on file with the author).

31 ACCV, June 9, 1989, letter from Chair Lawton to HHS secretary (on file with author).

32 The current vaccine rules run about twenty-one pages and describe the entire process and requirements from initial filing to final decision: www.uscfc.uscourts.gov/sites/default/files/court_info/20130813_rules/13.08.30%20Final%20Version%20of%20Vaccine%20Rules.pdf.

33 ACCV, May 1989 meeting minutes (on file with the author).

34 Ibid.; ACCV, November 1989 meeting minutes (on file with the author).

35 ACCV, July 1989 meeting minutes (on file with the author).

36 September 1989 letter from HHS General Counsel to Claims Court Chief Judge.

37 ACCV, May 1989 meeting minutes (on file with the author).

38 ACCV, February 1990 meeting minutes (on file with the author).

39 ACCV, April 1990 meeting minutes (on file with the author).

40 Adult claimants are allowed and in fact make up the majority of claims. Vaccines for influenza and tetanus, for example, are recommended for children but commonly administered to adults.

41 ACCV, June 1992 meeting minutes (on file with the author).

42 All the major studies are discussed in detail in the 1994 edition of the physician's reference guide to vaccines. Mortimer, "Pertussis Vaccine."

43 Ibid., 127.

44 Offit, Deadly Choices, 35–40.

45 A. H. Griffith, "Permanent Brain Damage and the Pertussis Vaccination: Is the End of the Saga in Sight?," Vaccine 9 (1989): 199–210, discussing Loveday v. Renton and the Wellcome Foundation, Medical Law Reports 1 (1990): 117.

46 Ibid., 205.

47 Brahams, "Medicine and the Law," 906. About eight hundred compensations had been paid under the British compensation scheme, about three-quarters of them based on the pertussis vaccine.

48 Tarannum M. Lateef et al., "Seizures, Encephalopathy, and Vaccines: Experience in the National Vaccine Injury Compensation Program," Journal of Pediatrics 166 (2015): 576–81.

49 Christopher P. Howson and Harvey V. Fineberg, "The Ricochet of Magic Bullets: Summary of the Institute of Medicine Report," Pediatrics 89, no. 2 (1992): 318–24, discussing the report they edited, Institute of Medicine, Adverse Effects of Pertussis and Rubella Vaccines (Washington, DC: National Academies Press, 1991); Institute of Medicine, Adverse Events Associated with Childhood Vaccines: Evidence Bearing on Causality (Washington, DC: National Academies Press, 1994).

50 Institute of Medicine, *Adverse Events Associated with Childhood Vaccines*, vi.

51 Institute of Medicine, *Adverse Effects of Pertussis and Rubella Vaccines*, 322.

52 The reasons for the changes and responses to critics are explained in detail in Secretary of the Department of Health and Human Services, "National Vaccine Injury Compensation Program Revision of the Vaccine Injury Table," *Health Resources and Services Administration, HHS, Federal Register* 60, no. 26 (February 8, 1995).

53 National Childhood Vaccine Injury Act of 1986, 42 U.S. Code §300aa-14(b)(3)(A).

54 New definitions taken from Health Resources and Services Administration (HRSA), "Vaccine Injury Table," www.hrsa.gov.

55 Kevin Conway, interview with the author, March 5, 2011.

56 Curtis Webb, interview with the author, March 5, 2011.

57 Affidavit of Clifford J. Shoemaker, April 8, 2008, quoted in *Avila v. Secretary of Health and Human Services*, No. 05–685V, December 22, 2009, U.S. Court of Federal Claims, 16, emphasis original.

58 *King v. Aventis Pasteur, Inc.*, 210 F. Supp. 2d 1201 (D. Or. June 7, 2002); *Mead v. Aventis Pasteur*, 2002 U.S. District Court, LEXIS 25552 (D. Or. June 7, 2002).

59 Williams O'Leary LLC, "Vaccine Injuries Litigation: Vaccine Injuries," www.wdolaw.com, accessed October 9, 2014.

60 ACCV, June 2002 meeting minutes (on file with the author).

61 Ibid.

62 ACCV, September 2002 meeting minutes (on file with the author).

63 ACCV, June 2002 meeting minutes (on file with the author).

64 National Childhood Vaccine Injury Act of 1986, 42 U.S. Code §300aa-11(2)(A).

65 *Doe v. Ortho-Clinical Diagnostics, Inc.*, 440 F. Supp. 2d 465 (M.D.N.C. 2006) considered thimerosal in RhoGAM and *Redfoot v. B.F. Ascher & Co.*, 2007 WL 1593239 (N.D. Cal. June 1, 2007) was about a product called Ayr Saline Nasal Mist. These cases did not have to be filed in the vaccine court because the associated products are not vaccines, but they were dismissed on summary judgment for lack of a credible expert.

66 For example, *Reilly v. Wyeth*, 377 Ill. App. 3d 20 (Ill. App. Ct. 1st Dist. 2007).

67 National Childhood Vaccine Injury Act of 1986, 42 U.S. Code §300aa-22(b)(1).

68 *Schafer v. American Cyanamid Co.*, 20 F.3d 1 (1st Cir. Mass. 1994).

69 *King v. Aventis Pasteur, Inc*, 210 F. Supp. 2d 1201.

70 For example, a judge dismissed fifty-three thimerosal lawsuits in what was termed the Maryland Thimerosal Litigation, finding that the language of the vaccine act was very clear that claims needed to go first to the vaccine court and that thimerosal claims were vaccine-related. *Agbebaku v. Sigma Aldrich, Inc.*, 2003 WL 24258219 (Md. Cir. Ct. 2003).

71 *Troxclair ex rel. Troxlair v. Aventis Pasteur*, 374 N.J. Super. 374, 381 (App. Div. 2005). Prior cases finding that thimerosal was not an adulterant or contaminant but part of a vaccine and covered by the vaccine act by then included *Laughter v. Aventis Pasteur, Inc.*, 291 F. Supp. 2d 406, 410 (M.D.N.C. 2003); *Murphy v. Aventis*

Pasteur, Inc., 270 F. Supp. 2d 1368 (N. D. Ga. 2003); *Blackmon v. Am. Home Prods. Corp.*, 267 F.Supp.2d 667 (S. D. Tex. 2002); *Owens v. American Home Products*, 203 F.Supp.2d 748 (Dist. S. Tex. May 7, 2002); *Wax v. Aventis Pasteur, Inc.*, 240 F.Supp.2d 191 (E.D.N.Y. 2002); and *Cheskiewicz v. Aventis Pasteur, Inc.*, 843 A.2d 1258 (Pa. Super. 2004).

72 *Reilly v. Wyeth*, 27; 21 C.F.R. 610.15(a).

73 *Blackwell v. Wyeth*, 408 Md. 575 (Md. 2009).

74 Brian Vastag, "Congressional Autism Hearings Continue," *Journal of the American Medical Association* 285, no. 20 (2001): 2567–69.

75 ACCV, June 2002 meeting minutes (on file with the author).

76 Meyers, "Fixing the Flaws."

77 Ibid.

78 Webb interview.

79 National Vaccine Injury Compensation Program, ACCV, "Summary of 1998 Legislative Proposals," www.hrsa.gov, accessed October 9, 2014.

80 Barnes and Burke note that an extended statute of limitations at the vaccine court would have meant that claimants in the VICP would be able to reject their judgments and sue in federal court, in effect extending the statute of limitations in tort. Barnes and Burke, *How Policy Shapes Politics*, 174. As petitioners' attorney Curtis Webb put it, "And then, of course, no one in the drug companies or the public health community was interested in extending the statute if it would preserve those clients going back [to court]." Webb interview.

81 Vaccine Injury Compensation Reform Act, H.R. 1003, 106th Cong. (1999); Vaccine Injury Compensation Program Corrective Amendments of 2000, H.R. 5330, 106th Cong. (2000); Vaccine Injury Compensation Program Improvement Act of 2000, H.R. 5579, 106th Cong. (2000); Vaccine Injured Children's Compensation Act of 2001, H.R. 1287, 107th Cong. (2001); National Vaccine Injury Compensation Program Improvement Act of 2002, H.R. 3741, 107th Cong. (2002); Improved Vaccine Affordability and Availability Act, H.R. 5282, 107th Cong. (2002). Rep. Tom Tancredo introduced a bill in 1999 that would have removed the excise tax on vaccines and thus made it impossible to pay compensations, but his effort was part of a general anti-tax effort and showed no understanding of its implications for vaccine injury payments. Top Ten Terrible Tax Act of 1999, H.R. 2414, 106th Cong. (1999).

82 ACCV, December 2001 meeting minutes (on file with the author). I do not think this different standard would result in much difference in actual decisions, however, because the evidentiary gaps are too big to be spanned by changing "preponderance of the evidence" to "positive association." Moreover, "positive association" sounds like it would amount to requiring an epidemiological study in the petitioners' favor, and they almost never have these, as I describe in Chapter 5.

83 ACCV, December 2001 meeting minutes (on file with the author).

84 Improved Vaccine Affordability and Availability Act, S.B. 2053, 107th Cong. (2002).

85 Kirby, *Evidence of Harm*, 226–28.

86 Ibid., 228 (citing an interview with a Kennedy staffer).

87 Children's Health Act of 2000, H.R. 4365, 106th Cong. (2000).

88 Homeland Security Act of 2002, Pub. L. No. 107–296, § 1716, 116 Stat. 2135, 2320–21, 107th Cong. (2002) (repealed 2003).

89 *Ferguson v. Aventis Pasteur, Inc.*, 444 F. Supp. 2d 755, 757 (E.D. Ky. 2006).

90 Kirby, *Evidence of Harm*, 4.

91 Ibid., 237 (quoting a Christian Broadcast Network interview that is no longer available online). See also Joel Roberts, "The Man Behind the Vaccine Mystery," CBS News, December 12, 2002, www.cbsnews.com, accessed October 9, 2014.

92 Kirby, *Evidence of Harm*, 4–5.

93 Brian Vastag, "Thimerosal Provision Repealed," *JAMA Capital Health Call* 289, no. 5 (February 5, 2003): 539.

94 *Troxclair ex rel. Troxlair v. Aventis Pasteur, Inc.*, 374 N.J. Super. 374 (App. Div. 2005).

CHAPTER 3. HEALTH AND RIGHTS IN THE VACCINE-CRITICAL MOVEMENT

1 Colgrove, *State of Immunity*; Durbach, *Bodily Matters*; Johnston, "Anti-Vaccine Movements"; Michael Willrich, "'The Least Vaccinated of Any Civilized Country': Personal Liberty and Public Health in the Progressive Era," *Journal of Policy History* 20, no. 1 (2008): 76–93.

2 Charles L. Jackson, "State Laws on Compulsory Immunization in the United States," *Public Health Reports* 84 (1969): 792. I thank an anonymous reviewer for this reference.

3 Matthew Browne et al., "Going against the Herd: Psychological and Cultural Factors Underlying the 'Vaccination Confidence Gap,'" *PLOS ONE* 10, no. 9 (September 1, 2015): e0132562.

4 Elizabeth A. Armstrong and Mary Bernstein, "Culture, Power, and Institutions: A Multi-institutional Politics Approach to Social Movements," *Sociological Theory* 26, no. 1 (2008): 75–78.

5 Abigail C. Saguy and Kevin W. Riley, "Weighing Both Sides: Morality, Mortality, and Framing Contests over Obesity," *Journal of Health Politics, Policy, and Law* 30, no. 5 (2005): 869–921.

6 Steven Epstein, *Impure Science: AIDS, Activism, and the Politics of Knowledge, Medicine and Society* (Berkeley: University of California Press, 1996).

7 Maren Klawiter, *The Biopolitics of Breast Cancer: Changing Cultures of Disease and Activism* (Minneapolis: University of Minnesota Press, 2008).

8 Jeffrey R. Dudas, *The Cultivation of Resentment: Treaty Rights and the New Right* (Stanford, CA: Stanford University Press, 2008).

9 McCann, "Law and Social Movements," 25–26.

10 McCann, *Rights at Work*.

11 Coulter and Fisher, *A Shot in the Dark*; Offit, *Deadly Choices*.

12 National Childhood Vaccine Injury Act of 1986, 42 U.S.C. §§ 300aa-1 to 300aa-34, 42 U.S.C. Public Law 99–660 (1986).

13 National Vaccine Information Center, "About National Vaccine Information Center," www.nvic.org, accessed March 10, 2011.

14 Johnston, "Anti-Vaccine Movements," 260.

15 Heller, *Vaccine Narrative*, 100–102.

16 Epstein, *Impure Science*.

17 Johnston, "Anti-vaccine Movements," 271.

18 Heller, *Vaccine Narrative*, 93.

19 SafeMinds, "Welcome," accessed March 17, 2011, www.safeminds.org.

20 Coalition for Vaccine Safety, "Newly Formed Coalition for Vaccine Safety Speaks with a Unified Voice," US Newswire press release, 2010.

21 The Canary Party, www.canaryparty.org, accessed January 1, 2015.

22 The Canary Party, "The Canary Party Position Paper," last modified May 27, 2011, http://canaryparty.net, accessed January 1, 2015.

23 Rob Schneider, "Do Vaccines Cause Autism?," YouTube video, 5:19, posted by "Canary Party," September 7, 2013, www.youtube.com.

24 Elizabeth Birt Center for Autism Law & Advocacy, "Our Mission," www.ebcala. org, accessed January 1, 2015.

25 "Bruesewitz v. Wyeth—Vaccine Press Conference," YouTube video playlist, 25:00, from a press conference held on March 3, 2011, in front of the U.S. Supreme Court, posted by "zenworksproductions," March 10, 2011, www.youtube.com.

26 Kevin Conway, interview with the author, March 5, 2011.

27 Dan M. Kahan, Hank Jenkins-Smith, and Donald Braman, "Cultural Cognition of Scientific Consensus," *Journal of Risk Research* 14, no. 205 (2010): 148, emphasis original.

28 J. B. Handley, interview transcript, *Frontline*, PBS, www.pbs.org, accessed January 4, 2015.

29 Barbara Loe Fisher, "2009 NVIC Conference Keynote Address" (speech, NVIC Fourth International Public Conference on Vaccination, Reston, VA, October 2–4, 2009).

30 Sallie Bernard, public comments at NVAC Vaccine Safety Working Group meeting, June 13, 2011 (notes on file with the author).

31 Mary Holland, "Reconsidering Childhood Vaccine Mandates," New York University Public Law and Legal Theory Working Papers Series (NELLCO Legal Papers Repository, 2010).

32 Fisher, "2009 NVIC Conference Keynote Address."

33 Vicky Debold, "Vaccinated versus Unvaccinated" (speech, NVIC Fourth International Public Conference on Vaccination, Reston, VA, October 2–4, 2009).

34 Centers for Disease Control and Prevention, "National, State, and Local Area Vaccination Coverage among Children Aged 19–35 Months—United States, 2012," *Morbidity and Mortality Weekly Report* 62 (2013): 733–40.

35 National Vaccine Advisory Committee (NVAC), "Recommendations on the Centers for Disease Control and Prevention Immunization Safety Office Draft 5-Year Scientific Agenda" (Washington, DC: U.S. Department of Health and Human Services, 2009), 82.

36 Institute of Medicine, *Childhood Immunization Schedule and Safety*, 196.

37 Sara Shostak, *Exposed Science: Genes, the Environment, and the Politics of Population Health* (Berkeley: University of California Press, 2013).

38 Barbara Loe Fisher, "Measles Reports in America: What Does It Mean?," *Vaccine Awakening*, September 24, 2013, http://vaccineawakening.blogspot.com, accessed November 20, 2013.

39 Institute of Medicine, *Childhood Immunization Schedule and Safety*.

40 Barbara Loe Fisher, Public Comments on Vaccine Safety Working Group Draft, June 13, 2011; NVAC, Sallie Bernard, Public Comments on Vaccine Safety Working Group Draft, June 13, 2011.

41 Holland, "Reconsidering Childhood Vaccine Mandates," 1–44; Marguerite Willner, "Brief of Amicus Curiae Marguerite Willner in Support of Petitioners, *Bruesewitz v. Wyeth*," American Bar Association, www.americanbar.org, accessed October 7, 2014.

42 Robert D. Benford and David A. Snow, "Framing Processes and Social Movements: An Overview and Assessment," *Annual Review of Sociology* 26 (2000): 614.

43 Opinion of Reva Siegel in Jack Balkin, ed., *What Roe v. Wade Should Have Said* (New York: New York University Press, 2005); MacKinnon, "Privacy v. Equality."

44 Nancy Appleton, *Rethinking Pasteur's Germ Theory: How to Maintain Your Optimal Health* (Berkeley, CA: Frog Ltd., 2002); Arthur M. Baker, *Awakening Our Self-Healing Body: A Solution to the Health Care Crisis* (Los Angeles: Dennis Nelson, 1994); William P. Trebing, *Goodbye Germ Theory: Ending a Century of Medical Fraud* (Bloomington, IN: Xlibris Corporation, 2004).

45 Glenda Wiese, "Chiropractic's Tension with the Germ Theory of Disease," *Chiropractic History* 16, no. 1 (1996): 72–87.

46 Johnston, "Anti-Vaccine Movements," 279.

47 James B. Campbell, Jason W. Busse, and H. Stephen Injeyan, "Chiropractors and Vaccination: A Historical Perspective," *Pediatrics* 105, no. 4 (2000): e43.

48 Ibid., e43.

49 Baker, *Awakening Our Self-Healing Body*; Arthur M. Baker, "Exposing the Myth of the Germ Theory," *College of Practical Homeopathy* (2005): 1–10, www.mednat.org.

50 Susan Sered and Amy Agigian, "Holistic Sickening: Breast Cancer and the Discursive Worlds of Complementary and Alternative Practitioners," *Sociology of Health and Illness* 30, no. 4 (2008): 616–31.

51 Christian Warren, *Brush with Death: A Social History of Lead Poisoning* (Baltimore: Johns Hopkins University Press, 2000).

52 For example, Mark R. Geier and David A. Geier, "Thimerosal in Childhood Vaccines, Neurodevelopmental Disorders, and Heart Disease in the United States," *Journal of American Physicians and Surgeons* 8 (2003): 6–11; and Mark R. Geier and David A. Geier, "Early Downward Trends in Neurodevelopmental Disorders Following Removal of Thimerosal-Containing Vaccines," *Journal of American Physicians and Surgeons* 11 (2006): 8–13.

53 As Rosalind Petchesky observes, social movements invoke human rights language in many ways. Rosalind Petchesky, *Global Prescriptions: Gendering Health and Human Rights* (New York: Zed Books, 2003). I suspect vaccine critics will not be able to harness a human rights frame in a national and international public health context in which vaccines are understood as safe and effective globally and where fair access in poor countries is more likely to seen as the real problem.

54 Brown, *Toxic Exposures.*

55 Science and Environmental Health Network, "Precautionary Principle," www.sehn.org, accessed December 4, 2013.

56 Science and Environmental Health Network, "Wingspread Conference on the Precautionary Principle," January 26, 1998, www.sehn.org.

57 François Ewald, "The Return of Descartes's Malicious Demon: An Outline of a Philosophy of Precaution," in *Embracing Risk: The Changing Culture of Insurance and Responsibility,* ed. Tom Baker and Jonathan Simon (Chicago: University of Chicago Press, 2002), 282–84.

58 National Vaccine Information Center, 2011 Annual Report, 2, www.nvic.org, accessed April 13, 2016.

59 Adams, "What's Really in Vaccines?"

60 Lillvis et al., "Power and Persuasion in the Vaccine Debates."

61 Pollan, *Food Rules.*

62 SafeMinds, "SafeMinds Energy Policy," last modified November 9, 2009, www.safeminds.org, accessed October 7, 2014.

63 Fisher, "2009 NVIC Conference Keynote Address."

64 Barbara Loe Fisher, "Vaccination during Pregnancy: Is It Safe?," *Vaccine Awakening,* November 12, 2013, http://vaccineawakening.blogspot.com.

65 The Canary Party, "Do Vaccines Cause Autism?," last modified August 24, 2014, http://canaryparty.net, accessed October 7, 2014.

66 Fisher, "2009 NVIC Conference Keynote Address."

67 Benjamin, *People's Science,* 154.

68 Dorothy Roberts, *Fatal Invention: How Science, Politics, and Big Business Re-Create Race in the Twenty-First Century* (New York: New Press, 2011).

69 Rosemarie Garland-Thomson, "Feminist Disability Studies," *Signs: Journal of Women in Culture and Society* 30, no. 2 (2005): 1557–87.

70 Parthasarathy, "Breaking the Expertise Barrier."

71 Lillvis et al., "Power and Persuasion in the Vaccine Debates."

CHAPTER 4. KNOWING VACCINE INJURY THROUGH LAW

1 Bruno Latour, *The Making of Law: An Ethnography of the Conseil d'Etat* (Cambridge: Polity, 2010), 221.

2 Ibid., 228, emphasis original.

3 Riles, *Collateral Knowledge*, 20.

4 Anderson, "Democracy, Public Policy, and Lay Assessments," 146.

5 Even claims of negligent vaccine administration by doctors (such as giving a second or third dose after an adverse reaction to the first one, resulting in injury) have been routed out of civil court to the compensation program. *Quigley v. Rider*, 357 S.C. 477, 593 S.E.2d 476 (Ct. App. 2003).

6 *Bruesewitz v. Wyeth*, 131 S.Ct. 1068 (2011). The losing petitioners in the autism cases hoped to be able to sue in state courts with the claim that thimerosal in vaccines constituted a design defect. The vaccine act states that "[n]o vaccine manufacturer shall be liable in a civil action for damages arising from a vaccine-related injury or death associated with the administration of a vaccine after October 1, 1988, if the injury or death resulted from side-effects that were unavoidable even though the vaccine was properly prepared and was accompanied by proper directions and warnings." 42 U. S. C. §300aa-22(b)(1). Manufacturers are still liable for claims based on defective manufacturing and inadequate directions or warnings, but these are not problems that critics have mobilized against. Manufacturers are subject to detailed regulations about labeling as well as inspections of facilities, and managing these liabilities is well within their control.

7 Health Resources and Services Administration, "Vaccine Injury Table."

8 The Canary Party, "Do Vaccines Cause Autism?"

9 *Riggins v. Secretary of HHS*, No. 99–382V (June 15, 2009) and *King v. Secretary of HHS*, 2011 U.S. Claims LEXIS 2233.

10 Sean Farhang, *The Litigation State: Public Regulation and Private Lawsuits in the U.S.* (Princeton, NJ: Princeton University Press, 2010), 4.

11 Sean Farhang and Douglas M. Spencer, "Legislating Incentives for Attorney Representation in Civil Rights Litigation," *Journal of Law and Courts* 2 (2014): 241–71.

12 Herbert M. Kritzer, *Risks, Reputations, and Rewards: Contingency Fee Legal Practice in the United States* (Stanford, CA: Stanford University Press, 2004).

13 *Riggins v. Secretary of HHS*, No. 99–382V (June 15, 2009).

14 Vaccine Rules of the U.S. Court of Federal Claims, www.uscfc.uscourts.gov, 129.

15 *Knudsen v. Secretary of Health and Human Services*, 35 F.3d (Fed. Cir. September 9, 1994), 548.

16 Vaccine Rules of the United States Court of Federal Claims, Rule 8(b)(1), www.uscfc.uscourts.gov, accessed October 23, 2013.

17 Legal Information Institute, "National Childhood Vaccine Injury Act of 1986, U.S. Code, Title 42, Chapter 6A, Subchapter XIX, Part 2, Subpart d, § 300aa-12(d)(3)

(B)," *Cornell University Law School* (1988), www.law.cornell.edu, accessed February 5, 2015.

18 Dr. Evans shared a chart with me that he kept to summarize these major periods in the program's history and the major events, such as Table changes and Institute of Medicine (IOM) reviews. I draw this periodization from his chart (on file with the author). The founding era was defined by a fairly permissive approach to compensation. The special masters compensated for adverse events following pertussis vaccination that medical authorities have since declared were unrelated or not backed by sufficient evidence but that parents insisted were related, such as SIDS, episodes of unresponsiveness followed by death, and seizure disorders and other chronic neurological conditions. Derry Ridgway, "Disputed Claims for Pertussis Vaccine Injuries under the National Vaccine Injury Compensation Program," *Journal of Investigative Medicine* 46, no. 4 (1998): 168–74. Chapter 6 analyzes the Omnibus Autism Proceeding in detail.

19 National Vaccine Injury Compensation Program, "National Vaccine Injury Compensation Program Data Report," April 1, 2016, Health Resources and Services Administration, www.hrsa.gov.

20 Martin Shapiro, *Courts: A Comparative and Political Analysis* (Chicago: University of Chicago Press, 1981), 1.

21 Ibid., 63.

22 Center for Personal Rights, "Vaccine Justice Press Conference."

23 "Judges—Biographies," U.S. Court of Federal Claims, www.uscfc.uscourts.gov, accessed February 13, 2015. Of the currently sitting eight special masters, four previously worked in the Department of Justice. They formerly worked in the tax division, the commercial litigation division, and the torts division. Half of the current special masters are men, and half are women. A few have been appointed at relatively young ages, but the more typical pattern has been to appoint someone with many years of legal practice experience. A recent chief special master, Denise Vowell, is a former chief trial judge in the Army, and another special master previously served as a municipal judge and administrative law judge in Colorado. One special master was both a tax litigator in the Department of Justice and a former partner in a private law firm, and two of the more recently appointed special masters are former litigators from private law practice who handled civil litigation defense and complex tort claims. The special masters who have been on the court longer are more likely to have come from the Department of Justice, and the four appointments made in 2013–2014 all came from private law firm practice or a state judgeship.

24 Lawrence Baum, *Specializing the Courts* (Chicago: University of Chicago Press, 2011).

25 Ibid., 32–40.

26 Nora Freeman Engstrom, "A Dose of Reality for Specialized Courts: Lessons from the VICP," *University of Pennsylvania Law Review* 163 (2015): 1631–1717.

27 Sheila Jasanoff, *Designs on Nature: Science and Democracy in Europe and the United States* (Princeton, NJ: Princeton University Press, 2007), 7.

28 There have been other IOM panels established to study vaccine-related issues, including safety, so this count is a conservative one. Institute of Medicine, *Immunization Safety Review: Vaccinations and Sudden Unexpected Death in Infancy* (Washington, DC: National Academies Press, 2003); Institute of Medicine, *Immunization Safety Review: SV40 Contamination of Polio Vaccine and Cancer* (Washington, DC: National Academies Press, 2002), Institute of Medicine, *The Anthrax Vaccine: Is It Safe? Does It Work?* (Washington, DC: National Academies Press, 2002); Institute of Medicine, *Immunization Safety Review: Thimerosal-Containing Vaccines and Neurodevelopmental Disorders* (Washington, DC: National Academies Press, 2001); Institute of Medicine, *Immunization Safety Review: Hepatitis B Vaccine and Demyelinating Neurological Disorders* (Washington, DC: National Academies Press, 2002); Institute of Medicine, *Immunization Safety Review: Vaccines and Autism*; Institute of Medicine, *Immunization Safety Review: Measles-Mumps-Rubella Vaccine and Autism* (Washington, DC: National Academies Press, 2001); Institute of Medicine, *Immunization Safety Review: Multiple Immunizations and Immune Dysfunction* (Washington, DC: National Academies Press, 2002); Institute of Medicine, *Childhood Immunization Schedule and Safety*; Institute of Medicine, *Immunization Safety Review: Influenza Vaccines and Neurological Complications* (Washington, DC: National Academies Press, 2003); Institute of Medicine, *Adverse Effects of Vaccines: Evidence and Causality* (Washington, DC: National Academies Press, 2012).

29 Health Resources and Services Administration, "How to File a Claim," www.hrsa.gov.

30 In this case, if a person sought medical treatment for a child or herself and the treatment was entered into electronic records, evidence of the condition and its closeness in time to the vaccinations would be part of the record to be studied later in a large epidemiological study to look for temporally related problems. This mode of research does not depend on anyone recognizing a vaccine injury at the time.

31 The vaccine program at HRSA contracted in 2010 with a communications company, Banyan Communications, to develop a national marketing plan. Options such as television advertising were part of that plan, but such a broad approach would be likely to alarm people as much as educate them. There was more support for targeted outreach to doctors and other elites who would be in a position to recognize possible vaccine reactions. Since then HRSA has worked to make itself more visible online and at professional events, and its outreach plan for 2015 included trying to inform health care providers, parents and expectant parents, adults over fifty, and attorneys. U.S. Government Accountability Office (GAO), "Vaccine Injury Compensation: Most Claims Took Multiple Years and Were Negotiated through Settlement" (Washington, DC: GAO, November 2014), 32. The VICP is explained on the Vaccine Information Statement (VIS) sheet accompanying every vaccine administration, but the sheet may have long been discarded by the time someone considers the idea of vaccine injury.

32 Vaccine Adverse Event Reporting System (VAERS), "Frequently Asked Questions," http://vaers.hhs.gov, accessed October 21, 2013.

33 Michael J. Goodman and James Nordin, "Vaccine Adverse Event Reporting System Reporting Source: A Possible Source of Bias in Longitudinal Studies," *Pediatrics* 117, no. 2 (2006): 387–90.

34 There may still be some dispute over what the compensation should be. For example, the government and the petitioners may secure a professional called a life care planner, whose job is to estimate what it will cost to care for a child with a lifelong disability, for example. Opposing life care planners may set out more or less generous compensation plans and the parties negotiate a settlement.

35 I draw my account of recognized injuries both from the official Vaccine Injury Table but also from the IOM's 2012 review of adverse events. The Table is in the process of being revised to include IOM-identified adverse events. HRSA, "Vaccine Injury Table"; IOM, *Adverse Effects of Vaccines*.

36 Conditions such as temporary soreness at the injection site are widely agreed-upon vaccine injuries but are too minor to qualify for compensation. The vaccine act requires that the person "suffered the residual effects or complications of such illness, disability, injury, or condition for more than 6 months after the administration of the vaccine." 42 U.S.C. § 300aa-11(c)(1)(D)(i). In one case, for example, a man claimed that the flu vaccine gave him a rash, but his case was dismissed after he was unable to gather evidence that the rash lasted for the required amount of time. *Backes v. Secretary of Health and Human Services*, No. 14–871V, 2015 U.S. Court of Federal Claims.

37 *Sand v. Secretary of Health and Human Services*, No. 08–632V, 2009 U.S. Court of Federal Claims.

38 *Kara McLaughlin v. Secretary of Health and Human Services*, No. 08–747V, August 10, 2009, U.S. Court of Federal Claims.

39 IOM, *Adverse Effects of Vaccines*, 153, 211, 337, 356, 579.

40 GAO, "Vaccine Injury Compensation," 13.

41 Special masters at the vaccine court have negotiated settlements as well as found for petitioners claiming that vaccines caused multiple sclerosis, for example, although these cases are not routinely settled. *W.C. v. Secretary of Health and Human Services*, No. 07–456V, February 22, 2011, U.S. Court of Federal Claims, denied a man's claim for multiple sclerosis after the flu vaccine, but *Jane Doe 74 v. Secretary of Health and Human Services*, [redacted] V, July 13, 2010, U.S. Court of Federal Claims, www.uscfc.uscourts.gov, affirmed compensation for multiple sclerosis after tetanus and MMR vaccines.

42 Guillain-Barré syndrome (GBS) occurs when the immune system attacks the peripheral nerves, damaging the myelin sheath insulating the nerve and causing paralysis beginning in the hands and feet and spreading in toward the trunk. Most people recover completely, but it can become life-threatening if respiratory paralysis sets in. GBS has several variations and may also be termed acute

inflammatory demyelinating polyneuropathy, Fisher syndrome or Miller-Fisher syndrome, acute motor axonal neuropathy, or acute motor and sensory axonal neuropathy. Almed Calvo, "Updating the Vaccine Injury Table: Guillain-Barré Syndrome (GBS) and Seasonal Influenza Vaccines" (presentation, Advisory Commission on Childhood Vaccines, September 5, 2013), www.hrsa.gov, accessed October 16, 2014.

43 *Froelick v. Secretary of Health and Human Services*, No. 11–01V, December 18, 2013, U.S. Court of Federal Claims, is an example of a stipulation in a case involving multiple sclerosis and acute disseminated encephalomyelitis.

44 IOM, *Adverse Effects of Vaccines*, 327. The 2009 H1N1 flu vaccine—prepared specially for this strain and covered not under the VICP but instead under the Countermeasures Injury Compensation Program—has been linked to a small increase in GBS cases (1.6 additional cases per million people vaccinated). Daniel Salmon et al., "Association between Guillain-Barré Syndrome and Influenza A (H1N1) 2009 Monovalent Inactivated Vaccines in the USA: A Meta-Analysis," *The Lancet* 381 (2013): 1461–68.

45 Barnes and Burke, *How Policy Shapes Politics*.

46 Kagan, *Adversarial Legalism*, 3.

47 Those countries are (in order of the establishment of the program) Germany (1961), France (1963), Switzerland (1970), Denmark (1972), Austria (1973), New Zealand (1974), Japan (1976), Sweden (1978), the United Kingdom (1979), Finland (1984), Quebec, Canada (1985), the United States (1986), Taiwan (1988), Italy (1992), Republic of Korea (1994), Norway (1995), Iceland (2001), Slovenia (2004), and Hungary (2005). Clare Looker and Heath Kelly, "No-Fault Compensation Following Adverse Events Attributed to Vaccination: A Review of International Programmes," *Bulletin of the World Health Organization* 89 (2011): 371–78. I have adjusted some dates based on subsequent research. Australia, Canada, and Ireland are under pressure to establish schemes, and China is reportedly considering it. Ibid., 372. The U.S. program administrators have a keen interest in what other nations are doing around vaccine injury compensation. The VICP then-director, Dr. Geoffrey Evans, conducted a 1999 study of other vaccine injury compensation programs worldwide and published a summary. Geoffrey Evans, "Vaccine-Injury Compensation Programs Worldwide," *Vaccine* 17 (1999): S25–35. The office maintains an unpublished chart (2005, on file with the author).

48 Looker and Kelly, "No-Fault Compensation," 375.

49 Ibid., 374.

50 Shin-Yi Wang et al., "Comparison Analysis of Taiwan/Japan Vaccine Injury Compensation Program," *Taiwan Epidemiology Bulletin* 29 (2013).

51 Yu-Chen Hsu et al., "An Analysis of Taiwan's Vaccination Services in Public Health Centers and Contracted Medical Institutions and Applications for Vaccine Injury Compensations," *Taiwan Epidemiology Bulletin* 30 (2014): 85.

52 Looker and Kelly, "No-Fault Compensation," 373.

53 Ibid.

54 Wang et al., "Comparison Analysis of Taiwan/Japan Vaccine Injury Compensation Program," 6–8.

55 Yu-Chen Hsu et al., "Analysis of Taiwan's Vaccination Services," 85.

56 ACCV, September 2002 meeting minutes (on file with the author).

57 See www.vcf.gov/pdf/VCFStatute.pdf.

58 Kenneth Feinberg, *What Is Life Worth? The Unprecedented Effort to Compensate the Victims of 9/11* (New York: Public Affairs, 2006).

59 Meyers, "Fixing the Flaws," 838.

60 See www.vcf.gov/genProgramInfo.html.

61 The Biomaterials Access Assurance Act of 1998 is another example of an industry-protecting ongoing scheme. The law protects suppliers of raw materials used in implanted medical devices from civil liability in order to ensure that they will not be driven out of business and thus interrupt the manufacturing of needed medical devices. Biomaterials Access Assurance Act of 1998, 21 U.S.C. 1601.

62 Lawrence M. Friedman, *A History of American Law*, 3rd ed. (New York: Simon & Schuster, 2005), 516.

63 James M. Anderson et al., *The U.S. Experience with No-Fault Automobile Insurance: A Retrospective*, Rand Corporation Monograph Series (Santa Monica, CA: RAND, 2010).

64 Radiation Exposure Compensation Act, Public Law 101–426, 104 Stat. 920 (1990).

65 Civil Liberties Act of 1988, Public Law 100–383.

66 In re Agent Orange Prod. Liab. Litig., 818 F.2d 145 (2d Cir. 1987); Peter H. Schuck, *Agent Orange on Trial: Mass Toxic Disasters in the Courts* (Cambridge, MA: Harvard University Press, 1986). The Black Lung Benefits Act is an example of legislation that straightforwardly compensates workers who have contracted an occupational disease. The United Mine Workers secured its passage in Congress in 1969, and the health care and compensation program is run through the Department of Labor.

67 Agent Orange Act of 1991, Public Law 102–4. Veterans who missed out on the settlement and Vietnamese citizens have continued to bring lawsuits for injuries from Agent Orange, but these have not been successful.

68 U.S. Department of Veteran's Affairs, Military Exposures: Agent Orange, www.publichealth.va.gov.

69 According to the law, there is a positive association "if the credible evidence for the association is equal to or outweighs the credible evidence against the association." 38 U.S. Code § 1116(b)(3). The IOM understood the required association to be a statistical association with consistent direction and magnitude in studies free of bias and confounding, specifically with soft tissue sarcoma, non-Hodgkin's lymphoma, and Hodgkin's disease. Institute of Medicine, *Veterans and Agent Orange: Health Effects of Herbicides Used in Vietnam* (Washington, DC: National Academies Press, 1994), 8.

70 Jeb Barnes, *Dust-Up: Asbestos Litigation and the Failure of Common Sense Policy Reform* (Washington, DC: Georgetown University Press, 2011), 58.

71 Report to the Chairman, Committee on the Judiciary, House of Representatives, *Asbestos Injury Compensation: The Role and Administration of Asbestos Trusts* (Washington, DC: GAO, September 2011).

72 Ibid., 15–16.

73 Barnes, *Dust-Up*, 93–97.

74 Ibid., 25–29.

75 Farhang, *Litigation State*; Kagan, *Adversarial Legalism*.

76 Michael J. Bazyler, *Holocaust Justice: The Battle for Restitution in America's Courts* (New York: New York University Press, 2003), 202.

77 Ibid., 254–55.

78 Anne Schneider and Helen Ingram, "Social Construction of Target Populations: Implications for Politics and Policy," *American Political Science Review* 87 (1993): 334–47. I thank Aaron Ley for this point.

CHAPTER 5. WHAT COUNTS AS EVIDENCE?

1 Health Resources and Services Administration, "Vaccine Injury Table," www.hrsa.gov/, accessed October 21, 2014; Institute of Medicine, *Adverse Effects of Vaccines*.

2 Institute of Medicine, *Adverse Effects of Vaccines*, 10.

3 Ibid., 12.

4 Ibid.

5 Ibid., 13.

6 Ibid., 14.

7 Ibid., 15.

8 Stephen Hilgartner, *Science on Stage: Expert Advice as Public Drama* (Stanford, CA: Stanford University Press, 2000).

9 Institute of Medicine, *Childhood Immunization Schedule and Safety*, 3.

10 Transcript of Organizational Meeting of Immunization Safety Review Committee Closed Session, January 12, 2001 (on file with the author).

11 Jim Moody, public comments, ACCV, December 2011 meeting minutes; Institute of Medicine, *Adverse Effects of Vaccines*, 111.

12 See, for example, Geier and Geier, "Early Downward Trends," which used VAERS data as well as a California state developmental services database to argue that new diagnoses of autism decreased after thimerosal was removed from vaccines.

13 *Age of Autism*, "HPV Vaccine (Gardasil and Cervarix) VAERS Reports—Injury and Death Continue to Climb," December 4, 2010, www.ageofautism.com.

14 Department of Health and Human Services, "VAERS: Frequently Asked Questions," http://vaers.hhs.gov.

15 Institute of Medicine, *Adverse Events Associated with Childhood Vaccines*, 286.

16 "Requirements on Content and Format of Labeling for Human Prescription Drug and Biological Products," 21 Code of Federal Regulations 201.56.

17 Dawn Richardson, "State Organizing to Get and Protect Vaccine Choices" (remarks, National Vaccine Information Center Public Conference, Reston, VA, October 2–4, 2009).

18 ACCV, "Guiding Principles for Recommending Changes to the Vaccine Injury Table," March 9, 2006, www.hrsa.gov.

19 Neal A. Halsey, "The Science of Evaluation of Adverse Events Associated with Vaccination," *Seminars in Pediatric Infectious Diseases* 13, no. 3 (2002): 205. Vaccine agents should clear the body fairly soon (in a matter of days), and so finding the vaccine-strain virus still in the body long after the administration coupled with medical problems in those same parts of the body would be worrisome. Vaccine-strain measles virus has been found persisting in the body of immune-compromised children and people with HIV, for example, suggesting that their bodies were not able to clear the virus.

20 Ibid.

21 Institute of Medicine, *Vaccine Safety Research, Data Access, and Public Trust* (Washington, DC: National Academies Press, 2005), 2.

22 Kirby, *Evidence of Harm.*

23 Letter from Dr. Jeanne Santoli, National Immunization Program, CDC, to Leigh Pruneau, IRB Administrator at Northern California Kaiser Permanente, February 13, 2004 (on file with the author).

24 Institute of Medicine, *Vaccine Safety Research*, 58–59.

25 Centers for Disease Control and Prevention, "Accessing Data from the Vaccine Safety Datalink (VSD)."

26 The Court of Federal Claims has subpoena powers under its rules (RCFC 45). "Motion to Issue Third Party Subpoena," October 7, 2003, Omnibus Autism Proceeding online docket, www.uscfc.uscourts.gov. Special Master Hastings rejected most of the fees requested to produce the article, which had not even been introduced in the autism hearings. *King v. Secretary of HHS*, 03–584V (September 22, 2011). The petitioners asked for $447,044.02 in compensation for producing the article.

27 *Mostovoy v. Sec'y of HHS*, No. 02–10V, 2013 WL 3368236 (Fed. Cl. Spec. Mstr. June 12, 2013).

28 Ibid., 39–41.

29 *Castaneda v. Secretary of Health and Human Services*, 11–749V (Fed. Cl. 2013).

30 Robert F. Kennedy, "Deadly Immunity," *Rolling Stone* (2005): 57–63. Kennedy's article has been roundly criticized for its inaccuracies and was eventually retracted and no longer appears on the Salon.com website.

31 Thomas Verstraeten et al., "Safety of Thimerosal-Containing Vaccines: A Two-Phased Study of Computerized Health Maintenance Organization Databases," *Pediatrics* 112, no. 5 (2003): 1039–49.

32 Verstraeten responded to these accusations in an op-ed titled "Thimerosal, the Centers for Disease Control and Prevention, and GlaxoSmithKline," *Pediatrics* 113 (2004): 932.

33 Harland Austin and Cathy Lally, "A Re-Analysis of the Vaccine Safety Datalink (VSD) Project Conducted by the Centers for Disease Control and Prevention Pertaining to Safety Issues Related to Thimerosal-Containing Vaccines" (unpublished expert report, 2006). This document was filed into the Omnibus Autism Docket

as Exhibit 91 and made public on the website www.uscfc.uscourts.gov, accessed February 23, 2015.

34 Ibid., 3.

35 Ibid.

36 U.S. Senate Committee on Health, Education, Labor and Pensions, "Enzi Says Investigation Does Not Support Allegations of Misconduct in Autism Research," September 28, 2007, www.help.senate/gov, accessed April 13, 2016.

37 Centers for Disease Control and Prevention, "Vaccines and Autism: A Summary of CDC Conducted or Sponsored Studies," www.cdc.gov.

38 ACCV, March 2011 meeting minutes (on file with author).

39 Clinical Immunization Safety Assessment Project, "Mission," www.cdc.gov.

40 Phillip S. LaRussa et al., "Understanding the Role of Human Variation in Vaccine Adverse Events: The Clinical Immunization Safety Assessment Network," *Pediatrics* 127, suppl. 1 (2011): S66.

41 Centers for Disease Control and Prevention, "Vaccine Safety and Human Genetic Variations," www.cdc.gov, accessed November 5, 2013.

42 ACCV, March 2011 meeting minutes (on file with author).

43 Sarah Atanasoff, Tom Ryan, Robert Lightfoot, and Rosemary Johann-Liang, "Shoulder Injury Related to Vaccine Administration (SIRVA)," *Vaccine* 28, no. 51 (2010): 8049–52.

44 The people reported pain very soon after the vaccination, and many of them remembered thinking the injection had been given too high. Their medical records showed evidence of excess fluid and tissue damage in their shoulders, suggesting that perhaps the misdirected vaccine had irritated a preexisting muscle tear.

45 Kent Heckenlively, "Gov't Admits Vaccine Autism Link," *Age of Autism*, February 27, 2008, www.ageofautism.com. Generation Rescue also maintains a list of compensated cases it claims show that the vaccine court acknowledges vaccines as an environmental trigger for autism: see www.generationrescue.org/resources/vaccination/vaccine-related-court-cases/.

46 The *Age of Autism* blog published the full Rule 4(c) report recommending the Poling compensation at www.ageofautism.com/2008/02/full-text-autis.html.

47 *Poling v. Secretary of HHS*, No. 02–1466V (2011) (attorneys' fees and costs decision), 2. Subsequent claims for vaccine-induced or -aggravated mitochondrial disease have not been successful because the special masters distinguished the Poling compensation as a Table compensation and did not find sufficient causation evidence (*Holt v. Secretary of HHS*, No. 05–0136V [2015]), because the timing of onset did not support causation (*Paluck v. Secretary of HHS*, No. 07–889V [2013]), and because the petition was simply the same condition and causal mechanism that had been litigated already in the autism cases, just relabeled as encephalopathy and mitochondrial disorder rather than autism.

48 *Banks v. Secretary of HHS*, No. 02–0738V (2007).

49 Science and medical blogger David Gorski summarized the controversy on March 10, 2008, at Science-Based Medicine, www.sciencebasedmedicine.org.

50 Paul Offit, "Vaccines and Autism Revisited—The Hannah Poling Case," *New England Journal of Medicine* 358 (2008): 2089–91.

51 Mary Holland and Louis Conte, "Unanswered Questions from the Vaccine Injury Compensation Program: A Review of Compensated Cases of Vaccine-Induced Brain Injury," *Pace Environmental Law Review* 28, no. 2 (2011): 480–544.

52 Ibid., 482.

53 Sallie Bernard and Albert Enayati, "Autism: A Novel Form of Mercury Poisoning," *Medical Hypotheses* 56, no. 4 (2001): 462–71.

54 Special Master Gary Golkiewicz, Autism General Order #1, 7, www.uscfc.uscourts. gov.

55 299.00 Autistic Disorder, in *Diagnostic and Statistical Manual of Mental Disorders*, 4th ed. (Washington, DC: American Psychiatric Association, 2000).

56 Qualifications and Aids to Interpretation, Vaccine Injury Table.

57 Holland and Conte, "Unanswered Questions," 531.

58 Jim Moody, June 2011 ACCV meeting transcript. Sarah Hoiberg, the mother of the vaccine-injured daughter on the advisory committee, responded angrily, "For me, the vaccine injury compensation program has, in a way, given life back to my daughter. I have been able to get her therapy that I never would have been able to afford on my own. For these people to stand up and say and pretty much throw it in the face of the government that they messed up, that ha, ha, ha, you compensated an autistic child is just wrong. That is why I am angry, because I feel like the program did something good in compensating these people." Sarah Hoiberg, June 2011 ACCV meeting transcript.

59 For example, David Gorski, "When You Can't Win on Science, Invoke the Law . . . ," *Science-Based Medicine*, May 11, 2011, www.sciencebasedmedicine.org, accessed January 17, 2015.

60 Elizabeth Birt Center for Autism Law and Advocacy, "Chairman Issa Postpones VICP Hearing," www.ebcala.org. The report was published in 2014 as GAO, "Vaccine Injury Compensation."

61 Michelle Murphy, *Sick Building Syndrome and the Problem of Uncertainty: Environmental Politics, Technoscience, and Women Workers* (Durham, NC: Duke University Press, 2006), 10.

62 Decoteau and Underman, "Adjudicating Non-Knowledge in the Omnibus Autism Proceedings."

63 Institute of Medicine, *Adverse Effects of Vaccines*.

64 For the varicella vaccine, causal links were found with the following conditions: disseminated Oka VZV (the vaccine strain virus) without other organ involvement; disseminated Oka VZV with subsequent infection resulting in pneumonia, meningitis, or hepatitis; vaccine strain viral reactivation without other organ involvement; and vaccine strain viral reactivation with subsequent infection resulting in meningitis or encephalitis. For the MMR vaccine: measles inclusion body encephalitis and febrile seizures. For the MMR, varicella, influenza, hepatitis B, tetanus-containing, and meningococcal vaccines: anaphylaxis. And finally, the

IOM found that any vaccine could have injection-related related injuries, namely syncope (or fainting, not itself dangerous, but the fall from an exam table onto one's head has led to serious injuries and even death) and deltoid bursitis (what HRSA medical officers termed shoulder injury related to vaccine administration or SIRVA).

65 The four causal relationships given the slightly less robust affirmative judgment were between HPV and anaphylaxis, MMR and transient arthralgia in female adults, MMR and transient arthralgia in children, and certain trivalent inactivated influenza vaccines used in Canada and oculorespiratory syndrome.

66 The rejected relationships were between the MMR vaccine and type 1 diabetes, the DTaP vaccine and type 1 diabetes, the MMR vaccine and autism, the trivalent in-activated influenza vaccine (TIV) and asthma or reactive airway disease episodes, and TIV and Bell's palsy.

67 *Contemporary Pediatrics* Staff, "Reassure Worried Parents: Vaccines Rarely Have Serious Adverse Effects," *Contemporary Pediatrics*, September 1, 2011.

68 National Vaccine Information Center, "Statement of the National Vaccine Information Center (NVIC) on Adverse Effects of Vaccines: Evidence and Causality," last modified August 25, 2011, www.nvic.org, accessed August 20, 2012.

69 Yih et al., "Active Surveillance for Adverse Events."

70 "Update: Recommendations from the Advisory Committee on Immunization Practices (ACIP) Regarding Administration of Combination MMRV Vaccine," *Morbidity and Mortality Weekly Report* 57 (March 14, 2008): 258–60.

71 "Use of Combination Measles, Mumps, Rubella, and Varicella Vaccine: Recommendations of the Advisory Committee on Immunization Practices (ACIP)," *Morbidity and Mortality Weekly Report* 59 (2010): 1–12.

72 Yih et al., "Active Surveillance for Adverse Events," S60–61.

73 Ibid., S61.

74 In one study monitoring the safety of the meningococcal conjugate vaccine (MCV) with Rapid Cycle Analysis in the VSD, for example, outcomes of interest were selected based on whether they were clinically well defined, whether they were serious enough to generate a hospital or specialist follow-up record, whether they had already appeared in passive surveillance reports, and whether they were plausible as a consequence of vaccination with MCV because they were either associated with similar vaccines or biologically plausible. Tracy A. Lieu et al., "Real-Time Vaccine Safety Surveillance for the Early Detection of Adverse Events," *Medical Care* 45 (2007): S90.

75 *Stevens v. Secretary of HHS*, No. 99–594V, March 30, 2001, U.S. Court of Federal Claims, 17.

76 Ibid., 20.

77 Meredith Daniels, "Special Masters in the National Vaccine Injury Compensation Program: Placing a Heightened Burden on Vaccine Program Petitioners by Straying from Precedent and Congressional Intent," *Journal of Health and Biomedical Law* 6 (2010): 87.

78 *Stevens v. Secretary of HHS*.

79 *Althen v. Secretary of HHS*, 418 F.3d 1274 (Fed. Cir. July 29, 2005), 1278.

80 Ibid., 1280; *Capizzano v. Secretary of HHS*, 440 F.3d 1317 (Fed. Cir. March 9, 2006).

81 Daniels, "Special Masters in the National Vaccine Injury Compensation Program," 90–93.

82 Conway interview.

83 *Moberly v. Secretary of HHS*, 592 F.3d (Fed. Cir. January 13, 2010), 1322; *Broekelschen v. Secretary of HHS*, 618 F.3d 1339 (Fed. Cir. 2010), 1345–46.

84 *Waters v. Secretary of HHS*, No. 05–0872V, December 23, 2013, U.S. Court of Federal Claims.

85 *Mathis v. Secretary of HHS*, No. 09–467V, June 7, 2013, U.S. Court of Federal Claims. In another case, a family had received a favorable ruling from a special master that they were entitled to compensation, but as their child's case moved into the compensation phase, newly discovered medical records showed that the child had indeed tested positive for SCN1A. The Department of Justice moved to reopen the compensation decision, arguing that the SCN1A mutation was the true cause of the child's condition. Another special master reheard the case and denied compensation, finding that the SCN1A gene mutation, not a vaccine, was the cause of the child's seizures and developmental problems. *Deribeaux v. Secretary of HHS*, No. 05–306V, June 4, 2012, U.S. Court of Federal Claims.

86 *Daubert v. Merrell Dow Pharmaceuticals*, 509 U.S. 579 (1993).

87 As I noted in Chapter 2, vaccine toxic tort cases that have managed to get to court (because the vaccination occurred before the statute became effective or because they were aimed at thimerosal sources outside the childhood vaccine schedule, such as RhoGAM shots given to Rh-negative pregnant women) were stymied by *Daubert* rulings. Memorandum opinion excluding all expert testimony, including that of Dr. Mark Geier in *Doe v. Ortho-Clinical Diagnostics, Inc.*, 440 F. Supp. 2d 465 (Middle Dist. N.C., July 6, 2006).

88 *Daubert*, 593–94.

89 Jasanoff, "Law's Knowledge," S52.

90 Ibid., S54.

91 Myron Levin, "Witnesses for Petitioners Are Often Tough to Find," *Los Angeles Times*, November 29, 2004.

92 *Peugh v. Secretary of HHS*, No. 99–638V, May 8, 2007, U.S. Court of Federal Claims. Special Master Millman was the noted favorite special master of the attorneys on the petitioners' side, often discussed as the most willing to compensate in contested cases.

93 *Werderitsh v. Secretary of HHS*, No. 99–310V, May 26, 2006, U.S. Court of Federal Claims.

94 *Gilbert v. Secretary of HHS*, No. 04–455V, March 30, 2006, U.S. Court of Federal Claims.

95 *Stevens v. Secretary of HHS*, No. 99–594V, February 24, 2006, U.S. Court of Federal Claims.

96 Institute of Medicine, *Adverse Effects of Vaccines*, 447. These processes describe how microbial agents or viruses can induce the body's immune system to attack itself and damage nerves, and if a wild virus could do it, then a vaccine-strain virus might be able to do it, too. Molecular mimicry, one theory cited in the mainstream literature as "a viable hypothesis" and frequently raised at the vaccine court, is one of these theories describing a similarity between molecules from different genes, such as when two different kinds of molecules have the same amino acid sequences. Michael B. A. Oldstone, "Molecular Mimicry and Immune-Mediated Diseases," *Journal of the Federation of American Societies for Experimental Biology* 12, no. 13 (1998): 1255–65. An immune response can then cross-react and damage other body cells. Molecular mimicry has been studied at the molecular and animal levels, but it is difficult to observe in people with naturally arising disease.

97 Paul Offit, "Inoculated Against Facts," *New York Times*, March 31, 2008, www.nytimes.com.

98 *Borrero v. Secretary of HHS*, No. 01–417V, September 24, 2008, U.S. Court of Federal Claims, 30.

99 Ibid., 33.

100 In *Ogletree v. Secretary of HHS*, No. 11–731V, December 7, 2013, U.S. Court of Federal Claims, for example, Special Master Millman signed a stipulation for a $575,000 payment to a man with MS. Like all such stipulations from the vaccine court, it notes that "[t]his Stipulation shall not be construed as an admission by the United States or the Secretary of Health and Human Services that the Hepatitis B vaccine caused petitioner to suffer multiple sclerosis or any other injury."

101 Webb interview.

CHAPTER 6. THE AUTISM SHOWDOWN

1 Epstein, *Impure Science.*

2 The autism petitions peaked in 2003 with 2,437 filings. At the time, the court normally got about 200 claims per year (now up to about 600).

3 There was originally to be a set of cases for a third theory that the MMR alone causes autism, but it was withdrawn presumably because all the relevant evidence was introduced in the first theory and there would have been no chance of success.

4 *Cedillo v. Secretary of HHS*, No. 98–916V (2007), 20.

5 *King v. Secretary of HHS*, No. 03–584V (2008), 17; *Mead v. Secretary of HHS*, No. 03–215V (2008), 24–25.

6 Handley, interview transcript, *Frontline.*

7 Kristin Bumiller cautions that this "geneticization of autism" may contribute to laxity in the search for environmental causes and increase the feelings among

autistic people of being eugenically targeted. Kristin Bumiller, "The Geneticiza-tion of Autism: From New Reproductive Technologies to the Conception of Genetic Normalcy," *Signs: Journal of Women in Culture and Society* 34, no. 4 (2009): 893.

8 Testimony of the government's genetic psychiatry expert, Dr. Edwin Cook, quoted in *Cedillo v. Secretary of HHS*, 1491. Dr. Cook noted that the other twin without autism seems to be affected, noting a study that showed that only one out of twenty-five siblings had formed an intimate adult relationship of any kind. Ibid., 1492. He estimated the overall genetic factors for autism at about 90 percent. Ibid., 1494.

9 Ibid., 94.

10 *Mead v. Secretary of HHS*, 30–37.

11 Testimony of Dr. Rodier quoted in *King v. Secretary of HHS*, 3326–27.

12 Testimony of Dr. Kemper quoted in *Mead v. Secretary of HHS*, 2807–9.

13 Testimony of Dr. Kemper quoted in *Mead v. Secretary of HHS*, 2412.

14 Testimony of Dr. Rodier quoted in *Mead v. Secretary of HHS*, 3032.

15 *Cedillo v. Secretary of HHS*, 98, emphasis original.

16 Ibid., 95.

17 Applied behavioral analysis (ABA) is the mainstream treatment for autism, in which a teacher drills a child over and over to achieve developmental goals. Its effectiveness is nonetheless questioned, and some insurance companies refuse to cover it on the grounds that it remains experimental. Daniela Caruso, "Autism in the U.S.: Social Movement and Legal Change," *American Journal of Law and Medicine* 36 (2010): 528. Drugs for anxiety and depression are also used with mainstream approval. Biomedical interventions, such as a gluten-free, casein-free (no milk or wheat) diet, secretin, hyperbaric chambers, and chelation therapy either have not been sufficiently well studied in clinical trials or, when studied, have not been shown to be effective, so there is little mainstream support for these interventions. Susan E. Levy and Susan L. Hyman, "Complementary and Alternative Medicine Treatments for Children with Autism Spectrum Disorders," *Child and Adolescent Psychiatric Clinics in North America* 17, no. 4 (2008): 803–20. Advocates of the injury framework insist they are effective, however, and many parents recount improvements in their children after using them.

18 Eric Fombonne, "Is There an Epidemic of Autism?," *Pediatrics* 107 (2001): 411–13.

19 *Mead v. Secretary of HHS*, 3282.

20 Ka-Yuet Liu, Noam Zerubavel, and Peter Bearman, "Social Demographic Change and Autism," *Demography* 47, no. 2 (2010): 327–43; Marissa D. King and Peter S. Bearman, "Diagnostic Change and the Increased Prevalence of Autism," *International Journal of Epidemiology* 38 (2009): 1224–34; Ka-Yuet Liu, Marissa D. King, and Peter S. Bearman, "Social Influence and the Autism Epidemic," *American Journal of Sociology* 115, no. 5 (2010): 1387.

21 *Mead v. Secretary of HHS* and *King v. Secretary of HHS*, 500–523.

22 Ibid., 513–14.

23 Michael Aschner et al., "Involvement of Glutamate and Reactive Oxygen Species in Methylmercury Neurotoxicity," *Brazilian Journal of Medical and Biological Research* 40, no. 3 (2007): 285–91.

24 *Cedillo v. Secretary of HHS*, 92, 115, 129–31.

25 Ibid., 95.

26 Amy S. Holmes, Mark F. Blaxill, and Boyd E. Haley, "Reduced Levels of Mercury in First Baby Haircuts of Autistic Children," *International Journal of Toxicology* 22, no. 4 (2003): 277–85. He also argued that chelation therapy helps cure autism, which must be because it removes the mercury, based on studies such as Jeff Bradstreet et al., "A Case-Control Study of Mercury Burden in Children with Autistic Spectrum Disorders," *Journal of American Physicians and Surgeons* 8, no. 3 (2003): 76–79.

27 *Miller v. Secretary of HHS*, 02–235V (2015), 12.

28 *Dwyer v. Secretary of HHS*, 03–1202V (2010), 257.

29 Ibid., 224.

30 Warren, *Brush with Death*.

31 Much of what we know about mercury poisoning comes from case studies of disasters, most notably a widespread poisoning in the 1970s in which farmers in Iraq ate seed contaminated with methyl mercury used as a fungicide, and the Minamata Bay industrial pollution case in Japan in the 1950s and 1960s in which factory waste contaminated with methyl mercury was dumped into local fishing waters. The symptoms of methyl mercury poisoning documented in these cases are paresthesia (feeling "pins and needles"), ataxia (uncoordinated movement), dysarthria (slurred speech), and loss of vision. *Mead v. Secretary of HHS*, 86. Ethyl mercury poisoning most frequently manifests with muscle weakness, loss of appetite, and dizziness. Ibid., 86.

32 Babies are born with mercury in their bodies already from their mothers, and one study estimated that in their first 180 days of life breast-fed infants get 290 μg from their mother's milk. Rejane C. Marques et al., "Hair Mercury in Breast-Fed Infants Exposed to Thimerosal-Preserved Vaccines," *European Journal of Pediatrics* 166, no. 9 (2007): 935–41. The 1990s vaccine schedule delivered up to 187.5 μg. A government toxicologist estimated that the full course of thimerosal-containing vaccines would add two to three parts per billion to the brain burden of mercury. *King v. Secretary of HHS* and *Mead v. Secretary of HHS*, 1810–11, 1818–19, 4335.

33 A can of tuna has about 0.17 parts per million of methyl mercury (or 170 parts per billion), though most of that would be excreted rather than remain in the body. N. J. Yess, "U.S. Food and Drug Administration Survey of Methyl Mercury in Canned Tuna," *Journal of AOAC International* 76, no. 1 (1993): 36–38. One popular form of reassurance has thus been to point out that there is more mercury in a tuna sandwich than in a vaccine. *King v. Secretary of HHS*, 36.

34 *King v. Secretary of HHS*, 106–7.

35 *Mead v. Secretary of HHS* and *King v. Secretary of HHS*, 1533; *Dwyer v. Secretary of HHS*, 164–76.

36 *Mead* and *King* transcript, 1161.

37 American College of Medical Toxicology, "Position Statement on Post-Chelator Challenge Urinary Metal Testing," *Journal of Medical Toxicology* 6, no. 1 (2010): 74–75.

38 *Mead* and *King* transcript, 1517–18.

39 *Snyder v. Secretary of HHS*, 01–162V (2009), 241–42.

40 *Dwyer* transcript, 180.

41 Marie Vahter et al., "Speciation of Mercury in the Primate Blood and Brain Following Long-Term Exposure to Methyl Mercury," *Toxicology and Applied Pharmacology* 124, no. 2 (1994): 221–29.

42 Thomas M. Burbacher et al., "Comparison of Blood and Brain Mercury Levels in Infant Monkeys Exposed to Methylmercury or Vaccines Containing Thimerosal," *Environmental Health Perspectives* 113, no. 8 (2005): 1015–21. Burbacher is an environmental toxicology and children's health researcher at the University of Washington who received funding for his work from the National Autism Association, a group that supports the injury frame from autism, including vaccine-linked causation. Burbacher hinted at his sympathies in the closing paragraphs of the article, criticizing the IOM for its attempt at closure in 2004 with its finding that evidence did not support an association between thimerosal and autism. "This approach is difficult to understand," he wrote, "given our current limited knowledge of the toxicokinetics and developmental neurotoxicity of thimerosal, a compound that has been (and will continue to be) injected in millions of newborns and infants." Ibid., 1021.

43 *King v. Secretary of HHS*, 65–66.

44 *Dwyer v. Secretary of HHS*, 68, 257.

45 Parthasarathy, "Breaking the Expertise Barrier."

46 Testimony of Dr. Kemper quoted in *King v. Secretary of HHS* and *Mead v. Secretary of HHS*, 2851–54.

47 Letter from Dr. Pardo to Dr. Kemper, May 13, 2008, available in the online docket of the Omnibus Autism Proceeding, www.uscfc.uscourts.gov.

48 Ibid.

49 *King v. Secretary of HHS*, 49.

50 Ibid., 50.

51 Kirby, *Evidence of Harm*.

52 S. Jill James et al., "Metabolic Biomarkers of Increased Oxidative Stress and Impaired Methylation Capacity in Children with Autism," *American Journal of Clinical Nutrition* 80, no. 6 (2004): 1611–17.

53 S. Jill James et al., "Metabolic Endophenotype and Related Genotypes Are Associated with Oxidative Stress in Children with Autism," *American Journal of Medical Genetics Part B: Neuropsychiatric Genetics* 141B, no. 8 (2006): 947–56.

54 Mady Hornig et al., "Neurotoxic Effects of Postnatal Thimerosal Are Mouse Strain Dependent," *Molecular Psychiatry* 9, no. 9 (2004): 833–45.

55 Mark Blaxill, "Rat on a Hot Tin Plate: New Evidence Shows Ethyl Mercury from Vaccines Causes Abnormal Brain Development in Infants," *Age of Autism*, November 3, 2009.

56 *Dwyer v. Secretary of HHS*, 224.

57 *Mead v. Secretary of HHS*, 111.

58 *Dwyer v. Secretary of HHS*, 225.

59 *Mead v. Secretary of HHS*, 117.

60 Jasanoff, *Science at the Bar*; Gieryn, *Cultural Boundaries of Science*; Gary Edmond, "The Law-Set: The Legal-Scientific Production of Medical Propriety," *Science, Technology, & Human Values* 26, no. 2 (2001): 191–226.

61 When asked under cross-examination whether "any substance is either toxic or non-toxic based upon the dose," Dr. Aposhian replied, "No. This is an ancient form of quotation that until recently we taught in medical schools. . . . We no longer believe that the dose determines the poison. This is an antiquated belief in this modern age because now we know about genetics and the hypersusceptibility of some people." *Cedillo v. Secretary of HHS*, 129.

62 *King v. Secretary of HHS* and *Mead v. Secretary of HHS*, 3968.

63 Ibid., 3976.

64 Ibid., 591.

65 Cross-examination of Dr. Deth in *King v. Secretary of HHS* and *Mead v. Secretary of HHS*, 588–98.

66 *King v. Secretary of HHS*, 74.

67 *Mead v. Secretary of HHS* and *King v. Secretary of HHS*, 917.

68 Sander Greenland, interview with the author, April 7, 2011.

69 Greenland interview.

70 *King v. Secretary of HHS* and *Mead v. Secretary of HHS*, 76.

71 Dr. Greenland's point about vulnerable subpopulations was treated as a statistical truism that would apply to any study. He could not advance the affirmative case for vaccine-induced damage. Ibid., 127.

72 On the witness stand, Dr. Goodman agreed with Dr. Greenland on these points. *King v. Secretary of HHS* and *Mead v. Secretary of HHS*, 3100.

73 Wakefield et al., "Ileal-Lymphoid-Nodular Hyperplasia," 637–41.

74 Brian Deer, "How the Case against the MMR Vaccine Was Fixed," *British Medical Journal* 342 (2011): c5347.

75 Day and Kelleher, "Lessons from MMR."

76 Conway interview.

77 *Cedillo v. Secretary of HHS*, 52.

78 Testimony of Nicholas Chadwick in ibid., 2284.

79 Andrew J. Wakefield et al., "Enterocolitis in Children with Developmental Disorders," *American Journal of Gastroenterology* 95, no. 9 (2000): 2285–95.

80 Wakefield, *Callous Disregard*.

81 Anderson, "Democracy, Public Policy, and Lay Assessments."

82 *Cedillo v. Secretary of HHS*, 85, emphasis original.

83 Testimony of Brian J. Ward in ibid., 1853. Replication attempts include M. A. Afzal et al., "Absence of Detectable Measles Virus Genome Sequence in Blood of Autistic Children Who Have Had Their MMR Vaccination during the Routine Childhood Immunization Schedule of UK," *Journal of Medical Virology* 78, no. 5 (2006): 623–30; and Yasmin D'Souza et al., "No Evidence of Persisting Measles Virus in the Peripheral Blood Mononuclear Cells from Children with Autism Spectrum Disorder," *Pediatrics* 118, no. 6 (2006): 2608.

84 Ruling Concerning Motion for Discovery from Merck re MMR Vaccine, 2004, 16.

85 *Cedillo v. Secretary of HHS*, 112, emphasis original.

86 Ibid., 119–20.

87 Ibid., 2.

88 Ibid., 2.

89 Ibid., 145–46.

90 Ibid., 1716.

91 Ibid., 1416.

92 Kirkland, "Legitimacy of Vaccine Critics."

93 Rebecca Estepp, Estepp Statement at Judicial Conference, Washington, DC, 2010.

94 Donald G. McNeil, Jr., "3 Rulings Find No Link to Vaccines and Autism," *New York Times*, March 12, 2010, www.nytimes.com, accessed April 13, 2016.

95 Center for Personal Rights, "Vaccine Justice Press Conference."

96 Ibid.

CONCLUSION

1 Tal Golan, *Laws of Man and Laws of Nature: A History of Scientific Expert Testimony* (Cambridge, MA: Harvard University Press, 2004).

2 Marcia Angell, *Science on Trial: The Clash of Medical Evidence and the Law in the Breast Implant Case* (New York: Norton, 1996).

3 Joëlle Anne Moreno, "It's Just a Shot Away: MMR Vaccines and Autism and the End of the *Daubertista* Revolution," *William Mitchell Law Review* 35 (2009): 1532.

4 Mello, "Rationalizing Vaccine Injury Compensation."

5 Ibid., 41. The ethical argument does not tell us which people are actually injured by vaccines, however, which is the root of the disputes I take up here.

6 Tyler, *Why People Obey the Law*, 24.

7 Parent representative Sarah Hoiberg, ACCV, June 2011 meeting transcript.

8 GAO, "Vaccine Injury Compensation," 29–30.

9 *Jacobson v. Massachusetts*, 197 U.S. 11 (1905); The challenge to the vaccine court brought by parents who had been denied compensation in *Bruesewitz v. Wyeth* in 2011 was the most significant legal challenge to the immunization social order because it would have allowed the losing autism families to take their claims back to state civil courts, but it did not raise the foundational question of whether vaccination is a legitimate claim on individual liberty in the name of public health.

10 Baum, *Specializing the Courts*; Nora Engstrom, "Dose of Reality for Specialized Courts."

11 Engstrom, "Dose of Reality for Specialized Courts," 1633–34.

12 Edward K. Cheng, "Changing Scientific Evidence," *Minnesota Law Review* 88 (2003): 315–56.

13 Ibid., 336.

14 Ibid., 338–49. The doctrine of res judicata ("a matter judged") has been a pillar of jurisprudence, guaranteeing finality of judgments, promoting certainty, and avoiding needless repetition in litigation. It precludes resuing the same defendant on the same cause of action again or reopening an issue of fact that has been determined in a proceeding between the same parties. Cheng argues that current exceptions to res judicata Rule 60(b) would not be broad enough to provide post-judgment relief for changing science as currently written and interpreted, but that they at least indicate some flexibility and could be grounds for future reform.

15 1986 House Committee Report, H.R. 99–908, 17.

16 Whitney et al., "Benefits from Immunization."

17 Gerard F. Anderson et al., "Health Spending in the United States and the Rest of the Industrialized World," *Health Affairs* 24 (2005): 903–14.

18 Ibid., 909–10.

19 Ibid., 911.

20 *Aetna Health, Inc. v. Davila*, 542 U.S. 200 (2004).

21 Peter D. Jacobson, *The Role of ERISA Preemption in Health Reform: Opportunities and Limits* (Washington, DC: O'Neill Institute for National and Global Health Law, 2009).

22 Anderson, "Epistemology of Democracy," 17.

23 Anderson, "Democracy, Public Policy, and Lay Assessments," 145–46.

24 Ibid, 146.

25 Ibid., 152.

26 National Vaccine Information Center, "National Vaccine Information Center and Mercola.com on Times Square!," March 32, 2001, www.nvic.org.

27 Lillvis et al., "Power and Persuasion in the Vaccine Debates."

INDEX

abortion, cell lines for vaccine development obtained from, 53, 111, 227n52

accountability, 8–9, 75, 103, 105–106, 118, 200, 202, 211

active vaccine safety monitoring system, 59

adult claimants, 119, 121, 232n40

adversarialism at the vaccine court, 72–75, 124

adversarial legalism, 70, 72, 134, 137, 214

adverse event, terminology for, 20. *See also* vaccine injuries

Advisory Commission on Childhood Vaccines (ACCV), 15, 88–90, 136, 146, 213

Advisory Committee on Immunization Practices (ACIP), 45–48

Aetna Health, Inc. v. Davila, 257n20

Affordable Care Act, 46, 61, 63, 109

Agbebaku v. Sigma Aldrich, Inc., 233n70

Agent Orange, 141

Agent Orange Act of 1991, 90, 141, 244n67, 244n69

Age of Autism (blog), 100, 149

AIDS Vaccine Victims Compensation Fund, 139

allergies, 1, 45, 67, 103, 105, 113–14

alternative childhood vaccine schedule, 25, 104

alternative health, 25–26, 38, 96, 99, 110

Althen v. Secretary of HHS, 165–66

American Academy of Pediatrics (AAP), 12, 72, 90

American Medical Association, 70, 208

anaphylaxis, 1, 80, 131, 162, 231n25, 248n64, 249n65

Anderson, Elizabeth, 22, 118, 190, 211

anthrax vaccine, 60

anti-vaccine (terminology), 18–20. *See also* vaccine critics

Aposhian, Vasken, 180, 187, 255n61

applied behavioral analysis (ABA), 252n17

Armey, Dick, 93

arthritis, 1, 80, 114, 132

asbestos, 141–42

Asbestos Injury Compensation Act, 141

Association of American Physicians and Surgeons, 109

asthma, 45, 103, 113, 131–32, 176, 249n66

attention-deficit disorder (ADD), 1, 5, 130–31, 155–56

attorneys' fees, 6, 82, 88, 91, 118, 120, 122, 130, 196, 201, 213

Austin, Harland, 155

autism: cases in the vaccine court, 8, 65, 122, 127, 153, 158–60, 172–197; causes of, 176–78, 252n8; definitions of, 159, 175–76; as epidemic or increasing, 176–78; excluded as a vaccine injury, 132, 162; and gender, 223n92; as mobilizing anti-vaccinationism and vaccine critics, 7, 10, 38–39, 100–102; as most visible recent vaccine injury claim, 10; regressive, 177; and thimerosal cases, 82–87; vaccine causation claims about, 11–14, 101, 112, 179–80

Autism Action Network, 100

AutismOne conference, 100

autoimmune disorders, 82, 103, 133, 168–69, 185, 206

Aventis Pasteur, 92

Avila v. Secretary of HHS, 233n57

Backes v. Secretary of HHS, 242n36

Banks v. Secretary of HHS, 247n48

Banyan Communications VICP awareness plan, 241n31

Barnes, Jeb, 72, 142, 230n5

Baum, Lawrence, 124, 208

Bearman, Peter, 178

Bell's palsy, 132, 249n66

Benjamin, Ruha, 17, 115

Bernard, Sallie, 13, 102, 152

Bernier, Roger, 87

big data, 55, 64, 95. *See also* surveillance

biodiversity, 112, 115

Biologics License Application, 44

Biomaterials Access Assurance Act of 1998, 244n61

Birnbaum, Sheila, 139

black box, 34–35, 148

Black Lung Benefits Act, 244n66

Blackmon v. American Home Products, 234n71

Blackwell v. Wyeth, 234n73

Blaxill, Mark, 185

Bolton, John, 71

Borrero v. Secretary of HHS, 251n98

Bowen, Otis, 71

brachial neuritis, 1, 132

brain damage, 67, 79, 81, 159, 179, 183

Braman, Donald, 102

Brazil, domestic vaccine production in, 37

British vaccine litigation: over autism claims, 11, 153, 189; over whole cell pertussis vaccine, 67, 79, 232n47

broad no-fault schemes, 137, 140, 144, 210

Broekelschen v. Secretary of HHS, 250n83

Brown, Wendy, 10

Bruesewitz v. Wyeth, 101, 195, 210, 239n6, 256n9

Bumiller, Kristin, 252n7

Burbacher, Thomas, 183, 254n42

Burbacher infant monkey study, 182–83

burden of proof: compared to other countries' vaccine compensation systems, 135–36; in the U.S. vaccine court, 88, 122, 194. *See also* preponderance of the evidence standard

Burke, Tom, 67, 71–72, 230n5

Burton, Dan, 87, 90, 92–93

Bustin, Stephen, 189–90, 193, 196

Campbell-Smith, Patricia (special master), 186

Canary Party, 100–101, 111–13

Capizzano v. Secretary of HHS, 250n80

Carpenter, Laura, 3

Casper, Monica, 3

Castaneda v. Secretary of HHS, 246n29

Catholic Church, view of vaccination, 227n52

causation-in-fact, 81

Caviezel v. Great Neck Public Schools, 227n44

Cedillo, Michelle, 189, 192–93

Cedillo v. Secretary of HHS, 174–75, 178, 191

Center for Biologics Evaluation and Research, 43

Center for Personal Rights, 100

Centers for Disease Control and Prevention (CDC), 2–3, 45, 55–58, 126, 152–53, 155–57, 163

Centers for Medicare and Medicaid Services (CMS), 60–61

Cervarix, 150

Chadwick, Nicholas, 190–91, 212

chelation, 180, 182, 252n17, 253n26

Cheng, Edward, 208, 257n14

Cheskiewicz v. Aventis Pasteur, 234n71

chickenpox, 3, 41, 51

chickenpox vaccine (varicella), 46, 51, 132, 161–62, 227n52

children's health in vaccine-critical arguments, 112–14, 176–177

China, domestic vaccine production in, 37

chiropractors, 38, 99–100, 111

Christian Scientists, 38, 52, 55

Christie, Chris, 37

chronic inflammatory demyelinating polyneuropathy, 168, 172

Citizens' Council for Health Freedom, 109

civil defense, vaccines as, 144

civil rights, 24, 115–16, 120. *See also* minority rights language; racial disparities; whiteness

Clinical Immunization Safety Assessment (CISA) Project, 156–57, 204

close call (in a compensation decision), 170–71, 194, 231n23

Coalition for Vaccine Safety, 100

Cohn, Amanda, 48

Committee on Government Reform, 87

community immunity. *See* herd immunity

compensation rates: compared to other countries' vaccine compensation systems, 136; at the U.S. vaccine court, 121–22

conflict of interest, 105, 149, 225n23

Conis, Elena, 223n91

Conway, Kevin, 81, 102, 159, 166

co-production, 21–22, 35, 65

Countermeasures Injury Compensation Program, 144, 243n44

credibility: classic scientific presentation of, 149, 188; and expert witnesses, 166–67, 173, 187–88; failures of the vaccine-autism theories, 11, 14, 186–89, 191–93, 207; loss of because of autism claims, 207; past attainment of by vaccine critics, 53–55, 98–99; social construction of scientific, 22, 148–49; struggle, 173, 192–93; of vaccine court rulings, 2, 22, 73, 117–18, 160, 170

Crusaders, The (film), 66

Daubert v. Merrell Dow Pharmaceuticals, 34, 87, 167, 201–202

Debold, Vicky, 103–104

Decoteau, Claire, 11

Defeat Autism Now! (DAN!), 181,

Defense Medical Surveillance System, 60

defensive medicine, estimated costs of, 209–10

Deisher, Theresa, 154

delay (at the vaccine court), 82, 129, 160, 165, 173, 185, 196, 200–201, 209, 215

deltoid bursitis. *See* shoulder injury related to vaccine administration

Democrats, vaccine policy preferences of, 37–39, 90

demyelinating conditions, 82, 133, 169. *See also* middle-ground cases

Denmark, health system in, 36, 61, 64, 110

Department of Defense, vaccine safety surveillance by, 60–61

Department of Health and Human Services (HHS), 15, 68, 126, 147

Department of Health v. Curry, 227n48

Department of Justice: as background of special masters, 123, 240n23; as a party in vaccine cases, 14, 74–75, 76, 82, 120, 157, 166, 250n85

Deribeaux v. Secretary of HHS, 250n85

design defect claims, 85, 101, 119, 195, 239n6

Deth, Richard, 179–80, 185–87

diabetes, 67, 114, 131–32, 141, 249n66

diphtheria, tetanus, and acellular pertussis (DTaP) vaccine, 12, 49, 51, 132

diphtheria, tetanus, and pertussis (DTP) vaccine, 50–51, 65–69, 76, 231n25

disability: fear of, 5, 49; lack of social welfare support for, 122, 145, 199; as minority identity, 97, 115; and neurodiversity, 115, 176; as vaccine injury, 70–71, 73, 88, 100, 103, 112–13, 205, 242n34. *See also* children's health in vaccine-critical arguments disaster schemes, 137, 210

discovery, 75, 83, 85, 121, 137, 153–55, 195

Disneyland, measles at, 39, 217n10

Dissatisfied Parents Together, 66, 98–99

Doe v. Ortho-Clinical Diagnostics, 233n65

dose theory of toxicology, 108, 181, 255n61

Dravet syndrome, 167

drug and vaccine approval process, 43–45

DTP. *See* diphtheria, tetanus, and pertussis (DTP) vaccine

Dubrofsky, Rachel, 9

Dwyer v. Secretary of HHS, 175

eczema, 114

electronic medical records, 60–63, 241n30

Eli Lilly, 91–93

Elizabeth Birt Center for Autism Law and Advocacy (EBCALA), 100–101, 231n24

Employee Retirement Income Security Act (ERISA), 210

encephalitis, 1, 82, 119

encephalopathy, 79–82, 130, 156, 158–60, 231n25

Engel, David, 17

Engstrom, Nora Freeman, 124, 208

environmentalism, 110

Environmental Protection Agency (EPA), methyl mercury standard of, 12, 58, 87, 152

epidemiology: difficulty for petitioners to obtain, 153–54, 234n82; as evidence about vaccine causation of injury, 80, 125, 134, 169–70, 173, 188, 191; in hierarchy of evidence, 95, 146–50, 164–66, 191; in safety surveillance, 55, 60

epilepsy, 67, 71, 80, 89, 103, 167

epistemic responsibility, 118, 190, 211, 212, 215

epistemology of democracy, 22

Epstein, Steven, 99, 173

ERISA. *See* Employee Retirement Income Security Act

Estepp, Rebecca, 14, 194

ethics of vaccine injury compensation, 203–204

ethyl mercury. *See* SafeMinds; thimerosal

Evans, Geoffrey, 121, 125–26, 161, 240n18, 243n47

everyday citizenship, vaccination as, 41–42

evidence. *See* hierarchy of evidence

Ewald, François, 111

excise tax, 6, 77, 203–204, 218n13, 234n81

expertise: barrier, 24, 153, 184; lay, 28, 36, 99, 102, 116, 192; scientific, 21–22, 34–36, 75, 102, 148–49, 201, 211; as a virtue of specialized courts, 124

expert witnesses: in autism cases, 175, 187–92; difficulty obtaining, 82, 168; fees and costs paid, 118, 120; regular appearances by, 168, 188

factors unrelated, 89–91

failure to warn, 84

fainting. *See* syncope

Farhang, Sean, 120

febrile convulsions, 66

febrile seizures, 57, 79, 132, 163, 248n64

Federal Advisory Committee Act, 149

federalism, 30, 36

Federal Rules of Civil Procedure, 121

Federal Rules of Evidence, 74, 184, 202

Feinberg, Kenneth, 138

feminist health movement. *See* women's health movement

feminist surveillance studies, 9

Ferguson v. Aventis Pasteur, Inc., 235n89

fetal tissue in vaccine manufacturing, 53, 85, 111, 222n81, 227n52

fever, 66, 128, 132, 163

Fisher, Barbara Loe, 18–19, 72, 99, 102–103, 105, 111–115, 152, 220n48, 231n24

flu. *See* influenza

Fombonne, Eric, 192

Food and Drug Administration (FDA), 12, 27, 43–51, 56, 62–63, 69–70, 76, 126, 150, 218n13

formaldehyde, 53–54, 111
Freedom of Information Act (FOIA), 16, 155
freedom of religion, 52, 96
Frickel, Scott, 35
Friedman, Lawrence, 140
Frist, Bill, 91–92
Frist bill (legislation), 91–93
Froelick v. Secretary of HHS, 243n43
Frye-Reed standard, 87

Gardasil, 149–50, 154
Gastroenteritis, 57
gatekeeping: effect, 120; mission of the vaccine court, 202
Gates, Bill, 30, 50
Geier, David, 152, 201, 212
Geier, Mark, 152, 196, 201, 212
General Medical Council (UK), 12
Generation Rescue, 100, 102, 176, 247n45
genetically modified organisms, 111
genetic polymorphism, 185
genetics, 91, 115, 133, 176–77, 255n61
germ theory of disease, 25–26, 107–108
Gilbert v. Secretary of HHS, 251n94
Gilliom, John, 64
GlaxoSmithKline, 37, 47, 59, 92
Global Alliance for Vaccines and Immunization (GAVI Alliance), 59
global South, 30. *See also* international aspects of vaccines
glutamate, 179–80
Golan, Tal, 200
Golkiewicz, Gary (special master), 14, 159, 164–65, 174
Goodman, Steven, 188, 255n72
Gorski, David, 247n49
Government Accountability Office (GAO) reports, 160–61, 241n31
Grading of Recommendations, Assessment, Development and Evaluation, 45–46
Greenland, Sander, 188–89, 255n71

Green Our Vaccines (march), 54, 110, 213
Green Party, 101
Guillain-Barré syndrome (GBS), 57, 61–62, 133–34, 172, 242–243n42

Haemophilus influenzae type b (Hib) vaccine, 3, 12, 50, 218n13
Handley, J. B., 100, 102, 176
Hannah Poling case, 158
Hastings, George (special master), 178, 181, 185, 191–192, 246n26
Hazlehurst, Rolf, 123, 195
Hazlehurst v. Secretary of HHS, 174
health bureaucrats, 9, 45, 55, 88–90, 106, 125–26, 135, 147, 157, 196, 203, 213
health courts, 124–25, 208–10
health freedom, 31, 106, 109–10
Health Insurance Portability and Accountability Act (HIPAA), 63
health libertarianism, 24, 27, 110, 214
Health Resources and Services Administration (HRSA), vaccine program housed in, 126, 128–32, 136, 241n31, 249n64
health social movements, 20, 24
Healthcare Cost and Utilization Project, 63
Heller, Jacob, 99, 222n81
hemolytic anemia, 67
hepatitis, 248n64
hepatitis A vaccine, 3, 46, 50–51, 111, 161, 218n13, 227n52
hepatitis B vaccine, 3, 12, 40, 46, 49–50, 82, 161, 168–70, 218n13, 248n64, 251n100
herd immunity, 19, 26, 29, 34–35, 40–41, 69, 144
herpes vaccine (genital), 17, 47
hierarchy of evidence, 127, 146–53, 164, 168, 171, 183
Hilgartner, Stephen, 148–49
Hodgkin's disease, 141, 244n69
Hoiberg, Sarah, 156–57, 248n58

holistic health frame, 106–10
holistic moms, 28, 38
Holland, Mary, 7, 195
Hollywood, vaccine critics and, 39
Holmes baby haircut study, 180, 212
Holocaust looted art, 142–43
Holt v. Secretary of HHS, 247n47
Homeland Security Act of 2002, rider
    attached to, 92–93
homeopathy, 107–108
Hornig, Mady, 185–86
human papillomavirus (HPV), 43, 154,
    161, 217n8
human papillomavirus (HPV) vaccine, 3,
    50, 149–50, 154, 218n13, 249n64
human rights, 97–98, 110–11, 211, 238n53
Huntington's disease, 177
hyperactivity, 67
hypersusceptible subgroup (to vaccine
    injury), 103, 105, 107, 176, 183, 186, 204

immune dysfunction, 45
immunization registries, 36, 61–63, 109
Immunization Safety Office, 157
immunization social order: challenges to,
    7, 23, 158, 168; definition, 2–3; vaccine
    court role in upholding, 7, 9, 16, 23–24,
    65, 94, 118–19, 123, 125, 202–207; worth
    of, 3, 29; politics of, 33–37, 41
Improved Vaccine Affordability and
    Availability Act, 91
inactivated poliovirus vaccine (IPV),
    50–51
India, domestic vaccine production in, 37
Indian Health Service, 60
infantile spasms, 80
inflammation, 1, 114, 119, 132, 175, 182–86,
    189
inflammatory bowel disease, 113–14
influenza, 61, 144
influenza vaccine, 50, 61, 119, 121, 161,
    218n13, 226n33, 232n40, 248n64,
    249n65–66

informed consent, 98, 103, 106, 111
inquisitorial justice, 134, 138, 154
In re Christine M., 227n42
*In re Exemption from Immunization
    Requested by Susan Lepage v. State*,
    227n49
Institute of Medicine (IOM): conflict of
    interest policy of, 105–106; credibility
    of, 149, 155; reports on vaccines, 13, 63,
    80, 91, 94, 104–106, 125–27, 130, 134,
    141, 152–55, 161–62, 203, 213, 241n28;
    hierarchy of evidence of, 146–49, 160–
    62, 168–69, 242n35
international aspects of vaccines, 14,
    17–18, 29–30, 42–43, 50, 54, 58–59, 67,
    134–37, 217n2, 226n36, 238n53, 243n47
intussusception, 57–60, 92, 162
Issa, Darrell, 160

Jacobson v. Massachusetts, 206
Jain, Sarah Lochlann, 9
James, Jill, 185
James Zadroga 9/11 Health and Compen-
    sation Act of 2010, 139
Jane Doe 74 v. Secretary of HHS, 242n41
Jasanoff, Sheila, 7, 21–23, 34–35, 126, 167,
    200
Jenkins-Smith, Hank, 102
Jenner, Edward, 50
Johann-Liang, Rosemary, 157
Johnson v. American Cyanamid Co., 230n9
Johnston, Robert D., 98–99
jury, 69, 71–72, 120, 195, 202, 209

Kagan, Robert, 134–135
Kahan, Dan, 37–38, 102
Kaufman, Sharon, 26
Kemper, Thomas, 184
Kennedy, Robert, 155, 246n30
Kennedy, Ted, 92
King v. Aventis Pasteur, 83
King v. Secretary of HHS, 174–75
Kinsbourne, Marcel, 179, 187–88

Kirby, David, 18, 152
Knudsen v. Secretary of HHS, 239n15
Kritzer, Herbert, 120

Lally, Cathy, 155–56
Latour, Bruno, 117
Laughter v. Aventis Pasteur, Inc., 233n71
Leach, Melissa, 217n2
lead poisoning, 105, 108
learning disabilities, 5, 67, 103
Lederle, 69
legalization of vaccine injury, 3, 29, 119–25, 176, 212
Legal Services Commission (UK), 11
legitimacy, 18–19, 22–23, 27, 34–35, 41, 54, 186, 196–97
Ley, Aaron, 245n78
libertarianism. *See* health libertarianism
life care planner, 82, 242n34
liver disease, 40
loophole lawsuits, 85
loss of consortium claims, 84, 86, 91
Lyme disease and vaccine against, 47, 225n28

MacKinnon, Catharine, 106
Magnet, Shoshana Amielle, 9
Maryland Thimerosal Litigation, 233n70
Mason v. General Brown Central School District, 227n43
maternalism, 26. *See also* mothers and mothering
Mathis v. Secretary of HHS, 250n85
McCann, Michael, 23
McCarthy, Jenny, 39, 54, 100, 110, 213
McCarthy v. Boozman, 227n46
McLaughlin v. Secretary of HHS, 242n38
Mead v. Aventis Pasteur, 83–84, 233n58
Mead v. Secretary of HHS, 174–75
measles, 4, 12, 17–18, 37–40, 46, 50, 176, 179, 188–91, 217n10, 222n81, 246n19
measles-mumps-rubella (MMR) vaccine: adverse events linked to, 1, 132, 158, 163, 231n25, 248n64, 249n65; and autism, 11, 13, 93, 129, 149, 153, 162, 174–178, 189–193, 219n31, 229n82, 251n3; lack of racial disparity in uptake of, 29; Merck's U.S. provision of, 46; objections to, 28, 39; in recommended schedule, 50–51; early inclusion in VICP, 76, 160, 231n25
Medicaid, 9, 60, 122, 136, 204
medical exemptions to vaccination, 4, 55
Medical Hypotheses, 13
medical officer, 75, 125–26, 129–32, 136, 147, 158, 168, 249n64
Medicare, 60–61, 109, 136
Mello, Michelle, 203
meningitis, 44, 47–49, 226n31, 248n64
Meningitis Angels, 48–49
meningitis vaccine, 47–49
meningococcal conjugate vaccine (MCV4), 47, 249n74
meningococcal vaccine, 48, 218n13, 226n31, 248n64, 249n74
meningococcal disease, 48, 161, 217n8
Merck, 36, 46, 59, 69, 92, 154
Mercola, Joe, 162
mercury. *See* SafeMinds; thimerosal
Mercury-Free Vaccines Act, 54
Mertonian scientific norms, 192
methyl mercury. *See* SafeMinds; thimerosal
Meyers, Peter, 138, 231n23
middle-ground cases, 31, 133–34, 168–73, 194, 201, 215
migraine, 114
Miller v. Secretary of HHS, 253n27
Milley, Frankie, 48
Millman, Laura (special master), 168–69, 250n92, 251n100
Minamata Convention on Mercury, 54
Mini-Sentinel, 62–63
minority identity and vaccine criticism, 114–15
minority rights language, 28, 176–77

mission trips, disease outbreaks linked to, 38–39

mitochondrial disorder, 158, 247n47

Moberly v. Secretary of HHS, 250n83

molecular mimicry, 170, 251n96

Monahan, Torin, 64

Moody, Jim, 102, 160

Moreno, Joëlle Anne, 202

Moss, Randy, 84–86

Mostovoy v. Secretary of HHS, 246n27

mothers and mothering, 24–29, 49, 100, 214–15, 223n91

multiple sclerosis, 168–70, 242n41, 243n43, 251n100

Mumper, Elizabeth, 181–82

mumps, 4, 50

mumps vaccine, 1, 39, 50, 77, 161, 174, 218n13

Munger, Frank, 17

Murphy, Michelle, 161

Murphy v. Aventis Pasteur, Inc., 233–34n71

myeloma, 141

myth of transcription, 34, 167

Nadler, Jerrold, 90

National Academy of Science, 148, 211

National Autism Association, 100, 254n42

National Childhood Encephalopathy Study (NCES), 79

National Childhood Vaccine Injury Act (NCVIA) of 1986: context for the passage of, 6, 23, 69–70, 96, 143; questions in the design of, 68; requirements of, 57, 147, 213. *See also* Vaccine Injury Compensation Program (VICP)

National Hospital Discharge Survey, 63

national identification card, 33, 36, 64, 110

National Immunization Program, 87, 152

National Immunization Survey, 63

National Institute of Health, 154

National Transportation Safety Board, 105

National Vaccine Advisory Committee (NVAC), 15, 102, 213

National Vaccine Information Center (NVIC): characterizations of, 15–16, 18–19, 98–100, 105, 112, 162, 231n24; and chiropractors, 99, 107; conference, 109, 112, 220n48; dosage count of, 49, 226n33; founding of, 66, 98; features in common with pro-vaccine parent group, 48–49; and libertarian right, 38–39, 63, 97, 109, 115. *See also* Fisher, Barbara Loe

National Vaccine Injury Compensation Improvement Act of 2002, 90

National Vaccine Program Office, 156

Native Americans, 60. *See also* Indian Health Service

negligence, 83–84, 137

neoliberalism, 33, 97, 110

neurodiversity, 175–76

neuroinflammation, 175, 179, 182–86

New Zealand, injury compensation in, 68, 135–36

Nielsen, Laura Beth, 17

no-fault: auto insurance, 137, 140; contrasted to negligence lawsuits, 5, 67–68, 72. *See also* broad no-fault schemes

Novartis, 37, 226n31

nuclear power, 137, 139–40, 143, 210

OAP. *See* Omnibus Autism Proceeding

Obamacare. *See* Affordable Care Act

oculorespiratory syndrome, 132, 249n65

Offit, Paul, 19, 58, 79, 159, 169, 173

off-Table claims, 81–82, 94–95, 119, 121, 130, 165, 170–75

Ogletree v. Secretary of HHS, 251n100

Omnibus Autism Proceeding (OAP), 13, 158, 172–197; defining an era of the vaccine court, 121; after regular court filings of thimerosal claims, 83, 87, 93–94; losses as loss of support for autistic children, 122; and immunization social order, 202. *See also* autism

oral polio vaccine (OPV), 51, 69, 85, 132, 231n25

outbreaks of vaccine-preventable disease, 38–39, 41, 46, 217n10, 226n31
Oversight and Government Reform committee, 160
Owens v. American Home Products, 234n71
oxidative stress, 179–80, 185, 187

pace of decisionmaking, 117, 200–201. *See also* delay
Pace law review article, 159–61
package insert, 44–45, 53, 57, 150
Paluck v. Secretary of HHS, 247n47
paralysis, 132–133, 242n42
paralytic polio, 132, 231n25
Pardo, Carlos, 184–85
Pardo neuroinflammation study, 184–85
parent activists, 66–67, 91–92, 98–101
parental rights, 24, 53
Parkinson's disease, 141
Parthasarathy, Shobita, 24, 116
passive vaccine safety monitoring system, 56, 149–51, 249n74
Paul, Rand, 37
Paul, Ron, 111
PCR (polymerase chain reaction), 189–91, 193
Pell, Owen, 143
personal belief exemption. *See* philosophical exemption
pertussis, 4–5, 50, 54
pertussis vaccine, 6, 12, 30, 49–51, 61, 65–67, 73, 79–80, 99, 119, 132, 218n13, 232n47, 240n18
Petchesky, Rosalind, 238n53
petitioners' attorneys: and adversarial legalism, 134–36; and challenges of their work, 82, 88, 128–29, 166, 168, 170–71; as part of vaccine court community, 14, 16; payments to, 6, 90, 118, 120, 122; relationship to social movement, 101–102
Peugh v. Secretary of HHS, 250n92

Pfizer, 37
pharmaceutical companies: and lawsuits for vaccine injuries, 11, 67–72, 85–86, 91–93, 195, 239n6; mistrust of, 25, 38, 53, 67, 112, 150; and passage of the vaccine act, 67–70, 85; and the vaccine market, 3, 18, 36–37, 43, 46
philosophical exemption, 4–5, 51–55, 217n10, 227n48
pneumococcal conjugate (PCV13) vaccine, 50, 218n13
Poling, Hannah, 158–59, 247n46–47
Poling v. Secretary of HHS, 247n47
polio, 4, 19, 41–42, 49–51, 69, 85–86, 132, 222n81, 226n36
polio vaccine, 17, 19, 29, 50–51, 67, 69, 76, 85–86, 132, 218n13, 231n25
Pollan, Michael, 54
Polletta, Francesca, 15
positive association standard under the Agent Orange Act, 90, 141, 155, 169, 234n82, 244n69
Post-Licensure Rapid Immunization Monitoring System (PRISM), 61–62
postlicensure vaccine safety monitoring, 56, 61. *See also* Vaccine Safety Datalink (VSD)
precautionary principle, 110–11
preemption, 86, 119, 195, 210
preponderance of the evidence standard, 81, 119, 136, 165–66, 171, 234n82
Price-Anderson Nuclear Industries Indemnity Act of 1957, 139, 143
privilege, 9, 26, 28–29, 39, 97, 200, 214
protective and ongoing schemes, 137, 139–40, 144
prototype of courts, 123
public health powers, 36

Quigley v. Rider, 239n5

racial disparities, 28–29, 224n101
racism, 113–14

Radiation Exposure Compensation Act of 1990, 140–41

Rapid Cycle Analysis, 60, 163, 249n74

reactive airway disease, 132, 249n66

recommended childhood vaccine schedule: changes in, 51, 163, 225n28; construction of, 30, 40–51, 104, 126; deviations from, 26–27, 103; global effects of, 59; number of shots in, 49–50; mercury in, 12–14; removal of RotaShield from, 58; VICP coverage for, 6, 77, 119, 135, 218n13, 232n40; vaccines included in, 3–4, 49–51, 217n8

Redfoot v. B.F. Ascher & Co., 233n65

"regime of perceptibility," 161

Reich, Jennifer, 16, 26, 29

Reilly v. Wyeth, 233n66, 234n72

Reiss, Dorit, 227n40

religious exemptions, 52–53, 55, 227n40, 227n48

Republicans, 160; vaccine policy preferences of, 37–39, 54, 71, 87, 90–92

res judicata, 257n14

RhoGAM, 85, 233n65, 250n87

Richardson, Dawn, 53

Riggins v. Secretary of HHS, 239n9, 239n13

Riles, Annelise, 8, 117

Roberts, Dorothy, 115

Roberts, Jackson, 187

Rotarix, 59

RotaShield, 57–60, 88, 92, 212

RotaTeq, 59

rotavirus (RV), 4

rotavirus vaccine, 46, 49, 51, 57–59, 88, 92, 212, 218n13

rubella, 4, 222n81

rubella vaccine, 1, 37, 39, 50, 77, 80, 111, 132, 161, 174, 177, 218n13, 227n52

Rutter, Michael, 178

Sabin polio vaccine. *See* oral polio vaccine (OPV)

SafeMinds, 13, 91–93, 100, 102, 105, 110, 112, 152, 185–87

Salk polio vaccine. *See* inactivated polio vaccine (IPV)

Salmon, Daniel, 156–57

Sand v. Secretary of HHS, 242n37

Sanofi Pasteur, 37

Schafer v. American Cyanamid Co., 233n68

schizophrenia, 177

Schneider, Rob, 101, 113

school entry immunization requirements, 30

Schwartz, Jason, 58–59

"science versus policy," 78–82

scientific knowledge: from compensated cases, 156–58; from the IOM, 147–49, 162; as a resource for policymaking, 34, 65, 78–81, 133, 147, 158; as politicized, 25, 34–36, 167; represented by the Vaccine Injury Table, 78–82; as socially constructed, 113, 167; and vaccine critics, 102–106, 162

SCN1A gene mutation, 167, 250n85

seizures, 57, 67, 79–80, 128, 130, 132, 163, 166–167, 179, 248n64, 250n85

Senate Committee on Health, Education, Labor and Pensions, 156

Sentinel Initiative, 62

September 11th Victim Compensation Fund, 117, 122, 138–40

settlement: for Agent Orange, 141, 244n67; in civil cases, 74; as common mode of vaccine claim resolution, 9, 133–34, 157, 201, 242n34, 242n41; lack of for Holocaust art claims, 142. *See also* stipulation

Shapiro, Martin, 123

Sherr v. Northport-East Northport Union Free School District, 227n45

Shim, Janet, 17

shingles, 82, 227n52

Shoemaker, Clifford, 82

shoulder injury related to vaccine administration (SIRVA), 132, 158, 249n64
Siegel, Reva, 106
signal (of possible adverse event), 55–64, 150, 161–63
silicone gel breast implant litigation, 200–201
Silverman, Chloe, 16–17
Simpsonwood conference, 155–56
smallpox, 41, 50, 139, 144
Smallpox Vaccine Injury Compensation Program, 139
Smith, Derek, 168
SmithKline Beecham, 92
Snyder v. Secretary of HHS, 174, 254n39
Somali community in Minnesota, vaccine fears of, 39
Sorensen, Ward, 138
specialized courts, 124, 201–202, 207–208. *See also* health courts
special masters, 2, 120; backgrounds of, 240n23; criticisms of, 195; as judges, 74, 121, 123, 154, 203; informal role in vaccine court processes, 82; as non-scientists, 21, 124, 201; as part of small community at the vaccine court, 14–16, 206
state level childhood immunization laws, 2, 4, 30, 54–55, 96, 213
statute of limitations, 83–84, 88–90, 128–29, 207–209, 234n80
Stevens test, 165
Stevens v. Secretary of HHS, 165, 249n75, 250n78, 251n95
stipulation, 95, 173, 243n43, 251n100
strict liability, 70
sulfur metabolism in vaccine injury theory, 179–80
subpoena, 121, 153–54, 246n26
Sudden Infant Death Syndrome (SIDS), 67, 80, 130, 150, 166, 240n18
Supreme Court, 101, 119, 167, 195, 206, 220n53

surveillance: criticisms of, 9, 64; in federal vaccine safety system, 55–64; and knowledge production, 126, 147, 149, 151, 161; missing populations in, 29, 214; as state power needed to detect adverse events, 9, 35. *See also* feminist surveillance studies; signal
swine flu, 61, 230n13
swine flu compensation program, 139
swine flu vaccine, 61–62
syncope, 57, 131, 249n64

Table. *See* Vaccine Injury Table
Table injury, 79, 119, 129–30, 133, 158–59
Talk About Curing Autism (TACA), 14, 100
Tea Party, 101
terminology choices in the book, 18–20
tetanus, 4, 222n81, 225n15
tetanus, diphtheria, and acellular pertussis (Tdap), 49–50
tetanus vaccine, 1, 12, 30, 49–51, 65, 119, 132, 161, 168, 218n13, 232n40, 242n41, 248n64
Texas megachurch measles outbreak, 38–39
thimerosal: as adulterant or contaminant, 233n71; cases at the vaccine court, 174–75; 179–98; discovery of amount in vaccines, 12, 152; ethyl mercury versus methyl mercury, 183; lawsuits in the U.S., 13, 82–86, 90–93; in products other than vaccines, 85, 233n65; studies of, 155–56; remaining in the flu vaccine, 219n32. *See also* autism; Omnibus Autism Proceeding (OAP)
thrombocytopenia, 67
thrombocytopenic purpura, 1, 82, 132
thyroid disorders, 114
Times Square Jumbotron anti-vaccine message, 24, 213
Toner v. Lederle, 69, 230n9
"too many too soon" slogan, 38, 51

Top Ten Terrible Tax Act of 1999, 234n81
Tornatore, Carlo, 169–70
tort lawsuits, 119, 208, 210; as attempts to avoid vaccine court, 82–87. *See also* loophole lawsuits
toxins, 89, 108, 111–12, 184
transient arthralgia, 249n65
transnational. *See* international aspects of vaccines
transverse myelitis, 168–69, 172
trivalent inactivated influenza vaccines, 249n65-n66
Troxclair ex. Rel. Troxclair v. Aventis Pasteur, 233n71, 235n94
trust fund: balance of, 122; for other U.S.-based compensation programs, 141–42; vaccine court, 6, 74–77, 118, 120, 204. *See also* excise tax
Tyler, Tom, 6–7, 23, 205

unavoidably unsafe products, 70
uncertainty: compensations in spite of, 65, 122, 124, 134, 170, 201; of litigation, 70; and precaution, 111; promotion of by vaccine critics, 102; surrounding thimerosal, 12–13, 149, 155; ongoing conditions of, 7–8, 11, 98, 117, 188; in vaccine safety review studies, 161–62
Underman, Kelly, 11
Unigenetics laboratory, 189–93
unjust enrichment, 83
U.S. Court of Federal Claims, 15, 196

vaccine act. *See* National Childhood Vaccine Injury Act (NCVIA) of 1986
Vaccine Adverse Event Reporting System (VAERS): as basis for vaccine critics' research, 149–50, 157, 162, 201, 212; creation of, 61, 213; filing a report in, 56–57, 129, place in the evidence hierarchy, 151; as signal generator, 57–59, 150, 162
vaccine choice, 37, 99, 103–106, 115, 203, 213

vaccine compensation programs around the world, 134–36
vaccine critics, 96–116; as alternative health adherents, 25–26, 99, 107–109; and environmentalism, 110–12; as health social movement, 20–25, 27–28, 97; and libertarianism, 109–10; and maternalism, 27; political mobilization of, 53–54, 66–67, 98, 100; terminology for, 18–20; whiteness of, 28, 96, 114
Vaccine Damage Payments Act, 67
vaccine ingredients, 53–54, 111–12
Vaccine Injured Children's Compensation Act of 2001, 90, 234n81
vaccine injuries: acknowledged in the mainstream, 131–32, 248n64, 249n64; insufficient evidence to establish causation about, 161–62; rejected in the mainstream, 132–33, 162, 249n66. *See also* middle-ground cases
Vaccine Injury Compensation Program (VICP), 119–27, alternative designs for and attempted modifications of, 87–93, 199; compared to other domestic compensation programs, 137–45; counterparts in other countries, 134–36, 243n47; critiques of, 158–61; early days of, 73–78; evasion of in thimerosal case filings, 82–87; publicity for, 75, 128, 241n31; vaccines covered under, 218n13. *See also* special masters; Vaccine Injury Table
Vaccine Injury Compensation Program Corrective Amendments of 2000, 234n81
Vaccine Injury Compensation Program Improvement Act of 2000, 234n81
Vaccine Injury Compensation Reform Act, 234n81
Vaccine Injury Table, 73, 78–82, 119, 146–47, 231n25
vaccine mandates, 4–5

vaccine politics, 21, 33–43; in the states, 51–55, 62, 213, 217n10; transnational and global perspectives on, 14, 29–30, 58–59, 67, 134–36, 238n53. *See also* federalism

vaccine-related adverse event (terminology), 20, 64, 131

Vaccine Roulette (TV episode), 66

Vaccine Rules, The, 121, 232n32

vaccine safety: advocates, 18–20, 24, 98–102, 105, 130; IOM studies of, 126, 147–49, 203, 213; monitoring for, 55–64, 66, 105, 125–28, 147–57, 161–63; at the population level, 8, 55, 151, 169; requirements for governmental system of, 9, 35–36, 56–64, 128; and study design, 103–104, 152–53, 163. *See also* National Childhood Vaccine Injury Act; signal; surveillance

Vaccine Safety Datalink (VSD), 59–61, 63, 128, 151–55, 163, 249n74

Vaccines and Related Biological Products Advisory Committee, 44

Vaccines for Children (VFC) program, 46

Vargas autopsy study, 183–184

varicella vaccine, 46, 49–51, 82, 111, 132, 161, 163, 218n13, 227n52, 248n64

Verstraeten, Thomas, 246n32

Veterans Administration, 141

Veterans Affairs Database, 60

Vietnam, 141, 143, 244n67

Vowell, Denise (special master), 180, 186, 240n23

vulnerable minority identity, 31, 97, 106, 111, 114–16, 177. *See also* hypersusceptible subgroup; minority rights language

W.C. v. Secretary of HHS, 242n41

Wakefield, Andrew, 11–14, 54–55, 58, 189–94, 212, 219n30

Wallison, Peter, 71

Ward, Brian, 256n83

Waters v. Secretary of HHS, 250n84

Waxman, Henry, 70–72, 90

Wax v. Aventis Pasteur, Inc., 234n71

Webb, Curtis, 81–82, 88–89, 234n80, 170

Weldon, Dave, 90

Weldon-Nadler bill, 90

wellness programs in the workplace, 223n89

Werderitsh v. Secretary of HHS, 250n93

White Citizens' Councils, 109

whiteness, 26, 28–29, 39, 96–97, 109, 114–15, 214

whole-cell pertussis vaccine. *See* diphtheria, tetanus, and pertussis (DTP) vaccine

whooping cough. *See* pertussis

whooping cough vaccine. *See* pertussis vaccine

Williams O'Leary, 83

Wilson's disease, 180

Wingspread statement, 110–11 *See also* precautionary principle

withdrawal of counsel (DOJ), 75

Wiznitzer, Max, 192

women's health movement, 26–28, 223n91

workers' compensation, 68, 137, 140, 142, 144

World Health Organization (WHO), 13

World Trade Center Health Program, 139

Wyeth Laboratories, 57–59, 87, 92

ABOUT THE AUTHOR

Anna Kirkland is Arthur F. Thurnau Professor and Associate Professor of Women's Studies and Political Science at the University of Michigan. She holds a law degree and a Ph.D. from the University of California, Berkeley. She is the author of *Fat Rights: Dilemmas of Difference and Personhood* (New York University Press, 2008) and a co-editor, with Jonathan Metzl, of *Against Health: How Health Became the New Morality* (New York University Press, 2010).